Certain Frag

What is the relationship between performance and play?
Between performance and technology?
Between performance and death?

Certain Fragments is an extraordinary exploration of what lies at the heart of
contemporary theatre. Written by the artistic director of Forced Entertainment,
acknowledged to be 'Britain's most brilliant experimental theatre company'
(*Guardian*), *Certain Fragments* investigates the processes of devising
performance, the role of writing in an interdisciplinary theatre and the
influence of the city on contemporary art practice.

Tim Etchells' unique and provocative voice shifts from intimate anecdote
to critical analysis and back again. As in his theatre-making so in his book:
with *Certain Fragments* Etchells disrupts traditional notions of creative,
academic and intellectual work. The book is an exciting and radical fusion
of story-telling and criticism. It also makes available, for the first time,
four seminal Forced Entertainment texts by Tim Etchells.

Tim Etchells is a writer, director and artist best known for his work leading
Forced Entertainment. Based in Sheffield, he has written extensively on
new performance and installation. A collection of his short fiction, entitled
Endland Stories, was published in 1999.

Certain Fragments

Contemporary Performance and Forced Entertainment

Tim Etchells

Photographs by Hugo Glendinning

For Deborah, Miles and Seth

First published 1999 by Routledge
11 New Fetter Lane, London EC4P 4EE
Simultaneously published in the USA and Canada by Routledge
29 West 35th Street, New York, NY 10001

© 1999 Tim Etchells

Designed by Lewis Nicholson
Typeset in Janson and Scala Sans
Printed and bound in Great Britain by St Edmundsbury Press Ltd,
Bury St. Edmunds, Suffolk.

British Library Cataloguing in Publication Data
A catalogue record for this book is available from the British Library

Library of Congress Cataloging-in-Publication Data
Etchells, Tim, 1962–
Certain fragments : contemporary performance and forced entertainment /
Tim Etchells.
p.   cm.
Includes bibliographical references and index.
1. Experimental theater—Great Britain.
2. Forced Entertainment (Theater Group) l. Title.
PN2595 . 13 . E97E83   1999
792' .022—dc21   98–41450 CIP

ISBN 0–415–17382–5 (hb) ISBN 0–415–17383–3 (pbk)

Thanks

My first thanks are to the members, past and present, of Forced Entertainment. Without their input, argument, hard work and insight over fourteen years none of what is in this book could exist. To the core team of Deborah Chadbourn, Terry O'Connor, Cathy Naden, Robin Arthur, Richard Lowdon and Claire Marshall and to founder members Susie Williams and Huw Chadbourn special thanks are due. The company's work has drawn strength and inspiration from its collaborations with numerous others who've worked alongside us as performers, technicians, film-makers and administrators. Our work with long-term associates performers Tim Hall and Sue Marshall deserves special mention as does the rich and long-standing work we've undertaken with composer John Avery and lighting designer Nigel Edwards. Photographer Hugo Glendinning, whose images are seen throughout these pages, has also been a long-term and inspirational collaborator on many projects as well as a considerable help in clarifying ideas on innumerable occasions.

Talia Rodgers at Routledge took up the idea for this book with skill, enthusiasm and patience. Lewis Nicholson, whose work to design this book has been a major collaboration, worked with Forced Entertainment over a number of years to create text and graphics for the work—his input then and now has been invaluable. The writer and academic Adrian Heathfield made comments on the manuscript in draft form which were very helpful. His understanding critique and support for the work were as vital here as they have been on numerous occasions in rehearsals and on tour.

A diverse group of editors, conference organisers, live art promoters and academics first commissioned or suggested the pieces in this book and my thanks are due to all of them, especially to Lyn Gardener during her time at *City Limits* and to David Hughes at *Hybrid* and then *Live Arts* magazine. In a more general sense Joanna Scanlan, Andrew Quick, Claire MacDonald, Alan Read, Susan Melrose and Peggy Phelan have at different times been an unofficial (and sometimes unknowing) support to me in the diverse ways that they have tried to talk, write or think about new performance and in the ways that they talked to me about my work, about their own work and about the field of contemporary arts.

The members of Forced Entertainment's board and advisory board past and present all deserve more than thanks for the hard and rigorous work they've done in extending and clarifying the company's practice, structure and approach. My thanks are due to Stella Hall, Katie Sender, Alan Read, Helen Marriage, Noel Greig, Nicky Childs, Antonia Payne, Philip Bernaise, Colin Pons and Simon Shibli.

Over fourteen years many people have funded, commissioned and otherwise supported Forced Entertainment in Britain and beyond and a true thanks goes to all of them for their faith and commitment. There are certain promoters, producers and critics whose engagement with the work at various times has gone beyond the call of duty. Thanks are due to the team of people at Artsadmin between 1987 and 1993, to John Ashford and Jim Hiley, and also to the former team at ICA Live Arts headed by Lois Keidan and Katherine Ugwu, whose efforts made things possible for us, challenged us and built a frame in which the work could be seen. Lois said she would like to have stayed in the room for the durational performance *12am Awake & Looking Down* 'forever' — and so in the unlikely event that there is a heaven I'd like to wish her that performance, when the bad day finally comes. Nikki Milican and the team at New Moves / National Review of Live Art also deserve special thanks from us for helping to create a space in which we and many other artists have been able to question, frame and reinvent our work.

I could (to steal a line from Ritsaart Ten Caate) fill a book with the names of people whose performances have been a kind of unwitting and unspoken conversation, provocation and inspiration over the years. In the UK and, indeed, in mainland Europe, the community of people making new theatre and performance remains in many respects small and correspondingly vital — these artists and makers have provided a necessary daily reminder of what's worth doing and what's not, a reminder for which my thanks are more than due. As young artists the inspiration we found on-stage in the work of Impact Theatre was mirrored by a supportiveness and a generosity from them (practical and artistic) that does not have a name. In different ways the members of that group, especially Pete Brooks, Claire MacDonald, Richard Hawley, Steve Shill, Graeme Miller and Nicky Johnson, have stayed as shifting reference points in the navigation we have tried to make. Theirs is the thanks that fellow travellers get — the nod across a room which rarely finds its way into print. Since Impact there have been others who have walked the same route as us for a while, providing support, conversation and inspiration — my special thanks to David Gale, to Nick and Graham of Index, to Jo and Christine of Desperate Optimists, to Matt and Ju of Blast Theory, to Jolente, Frank, Thomas, Damian and Sara of Stan, to Michael Atavar and to Nancy and Fred Reilly-McVittie.

Finally a special thanks must go to Steve Rogers who as editor of *Performance* magazine in the early 1980s encouraged me to start writing about my work with the company and that of other people. Steve died along with his partner Mark of AIDS-related illnesses in 1988, and his own practice as an editor and a writer engaged in a community of artists set a better example than one could reasonably wish for. He told me one day about wanting to do an art project wrapping buildings in fairy lights. I wish I could do that for him now.

—Tim Etchells, 1999

Contents

Section III

Journalism and
Programme Notes

Journalism

Programme Notes

Performing Questions, Producing Witnesses

Peggy Phelan

I've never been to Sheffield, England but I feel as if I've seen the performance, thanks to the work of Forced Entertainment, the performance ensemble established there since 1984. In *Certain Fragments*, Tim Etchells, the company's director and writer, chronicles the aspirations and achievements of the group and charts his own solo work as an artist-critic, an interviewer, and essayist. Poised between empirical documentation of the work of the company and lucid exploration of the gap between the scenario of the dream and the boards of the live stage, Etchells' book recasts several histories. In addition to charting a history of Forced Entertainment's development (who left, who arrived, when funding was refused, when invitations to travel became routine), Etchells also composes a history of his illuminating talks and correspondence with his son Miles, and a history of some disparate trips, acts, and images that might resemble something we could, if we were feeling grandiose, call a culture. But it's difficult to sustain a grandiose mood while reading these pages for Etchells insists that Forced Entertainment wants to discover a way to stage questions rather than to stake claims. 'The themes we have returned to are love and fragmentation,' Etchells writes in his introduction, 'the search for identity, the edges of sexuality, the need to confess. There's been a long commitment not to specific formal strategies but simply to challenging and provocative art — to work that asks questions and fuels dreams.' Etchells rebels a little at the task of trying to summarize fourteen years of collective work, registering his resistance in the phrase 'a long commitment not to'. A long commitment not to notice certain boundaries — especially those around performance and life — has been generative for Forced Entertainment. Ranging from the claustrophobic terror of *Club of No Regrets*, to the obsessive confessions of *Speak Bitterness*, Forced Entertainment has produced a remarkable body of work that pulses with the blood of different genres, aesthetic categories, and political-philosophical dares.

Etchells the writer for the stage should not be confused with Etchells the writer for the page. While the two share many preoccupations and predilections, the man of the theatre has dedicated himself to the task of asking collective questions in the company, while the writer for the page indulges in that alluring cowardice writing offers all who romance it — staking claims. Among the most compelling claims Etchells makes here is that Forced Entertainment has struggled 'to produce witnesses rather than spectators.' Moreover, he views this aspiration as an ethical act. 'To witness an event is to be present at it in some fundamentally ethical way, to feel the weight of things and one's place in them, even if that place is simply, for the moment, as an on-looker.' Such a notion suggests that ethical action might not be completely dependent upon empirical truths. Such truths, Etchells reminds us, can rarely be separated from the fictional; witnessing a shooting on the street is framed by our many rehearsals of witnessing shootings in the cinema, on the television news, and indeed, in theatre itself.

Performance employs the concept and experience of the live event as a way to rehearse our obligations to the scenes we witness in realms usually labeled the representational or the mediated. Like the Chicago-based performance group, Goat Island, the New York-based group, The Five Lesbian Brothers, and the Barcelona-based company, La Fura, Forced Entertainment suggests that performance might be an arena in which to investigate a new political ethics in the dying days of this century. For as we attempt to understand the violently repetitive genocides of the twentieth century, we come face to face with the challenge of witnessing traumas whose sources are both psychically and politically unbearable. The trauma that has been the consistent political performance of this century has proven to be extraordinarily resistant to the logic of the empirical.

Influenced by the enigmas of Robert Wilson's lyrical images, Pina Bausch's dancers' frenzied yet perfectly measured movement performances, the intellectual curiosity of William Forsythe, and inspired most directly by the remarkable example of The Wooster Group, some contemporary performance ensembles have begun to forge a collective response to contemporary western culture's 'long commitment not to notice' the ethical responsibilities it has to its past. While The Wooster Group, under the fierce direction of Elizabeth LeCompte, has been intent on deconstructing dramatic (and usually, but not always, North American) classics that animate theatre history, more recently formed companies have been interested in creating new texts and movement performances that obscure the distinction between fact and fiction, truth and dream.

The investigations of contemporary performance companies are significant because they demonstrate that performance art, despite its difficult relation to documentation, tradition, and transmission of bodily knowledge, does have an ongoing history. More precisely, these contemporary companies have adapted the conventions of influential avant-garde theatre collectives in order to create performance art, a term that is too frequently associated exclusively with solo work. Recognizing the 'long commitment not to' be devotées of a particular theatrical guru, shaman, or 'genius,' that had been characteristic of the practice (if not the theory) of their avant-garde predecessors, these companies have managed to create a concentrated body of collective work, even while individual members pursue other interests and lives outside the company. Some teach;

some travel; some make houses; some perform solo; some make sentences; some sew. These companies tend to be less devoted to their leaders and more inspired by the possibilities of creating and 'producing witnesses.'

Certainly avant-garde theatre has a long and distinguished history of employing performance to ignite the conscience of an ethical observer. From medieval morality plays, to the Forum performances of Augusto Boal — to say nothing of the achievements of Brecht, Artaud, Beckett, Churchill, to name only a few European canonical authors of this century — some important western theatre has been dedicated to making explicit links between theatrical arts and social politics. Some theatre makers have left the link implicit; some have tried, unsuccessfully, to ignore it. Enmeshed now in a world that routinely consigns theatre and performance to the broad category of escapist 'entertainment,' Forced Entertainment's name helps us see the coercive interests involved in keeping art in 'show business' rather than in 'real' business. Residing within the distinction is the notion that 'the real world' operates in the realm of brute fact, free of illusion, while 'show business' traffics in fiction, illusion, and disguise. Much contemporary performance art has attempted to expose the illusions that prop up the fiction of 'the real world.' But Forced Entertainment has been especially literal about the way in which we suture our histories from scraps of fictions and reverberating echoes from 'the real world.'

Taking the map of a city as a structuring metaphor and a literal movement score for a bus journey, Forced Entertainment remapped Sheffield and Rotterdam with the stories of individual residents' memories and associations with particular physical places. The 'tour bus' drove through the same city while performers narrated shifting stories of the memories associated with specific sites. Reflecting on these performances in a 1994 piece entitled, *A Decade of Forced Entertainment*, Claire Marshall speaks of the strange ways in which affective history seeps across material space, forming geological-like layers which might be termed: Public Political, Intimate Romantic, and Professional Biography:

> They drew a map of the country [England] and marked on it the events of the last ten years—the sites of political and industrial conflict, the ecological disasters, the show-biz marriages and celebrity divorces. On the same map they marked the events of their own lives—the performances they'd given, the towns and cities where they stayed, the sites of injuries and fallings in and out of love. [...]

They drew a map of the country and marked on it events from the rest of the world. On this map the Challenger Space Shuttle had blown up in Manchester in 1985. The Union Carbide Bophal Chemical Works which had exploded in late 1984 was located in Kent. The siege of the Russian Parliament Building in 1991 had taken place in Liverpool.

What Forced Entertainment mapped, in other words, was that complex process by which a public event arrives in the spectator's consciousness. When the Challenger 'slipped the surly bonds of earth' it crashed in Manchester because someone in the company was there to witness it. Mapping space and time in this manner transforms history (and travel) into an actively composed set of personal stories and not a passively experienced set of external events and locations. When Marshall notes that the group marked on their map 'events of the rest of the world,' she recognizes that information from the rest of the world comes to them sizzling across fiber-optic cables, electronic pixels, wire services, and satellite dishes. But as these events go whizzing by, they cannot be 'read,' or made meaningful until they are processed by some reading-machine that can decipher these codes. This reading-machine is both technological and affective, both collective and personal. Forced Entertainment's primary interest lies in how individual readers suture this new information into ongoing narratives of their own affective and empirically specific histories.

Etchells, unusually candid about Forced Entertainment's willingness to 'forgo the suspect certainties of what other people call political theatre,' remains confident that the theatre they make is 'deeply and always political.' Their politics are rooted in the effort to stage 'the territory between the real and the phantasmatic.' This aspiration animates Etchells' second project in *Certain Fragments*: to create a performance on the page that echoes the performances he makes and sees on the stage. *Repeat Forever*, like a net flung and floating across two continents, three generations, and the slippery divide between life and death, attempts to capture both the empirical and affective force of death for witnessing bodies that are at once vital and mortal. An exemplary illustration of the strengths of performative writing, *Repeat Forever*, underlines the connection between the live and the mediated, the fusion that allows a mechanical pump to keep our otherwise irregular hearts beating.

Etchells asks you, dear reader, to become a witness to events that you may encounter only here on the pages of this book. In 'Replaying the Tapes of the Twentieth Century,' he records an interview he did with the incomparable

actor, Ron Vawter, who died in 1994. Inserted within the transcript are quotations from performances Vawter did with The Wooster Group and as a solo
performer. Reading what is in a certain sense a posthumous publication, re-
encountering the voice of a dead artist on the pages of another artist's book,
one begins to glean the essential nature of witnessing itself: to continue a
conversation that without your intervention would cease. Etchells reanimates
Vawter's voice in order to prompt our collective re-encounter with it. Witnessing allows the dead, the disappeared, the lost, to continue to live as we redis-
cover their force in our ongoing present. Etchells understands that to 'produce
witnesses' in his theatre, requires the active solicitation of his own moments of
witnessing in the theatre of the other. His critical reviews of other artists are
snapshots of this practice.

In the spirit of performing questions, it's useful to raise a query about the kind
of solicitation of a witness contemporary performance undertakes. For one ought
to summon a witness only when one actually needs one; one wants to respond only
to genuine calls. Sometimes staging a body in extreme pain will, in and of itself,
solicit spectators' compassion. But compassion is not necessarily ethical and pain
voluntarily endured is a different act than, say, torture. Similarly, an actor who literally pulls the spectator onto the stage may or may not induce that spectator's
presence within the scene, and may or may not invoke the spectator's assent to the
scene's message. The 'production of witnesses' in the theatre cannot be like other
kinds of production. The 'product' will never be formed into an object, for witnessing, as a conscious, albeit belated, response to the messy truths that exceed the
empirical, prevents objectification.

The psychoanalytic account of witnessing trauma argues that witnessing only
occurs well after the trauma itself has ceased. That is, during the unfolding of the
live traumatic event the witness has no consciousness that he or she is becoming a
witness; one concentrates on surviving. To solicit an ethical witness in a theatre
event requires one to trust that the border of the performance exceeds its spatial
and temporal boundaries. While theatre has borrowed the understanding of witnessing from psychoanalysis and political ethics, it seems to me that theatre has
been somewhat shy in pursuing what it can add to the force of witnessing itself.
Witnessing in the theatre need not only be an ethical response to trauma, accident,
and death, but can also help us discover the capacity to respond to the equally
treacherous and equally urgent need to witness joy, pleasure, and the profundity of
delight we feel in our mortal bodies, flawed minds, imperfect hearts, and impover-
ished tongues. Forced Entertainment creates a space for the staging of cowardice

rather than courage, for exploring both loneliness and exuberance in the middle of the circus we can't seem to quit and can't seem to love.

Etchells notes that when Hugo Glendinning began to take photographs of Forced Entertainment's 1993 piece, *Club of No Regrets*, he 'shot without looking …never certain of what he'd get. But a part of the action.' Eliminating focus, Glendinning's photographs 'hunted' the performance without ever quite catching it. And yet precisely in the way in which Glendinning missed it, Forced Entertainment began to see 'what exactly we were doing.' Witnessing in the theatre might be likened to that strange collaborative process in which you and I are currently engaged: that process whereby one sends words, letters, e-mail, introductions, back and forth hoping to discover what one just wrote, what one just read. An early essay by Claire MacDonald, Etchells notes, provided Forced Entertainment with a language in which they might discover who they were in the process of becoming. Reading her words, they began to find their way. Witnesses create performance ensembles like readers create authors. I am happy to introduce you to an author whose acquaintance, dear reader, you might want to make.

Introduction

(1) A Party

San Francisco 1997. After the last performances ever of *Club of No Regrets* there's a party on the stage—a party that gets quite out of hand in a mixture of alcohol, exhaustion, exhilaration, and other things. I don't have pictures of the fire people started with bits of the set, the props and costumes at 3 in the morning, or of the smoke and sparks from the fire rising up and curling over the freeway overpass. I don't have any pictures of the company going straight to the airport at 7am, not having slept, still jumping, looking forward to 11 hours of flight.

But I do have pictures of the scene, must have been 2am, where two members of the audience—people we'd met in San Francisco who'd been helping out around the show—decided to enact a section of the piece in which, gagged and bound to chairs, the performers struggle to get out; a cross between escape artistry, brutal ballet and the climax of some well-dodgy thriller.

I think we had always known that people in the audience often felt drawn to get up and join in with this very physical and probably dangerous bit of *Club of No Regrets*—you could see it in the twitches and energy of people in their seats—so it was really refreshing to see it finally happen. I mean I don't want to get *too* romantic about people going mad and smashing furniture to pieces to incredibly loud music, but that night there was definitely a line crossed. I remember that once he had escaped Will was swinging his chair repeatedly onto the floor and smashing it and shards of wood and metal were splintering everywhere and people really near him were just staring and clapping and laughing. There was a weird and inexplicable feeling that everyone in the room that night was indestructible.

Perhaps that was the kind of performance we really dreamed of. Something beyond.

(2) A Decade

The first piece in this volume—the performance text titled *A Decade of Forced Entertainment*—might well serve both as an extended introduction to the company and its work and as a paradigm case of the kind of writing I am attempting to do about performance practice and process.

Decade was created late in 1994 as Forced Entertainment celebrated its 10th anniversary. The idea was to mark this occasion with a special one-off performance event that looked back on our work and on the years in which it had been made. In particular we wanted to use the piece to make some links between the work we'd created, the process and the UK landscape (cultural, geographical, psychic) in which we'd been operating. We'd always been keen to take part in the discussions and debates around new performance and felt that a piece like *Decade* could be a good way for us to contribute to that, whilst at the same time allowing us to shift the agenda of such discussions towards territory that we might find more fruitful.

Making *Decade* was a hurried business—time snatched from rehearsals and reworking on *Hidden J* (1994), the touring theatre piece we made that same year. For *Decade* we discussed the kind of information we wanted to include and set someone researching newspapers—looking for pictures, stories, 'facts' that might be of use to us. I wrote text. We told anecdotes, people wrote their own notes and added fragments of text. The tables in the rehearsal room were soon littered with sections of writings from previous shows, newspaper 'end of the year' trivia quizzes and so on.

Perhaps the most useful discovery was in the writing I did describing our work at a distance—referring always to 'they', writing as if Forced Entertainment were some distant, semi-fictional group of people in a country far away. The distance was useful—a fictionalising manœuvre that nodded to the versional nature of all history. Along with the distance came other discoveries—a way of intercutting different voices, different layers, eschewing a single line in favour of fragments arranged around a centre that is only ever implied. The strategies in *Decade*—cutting between the distance of 'he' and 'they' to the proximity of 'we' and 'I', jumping between chronicle and quotations from performances, between Britain and some fictional place—are strategies that come back again and again in the writing that follows. As if this hybrid form were really the natural way to speak truly of what we do.

(3) Forced Entertainment

We moved to Sheffield in 1984 and started making performance. There were seven of us. It was that time during Thatcherism when you could hide amongst 3–4 million unemployed and quietly get on with your work and being poor. Lots of artists did that—painters, musicians, performance makers, film-makers—in the North of England, in the South, everywhere. The culture of interplay between these people and between their 'audiences' was also tangible.

The first work we made was theatre, but *Jessica in the Room of Lights* (1984), with its soundtrack by the bassist of a local industrial noise band, its blurred 'storyline' about a cinema usherette whose real life gets mixed up with films she's absorbed at work and its first performances, in the upstairs gallery of an artist-run space, already had Forced Entertainment placed firmly at the margins of what most people might think of as 'British Theatre'. We were, on average, 24 years old, and being at the edges of the theatre didn't concern us too much since we knew we were in the centre of something else — a shared eclectic sensibility that seemed 'natural' to us and to others, to make work drawing on music, fine art, city life, cinema, science fiction, photography, graffiti, personal history, performance; trying, as we liked to say, 'to discuss the concerns of the times, in a language born out of them'.

(4) 84–98

It's an attempt that we continued, although in time the work has certainly shifted. Between 84 and 98 we made 16 full-scale touring theatre pieces — all of them devised, designed and performed by the group, addressing audiences in provocative and formally challenging ways. Throughout there's been a commitment to ensemble practice, to the building and maintaining of a group which shares a history, skills and an equal involvement in the process of making its work.

The process we've worked through (of which I'll say much more below) has always mixed improvisation with writing, argument, discussion and, latterly at least, a great deal of watching back through video-tapes of the previous day's work. It's a process in which no single aspect of the theatrical vocabulary is allowed to lead — so that set design, found costume, soundtrack, text fragment or idea for action might each just as well take the lead as a source or starting-point in a project. It's also a process which refuses to know, at the outset, what it is looking for. Remaining, rather, a journey undertaken, in which the territory unfolds, as much of a surprise to us as it may be to anyone else. We say without hesitation that it takes us time to find out what a certain piece of work might mean or even be concerned with, and that this discovery, if it comes at all, is made by doing — making, talking, touring — a discovery based on risk and uncertainty, not by our adherence to a plan.

At best, we say, the work (be it theatre, performance, installation or film) remains ahead of our thinking. It speaks of things that could not otherwise be spoken; it takes us somewhere. Less than that is simply not good enough.

(5) Witnesses

Imagine this: shot in the arm at close range by a friend and rushed from a gallery in Venice, California to hospital for his 1971 performance *Shoot*, the artist Chris Burden described those watching him that night not as an audience or as spectators, but as witnesses.

It's a distinction I come back to again and again and one which contemporary performance dwells on endlessly because to witness an event is to be present at it in some fundamentally ethical way, to feel the weight of things and one's own place in them, even if that place is simply, for the moment, as an onlooker.

The struggle to produce witnesses rather than spectators is present every-where in the contemporary performance scene. You can see it, in excess/epic style at least, in the public piercings and mutilations by American artist Ron Athey or the 'suspensions' on meat-hooks carried out by Stelarc, events in which extreme versions of the body in pain, in sexual play and in shock demand repeatedly of those watching — 'be here, be here, be here …'.

You can see it in much milder work too, and sometimes more clearly. In the rearrangements of audience space and contract repeatedly employed by the UK performance companies Station House Opera and Blast Theory, and by the US group Goat Island, whose physical vocabulary (of school gym class, nervous ticks, sports moves and intimate gestures) is itself a kind of witnessing — a writing of cultural biography in neglected physicality. You can see the plea for witnesses in the ritualistic slowness and simple presence of work by performance artist Alistair MacLennan, work that charts a landscape half public and politicised, half private and resolutely interior. You can see it in the durational performances of poet and artist Brian Catling, and in the use of personal and unlikely public spaces by Bobby Baker — kitchens, medical centres, schools. In each of these artist's work one gets, in very different ways, an invitation to be here and be now, to feel exactly what it is to be in this place and this time. This desire informed the decision we made for our own performance, *Speak Bitterness* (1995), to gently light those watching at all times. In this way the performers in the piece, whilst speaking the great litany of confessions both real and imaginary that make up its text, could see the public easily, and as individuals, not as a mass. If *Speak Bitterness* was a textual form of bearing witness to the dreams and failings of a culture, the light on those watching meant, above all, that eye contact was possible, so the two-way nature of every line was emphasised — something spoken, something heard — eye contact made and then broken again, eye contact offered, rejected, then offered again — a series of complex negotiations about complicity, about who has done what or who is implicated in what.

Twenty-six years after *Shoot* the audience/witness distinction remains vital and provocative since it reminds us to ask again the questions about where art matters and where it leaves its mark — in the real world or in some fictional one — and on whom it leaves its burden. The art-work that turns us into witnesses leaves us, above all, unable to stop thinking, talking and reporting what we've seen. We're left, like the people in Brecht's poem who've witnessed a road accident, still stood on the street corner discussing what happened, borne on by our responsibility to events.

(6) Sheffield, UK

Jurg Woodtli (a theatre programmer in Switzerland with whom we worked for several years) once said that he liked our work because it came so clearly from *is this so of our work?*

a particular place. In a world where too much contemporary art, dance and performance looks like it was born on the floor of a nameless, faceless Euro-Novotel, his comment was a real compliment. And if we sometimes laughed at the number of reviews beginning with lines like 'Forced Entertainment are from Sheffield and it shows' or 'Britain breeds football hooligans and theatre like this', we knew at least that the connection was tangible. When Claire MacDonald wrote the first critical piece of any length or substance about our work ('Unpicking Kentucky Fried City', *New Socialist*, September 1986), her statement that 'the media-glutted consumer culture of the city needs a new visual grammar to prise it open', not a 'worn out social realism', helped clarify and crystallise our understanding of what we were doing.

The theatre we dreamed of was concerned with ethics and identity, it was deeply and always political but, in embracing the fractured ambiguous landscape (social, cultural, psychic) of the 80s and 90s in Britain we knew it had to forgo the suspect certainties of what other people called political theatre, that it had to work the territory between the real and phantasmic, between the actual landscape and the media one, between the body and imagination. We worked with a growing confidence that a reliance on intuition, chance, dream, accident and impulse would not banish politics from the work but ensure its veracity—a certainty that old rules did not apply.

The landscape we've charted has been one of cities, late-night television, ghosts and half-remembered stories. The themes we have returned to are love and fragmentation, the search for identity, the edges of sexuality, the need to confess. There's been a long-term commitment, not to specific formal strategies but simply to challenging and provocative art—to work that asks questions and fuels dreams.

(7) Lineage

It works small, the history thing. Small things make big changes.

One night in 86 the house in S was filled up with ourselves and an entire Polish theatre company or two, a broken down bunch of people with a broken down van *en route* or off route to some festival, people who wanted to drink until 4 in any case and ask all the big questions. And, at a certain point (when talking became impossible or just too incoherent) we started playing them videos—a crash course taster in stuff we liked or loved, or stuff we thought might speak to our guests. Our lineage in random edit form.

A few fragments of Impact Theatre and Russell Hoban's *The Carrier Frequency*. A documentary on the Wooster Group with some sections of *L.S.D.*, another on Robert Wilson, another on Joseph Beuys. *Coyote*. Fast forward. Rewind. A piece by Bobby Baker. A piece by Station House Opera. Tables in the air. Pina Bausch. Can't find that tape. The Belgian choreographer Anne Teresa De Keersmaeker. Gary Stevens. Neil Bartlett. Spinning through the jumpcut influences, the likes, loves and dislikes of our 'world'. Tapes of poor quality and dubious origins. Tapes that said one thing but were really another. Third-generation copies. Incomplete tapes.

At dawn several persons were still awake, watching Tarkovsky's film *Mirror*, wide-eyed with sleeplessness, euphoric. No more vodka.

That night we were the curators of our own partial history—in performance terms at least—between the classicism, beauty and anguish of the European avant-garde, the postmodern formalism of American performance and the peculiar specificities of British performance itself—a small pile of videos and a whole lot of drunken stories. We loved the way that a chance encounter with this work or that (live or as anecdote) could change your own perspective for years and years to come, how one engaged in a strange conversation with people you might not ever meet, over oceans, between cities, over time.

(8) To Make an Introduction

This history, if it is one at all, on fast forward, parsing the landscapes—British, European, American—a growing list of Forced Entertainment tour dates, small shifts in personnel, exhaustions, discoveries, performances and endless rehearsals in rooms without windows. Meetings with other artists, encounters with other work, shocks, confrontations.

A slow expansion to projects outside of the theatre—from black-box spaces and studios to durational performances, interventions in unusual sites, guided tours, installations, works in photography, film and digital media, the latter often made in collaboration with photographer Hugo Glendinning. The kind of drifting across borders (national, artistic, intellectual) that is at the heart of so much art practice in the late twentieth century. But always, in the centre, theatre. And the notion of charting, somehow, the times in which we've lived.

I wanted to quote what journalist and novelist Michael Herr wrote in *Dispatches* (1968) about his experience of going to cover the Vietnam war. He wrote:

> I went to cover the war … behind the crude but serious belief that you had to be able to look at anything, serious because I acted on it and went, crude because I didn't know, it took the war to teach it, that you are as responsible for everything you saw as you were for everything you do. The problem was that you didn't always know what you were seeing until later, maybe years later, it just stayed stored there in your eyes …

We always loved the idea in this—of one's responsibility for events only seen. The strange responsibility of the city and its endless crowds and half-glimpsed lives, or of the media space with its images everywhere, always, already. That (lucky) experience of having seen only two real dead bodies and yet thousands upon thousands of TV corpses—real deaths and fictional deaths, mediated deaths. We wanted to speak of what it felt like to live in this space—of second-, third- and fourth-hand experience.

I'm not exactly telling our 'story' in this collection but I dare say anyone that wants to find it could do so between the lines of its pages.

(9) For the Record, in any case

Founder members: Tim Etchells (writer/director), Robin Arthur, Cathy Naden, Richard Lowdon (designer), Susie Williams, Huw Chadbourn and Deborah Chadbourn (administrator, now general manager).

Subsequent members: Terry O'Connor (since 1986) and Claire Marshall (since 1989).

Departures: Huw Chadbourn (1986), Susie Williams (1987).

Associates: John Avery (soundtracks, since 1984), Hugo Glendinning (photography and other projects, since 1985), Nigel Edwards (lighting design, since 1989), Sue Marshall (performer, since 1994), Tim Hall (performer, since 1994), Mary Agnes Krell and Todd Reidy (digital consultants, since 1995).

(10) What is it?

We knew that one worked in culture and through it, never outside of it. We knew that in addressing a site—library, theatre, gallery or tourist coach—one did so at best with an understanding and reference to the history or expectation of practices or events in such places. We knew that in the dancing with and around the expectations inherent in form and in place lay the possibility of meaning. In this sense everything we did was site-specific—a reaction to the history and properties of a certain arena. We made theatre, installation, digital media and publication in and around the rules. Sometimes we made things that could not easily be named. In Sheffield (1995) and Rotterdam (1997) we made a coach trip through a city, performers and audience on the bus. No action to speak of—just a finger pointing to the houses and the night.

What is it?

We operated in a culture where definitions of form were sometimes keenly policed, and where the work itself was constantly subject to the processes of calling, categorisation and containment. Boundaries are drawn, but for our own part we liked to shift them and to shift shape constantly. Because in shifting frames and shifting shape comes witnessing again—the sense that the watching is at the edges of its contract, on the edge of something more.

What is it?

The question could be fatal, because in the divisions of cultural practice called taste and politics art is divided from not-art, 'good' divided from 'bad', money divided from no-money. Weeks after the first performance of *Decade* the Drama Department of The Arts Council of England decided to refuse support for our next proposed project, *Speak Bitterness*. Swathed in concerns about aesthetics, 'poor-quality' productions, 'low production values' 'lack of development' and off-the-record questions about our status as drama or 'something else', the refusal meant more than a lost project—in economics it was a body blow and in critical terms it was a recognition (and an inscription) of a culture gap that had been widening for years. Surveying the bitter and fragmented performance *Hidden J*, hastily written ACE reports condemned its acting, its ugly set and its aggressive attitude to narrative coherence. Like much journalistic comment on the work the critique was largely a category error; being shamed for losing in a race that one had never entered. A set of assumptions—about what might be meant by terms like 'quality', 'structure', 'acting' and 'career development'—were rife and unjustified, as if drama were only one thing, as if Britain were one thing, as if there were really no dispute over beauty in the world. 'Surely...', implored some poor wounded soul in rhetorical biro after watching the piece, 'Surely the purpose of art is to bring people together, not just to rub their noses in the dirt?'

Well, maybe. And maybe not. We could only think of a quotation from a previous generation of British political dramatists—Trevor Griffiths' thug-comic Price in his best play *Comedians*:

National Unity? Up yours sunshine.

The problem of the work was a decision, not a mistake. Our 'funding crisis' became both a long and public battle (letters, meetings, lobbying) and a small but invaluable community-defining moment in which the value and diversity of non-literary theatrical forms in Britain were championed anew with passion by many people more articulate than ourselves. The Drama Department decision was, in the end, reconsidered, a revised application for our next project was submitted and the funding was granted anew.

(11) This Writing

'To be bound up with what you are doing, to be at risk in it, to be exposed by it...'

Alongside the work we've made there has always been talk and sometimes writing. About what we've done and why; about what others did and how. Writing as a partial trace of performances, or as a way of understanding what one did, or simply as another way of talking to people. Over 13 years the writing has gathered together for its own purposes theory, anecdote, observation, evidence and speculation and arranged them to open up a space—to raise questions and float possibilities about what performance is for us now.

The texts in this book range from what might be called theory, through observation, to criticism and performance texts. It is, however, writing always resolutely bound up with practice—with long hours of collaborative rehearsal room doing and talking on more or less countless performances. It is writing which I hope has dirty hands and with that a pragmatism and fluidity that comes from the making process in which an endless making-do is one's only hope for progress, in which dogma never prospers, in which the surprises of improvisation, mistakes and of changing one's mind are the only certainties worth clinging to.

Two of the pieces in this volume have multiple authors in a very straightforward sense. The performance text for *Speak Bitterness* contains a deal of material either written or made up by all of the performers in the piece as well by myself. *A Decade of Forced Entertainment* also contains material written or improvised by members of the company following initial writings by myself. The texts used in the other three performances— *(Let the Water Run its Course) to the Sea that Made the Promise* (1986), *Club of No Regrets* (1993/4) and *Emanuelle Enchanted* (1992)—documented in Section II were written by me but created deep in the context of group work. In this process, words (like everything else) were ordered and reordered, recontextualised and remade by the performers and myself as we worked in the rehearsal studio.

Even the critical and theoretical pieces which make up the bulk of this book are absolutely informed by the work I've done with Forced Entertainment and by the understanding of performance that we have jointly arrived at or stumbled into.

There are rules for the critical writing here (unspoken rules, only discovered afterwards): that it should open doors not close them; that it should in some way mirror the form of its object; that it should work with the reader as a performance might (playing games about position, status and kinds of discourse). That it should be, in short, a part of the work, not an undertaker to it.

With these rules in mind we felt that since the work we made or loved was often in fragments or layers (of image, sound, movement and text), so too the writing should be in fragments—fragments between which the reader must slip and connect if she is to get anywhere.

And since the work we made or loved was often concerned with the play between the real and the imaginary, fact and fiction—so the writing headed for this territory too, making drama from its shifts of voice, not always describing a situation so much as placing the reader in one.

Going in. At the deep end.

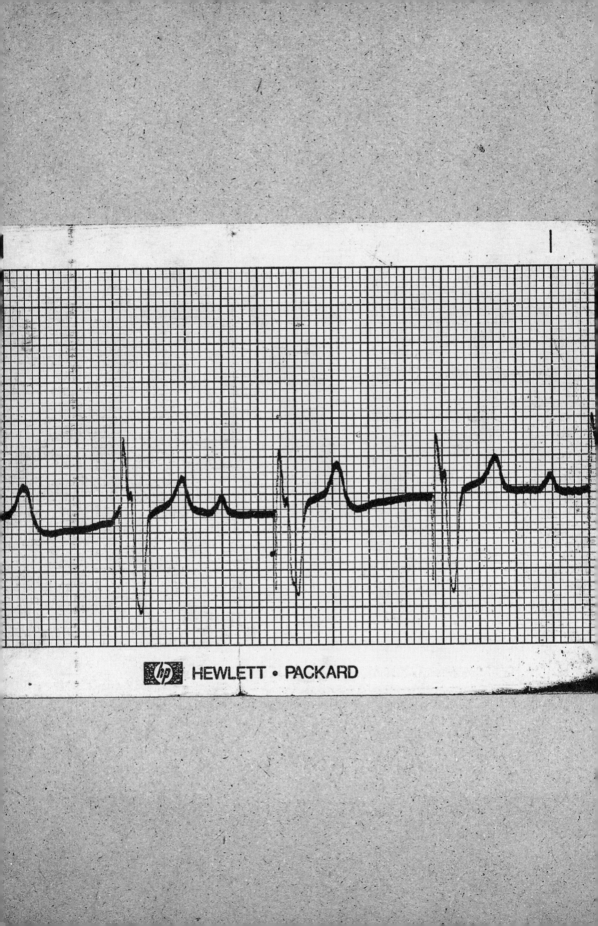

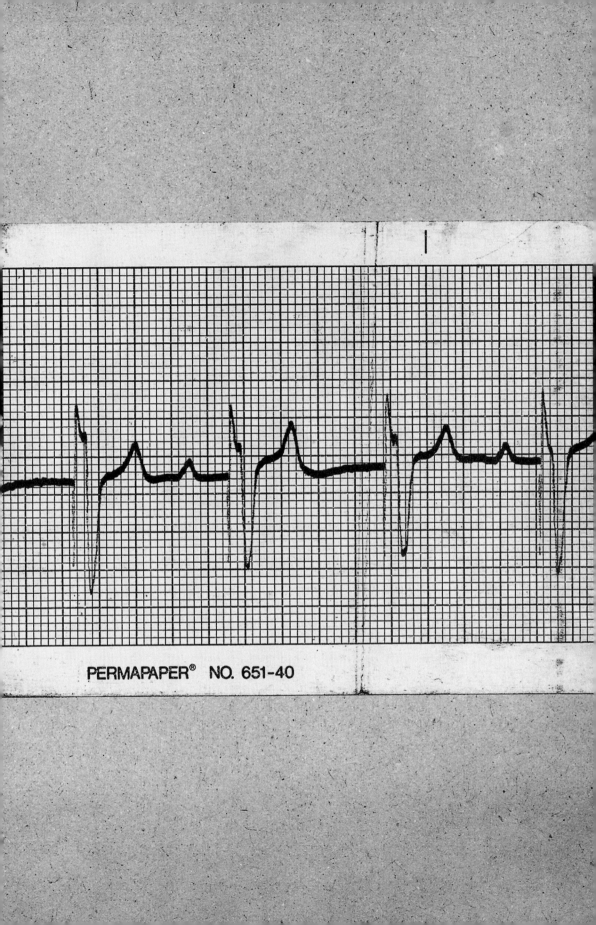

PERMAPAPER® NO. 651-40

Section I

Essays

A Decade of Forced Entertainment

Created to mark our 10th anniversary *A Decade of Forced Entertainment* is a speculative history of the company, a collage of fragments of previous works and a meditation on the place and processes of new performance. It was first performed on 3 December 1994: the six of us sat at a pair of long tables facing the audience in the ICA theatre, with a continuous cycle of Hugo Glendinning's images of the work and of Sheffield (and of a series of specially prepared maps of the UK bearing slogans) on three projection screens behind us.

The programme note described the work as 'part autobiography, part archive, part historical meditation and part theoretical speculation — a look back on ten years of the company's work and on ten years of change in the British urban culture from which it has sprung'.

Part One

Hans: Mike, Dolores, tell us a bit about the act.

Mike: Well, we did a thing quite a while ago now, it was a love show and everyone on the stage drank down a love potion that er, sent them all off to sleep and when they all woke up again they were all in love and no one felt sad.

Hans: I see.

Mike: Well, that's not the kind of work we want to do anymore.

(*Some Confusions in the Law about Love*, 1989)

Terry: We wanted to look back on the decade 1984–1994 — the ten years in which we've been making our work, and we knew that this looking back would have to include the things that hadn't happened as readily as those that had. We had in mind a map of the last ten years — a haunted map — a false map — and yet, in some ways, an accurate map.

And at some point we realised that this map-making, this charting of a time and a landscape, was what our work had often consisted of. A kind of mapping, a kind of temperature-taking.

Tim: 10 years of Forced Entertainment is 10 years finding notes in the street. When we first got to Sheffield we didn't know anyone — so the first months were very voyeuristic — months spent watching, trying to pick up the patterns of the place. In this time, above all others, we found notes and photographs in the street.

There was a note to a woman at a bus stop — along the lines of 'I see you every day but will never dare speak to you ...'. There was a letter from someone in prison, that had been torn into pieces as small as confetti but which were reassembled by us on the formica-topped table at 388 City Road.

All through the winter we found things. There was a photograph of the ground beside a Mediterranean swimming pool, there was page ripped out of a kid's cowboy book which had been vandalised so that where it once said 'Tex gunned the man down ...' it now said 'Tex bummed the man ...'.

There were discarded photographs, there were incomprehensible shopping lists, there was a note I found near the high-rise flats which said 'DAVE — I HAD TO GET OUT — THE GAS IS CUT OFF AND THE TV HAS GONE BAD — BACK THURSDAY'.

There was a map, showing how to get to the motorway.

Cathy: Working on *Nighthawks* (1985) we wanted to make a far-away country called America in the Movies — we were determined that nothing in the performance should be recognisably British. So, following this peculiar logic we made regular visits to the Chinese take-away on London Road to collect their old Chinese newspapers, which were thrown around on-stage. For the same show we made trips out to Manor Top Industrial Estate to pick up soda siphons; we caught the bus to Killamarsh to try and find three identical bar stools, we collected obscure liquor bottles from shit night-clubs all over town. Getting to know the city through trying to find a ramshackle collection of props and set.

> Unfortunately one day when we were driving a Cornflakes truck hit us doing 93. And I remember thinking how quiet the whole world seemed and still and wondering if you blacked out before you hit the windscreen.
>
> We died in the accident of course. I lost control of my bladder before we hit the Kellogg's truck so I didn't mind: my best suit was ruined anyway.

((Let the Water Run its Course) to the Sea that Made the Promise, 1986)

Claire: They drew a map of the country and marked on it the events of the last 10 years — the sites of political and industrial conflict, the ecological disasters, the showbiz marriages and celebrity divorces. On the same map they marked the events of their own lives — the performances they'd given, the towns and cities where they'd stayed, the sites of injuries and fallings in or out of love.

They drew a map of the country and marked on it the events of the previous 300, then 400, then 500 years. They kept on going until the beginnings of geological time. Until the map was scribbled over a thousand times — utterly black.

They knew something strange had happened to time. They drew a map of the country and marked on it events from the rest of the world. On this map the Challenger Space Shuttle had blown up in Manchester 1985. The Union Carbide Bophal Chemical Works which exploded late in 1984 was located in Kent. The siege of the Russian Parliament Building in 1991 had taken place in

Liverpool. The Democratic Party's recent set-backs in the mid-term elections had been most severe in the Isle of Dogs. The 1989 fatwa on Salman Rushdie had been issued from Tunbridge Wells.

> After the Kellogg's truck hit us and killed us we went to the hospital. There we were put in the capable hands of Dr Lyver who had plenty of money.
>
> Seeing as how we were dead they put sort of plastic taps in our arms and drained all the red sort of blood out of us into a sort of bucket. Then they got lots of other blood and pumped it into us through all possible entrances.
>
> This new blood they put in us was stuff they'd collected here and there from other people. The blood it mixed together all these people's blood and thoughts and everything and this was our biggest problem you see: because the blood moved inside us, changing and turning: one person then another, we dint know who the fuck shit piss we were, we'd say one thing then another, stand up, sit down, the blood moved, we didn't know.

((*Let the Water Run its Course) to the Sea that Made the Promise*, 1986)

Tim: We'd like two silences now. First one minute's silence for Steve Rogers — Steve was editor of *Performance* magazine in the mid-80s and was very important to us and the whole sector of live art and experimental performance here in the UK by way of energy and criticism and constant encouragement. Steve died, along with his partner Mark, of AIDS-related illnesses in 1988. One minute's silence please, for Steve and Mark.

And a minute's silence for Ron Vawter, who died in 1994, also of AIDS-related illnesses. Ron was a performer with The Wooster Group, and his performances, his energy and openness inspired all of us here.

> A: Howl! Howl! Wake it up poor dead person for we are upset and grieving angels.

> B: Oh we are distressed and sorrowful angels!

> A: And we have lamented of all and weighty things.

> B: We have wept on drinking and eternity and of dreams etc.

> A: We have cried for loving and of souls and of death.

> B: But we have never grieved as much as this before.

> A: Wake it up and think all hard of this … If you don't to get up who will shout and sing songs at the stupid moon?

> B: Who will to live in then your idiot house?

> A: Who will bang its walls and blood and bruise its stairs?

B: O we are drunk and dependable angels and we can to raise our friends from out the dead.

A: When we to say of now you will jump and rise and live again.

A&B: 1.2.3. Now!

(*200% & Bloody Thirsty*, 1988)

Part Two

Terry: We made work for 10 years in a country with a Conservative government. None of us ever voted in a general election that returned anything other than a Conservative government.

As things changed, the maps we made of the country had to be redrawn.

Richard: We noticed big changes to the country but could never date them precisely. When did the streets fill up with beggars? When did the great programmes of building, rebuilding and demolition begin? When exactly did the shopping malls and the 10-screen cinemas arrive? When did our city get its lift shaped like a rocket? From the day these places opened it seemed like they'd always been there.

As time went on we got more and more sure that the work should look thrown together — chaotic, out of control, unintended — so that, perhaps, when it did pull something out of the bag, one simply wasn't prepared. The chaos of the work was always running to catch up with the chaos and confusion of the times it came out of.

We admired the title of a Cady Nolan sculpture — a pile of aluminium baskets, mace canisters, and back issues of the magazine *Guns & Ammo* — she called it: *Bloody Mess*.

We liked that feeling that events on-stage were simply falling into place, that meaning was always an accident, although of course it rarely was.

Claire: Everything they seemed to use was brutal in some way. The materials were heavy steel, often rusted — the structures looked like buildings under construction, or buildings stripped of the walls. They used dirty untreated plywood, cardboard for writing on, cardboard to cover the floor. There was always the unreal beauty of electric light, the shabby mess of polythene and jumble-sale clothes.

In 1989 we made a show, not about Elvis Presley but about an Elvis Presley impersonator in Birmingham, England. We didn't want anything authentic, we wanted a third-rate copy — we loved that more dearly than anything original.

Robin: They were interested in the margins of life, never the centre. They tried not to talk about the people who made decisions but about those people who were affected by decisions made in other times and other places. They were provincial, by choice and by accident.

Is it true that the more desperate and depressed a city becomes the more exotic the names of its night-clubs and amusement arcades become? They thought so. Through the 80s and into the 90s the city they lived in had a bar called MILLION-AIRES and a casino called BONAPARTES — one night they heard a drunk boasting how he once paid five pounds for a sandwich in BONAPARTES — he thought it was great. They drew a map of the country and marked on it the amusement hall called GOLD RUSH, the discount shop called BARGAIN WORLD.

Terry: Is it true that the only way to see Britain properly is to see it drunk? They thought so. There were drunks in all of the shows, often drunks who were also dead.

Walking in the city they'd use an almost conscious confusion. What were they trying to solve — the latest show or the city itself? Eating pizza after late-night rehearsals they'd see a riotous hen party — a woman dancing on the table and pulling her tights off as she danced. They'd discover a blind man negotiating his way through the tangle of builders' scaffolding near their rehearsal space on the Wicker — the city's most notorious has-been street. They'd ask why aren't these things represented in the show? How could a map of the country include these things? Why isn't the texture of the show as desperate and gaudy and vital as these things? They laughed when the blind man told them (1) he'd just been to the match and (2) he was utterly pissed.

Tim: Beyond the city itself lay an alternative city too — not the one of night-clubs and blues clubs, but one of craters and broken ground. It seemed that during the Second World War the city lights had been blacked out and a decoy metropolis created in the hills using searchlights and halogen floods. So the hills took the pounding for the city and the Germans bombed the grass, stone and moor land into burning mud. So the city always had its twin — an empty space waiting for them to fill it.

Much of the rest of the city was empty anyway. Walking around in 1984 and 1985 you'd never seen so many disused factories and fields of rubble. Often on Sundays, in those days, they'd walk, exploring the city and these empty buildings; places still littered with time sheets and newspapers. Was it in one of these places that they saw the graffiti DOWN WITH CHILDHOOD and RAPE A TART TONIGHT?

> The night the rain stopped was wild and cold and full of strange noises and we did magic acts and were scared for each other and ourselves. We practised CLOSING BOTH EYES TIGHT WHILST DRIVING DOWN A ROAD, we practised EXHIBITION OF DUST. We practised HAUNTED GOLF. We worked on YOU'RE GOING HOME IN A FUCKING AMBULANCE.
>
> This is the life that we lived then, in the city, in the chaos and the dark …

(*Emanuelle Enchanted*, 1992)

Richard: They drew a map of the country and marked on it the locations for a hundred fictional events—here the house in which gangster James Fox goes into hiding in Nick Roeg and Donald Cammell's film *Performance*; here the wind-blown meadow from Tarkovsky's film *Mirror*; here the crack house from Victor Headley's novel *Yardie*; here the Mexican town rebuilt by a film crew as a Wild West town in Dennis Hopper's *The Last Movie*; here the New Rose Hotel from William Gibson's story of the same name.

They drew a map of the country and marked it with the street names they'd collected over years, some real, some from fiction, some dreamed up just because they sounded good. They marked on the map ESPERANTO PLACE, OCCUPATION AVENUE, METEORITE STREET and ALPHABET ROAD.

Claire: Was it really in the 80s that the naming of things became so wonderfully and inventively blunt? It seemed like it. They drew a map of the country and marked on it MR BUYRITE. Hi-Fi WORLD and BARGAIN LAND. They even saw a street somewhere called CAR PARK WAY. They marked this street on the map. At the end of this line lies I CAN'T BELIEVE THAT'S NOT BUTTER and a beer called THIS BEER IS THE BEST BEER I'VE EVER DRUNK IN MY WHOLE LIFE I SWEAR TO GOD. After the seductive power of ambiguous images it all comes back to hard sell. They marked on the map a bar they'd seen in Zurich (1988)—THE EVERYTHING A MAN COULD WANT BAR.

They drew a map of the country and marked on it roads named after Scargill, after Mellor and de Sanchez, after Reagan, North and Yeltsin. They marked roads named after Rodney King, after Arnold Schwarzenegger, after the Birmingham Six and the Guilford Four, they marked roads named after Diego Maradonna and Eric Morecambe. They marked a public park named after Nicolae Ceaucescu, and another named after Edwina Currie. They named a public square after the Russian cosmonauts who'd been circling the earth during the *coup*, unable to return and uncertain of what they'd come back to. They named bridges for deposed presidents, for kids on job-creation schemes and for the glue sniffers who'd graffitied on an abandoned house near where they lived, in big letters, a sign saying DAVE'S GLUE CLUB—EVERYONE WELCOME.

On the map they marked museums for love and drunkenness, museums for rioters, accidents, happenstance and luck.

Richard: On the map they marked the questions from a decade of end of year quizzes.

In what year did the European Single Market begin?

Who said and in what year 'I am Jesus Christ and I announce the end of the world'?

Did David Alton's Abortion Bill to cut the maximum age of the foetus to 18 weeks win or lose in the House of Commons?

Who said and in what year 'I am Jesus Christ and I announce the end of the world'?

Which won the Oscar as Best Film in 1987 — *Platoon, Hannah and Her Sisters, The Mission* or *A Room With A View*?

In which year did Rupert Murdoch move four newspapers into Wapping?

Who said 'We had a wonderful day ...'?
Was it:
(a) Class War after the Poll Tax Riots in 1990?
(b) Sir Geoffrey Howe after 152 Tory MPs voted Margaret Thatcher from the leadership position?
(c) Brian Keenan after his release in Damascus?

Gilbert, Joan and Ruby were lethal in 1988 — what were they?

Who said 'The master of the country has spoken'?
Was it:
(a) Gennady Gerasimov, announcing Moscow's rejection of separatist claims by the Baltic republics?
(b) Mikhail Gorbachov after the electorate voted for a new Soviet Assembly?
(c) Polish Premier Tadeusz Mazowieki, after an audience with Lech Walesa?
(d) Deng Xiaoping after the Tiananmen Square massacre?

In what way did Willie Horton affect the US election?

Who put out the flames of Piper Alpha?

Part Three

Cathy: At the start of the shows they'd lay bare the means they had at their disposal like a bunch of crap magicians keen to prove they had nothing up their sleeves. As if to say you can't believe this ridiculous pretending and yet against your better judgement you will believe in its outcome.

They told you so many times they weren't acting that when they did act they hoped you'd think it real. And on a good night that's what happened. They believed that suspension of disbelief was something you worked for, not took for granted.

They said they had faith in cities — even when all the evidence was against them. They believed that the architecture of the twentieth century worked best at night, with all the lights on.

They said they liked the media culture, the cargo cult of TV and movie

detritus, but perhaps it would be truer to say that that was the world in which they found themselves, and so, like everyone else, they did their best to make sense of it all.

Robin: They pretended to be dead. They pretended to be Elvis. They pretended to be drunk. They pretended to be angels. They pretended to be devils. They pretended to be cowboys. They pretended to be kung-fu fighters. They pretended to be opera singers. They pretended to be Lee Harvey Oswald. They pretended to be Marina Oswald. They pretended to be guilty. They pretended to be innocent. They pretended to be Mary, Joseph and the Angel Gabriel. They pretended to be lovers. They pretended to take drugs. They pretended to be foreign. They pretended to be stupid. They pretended to be clever. They pretended to be lost in the woods. They pretended to be cosmonauts. They pretended to be widows. They pretended to tell lies, they pretended to tell the truth. And often they pretended to be themselves.

Terry: Trying to think about the last 10 years we wanted to track both the real 10 years and the fictional one moving through it.

One day during rehearsals for *Marina & Lee* (1991) in a freezing cold abandoned school we plan to eat in the warm of the Meadowhall Shopping Centre and to talk about the show as we do.

By some unlucky chance it is Red Nose Day and Meadowhall is seething with fun-loving bastards dressed up to shake a bucket for a good cause. We try to eat at the Food Court—a Disney-esque Spanish village housing a feast of fast food from all over the world.

As we eat I notice that Mark and Robin are still wearing their Dixon's sales assistant costumes from the show. Claire's crude drawn-on beard is only half washed off. A plastic penis hangs between her legs. No one notices these anomalies, least of all the many shoppers.

In the noise and the crowds no one can concentrate and soon we're eating in silence, listening to the Red Nose Day fun quiz for which a line of pre-adolescents kids have been lined up on a crude stage, their images relayed to a video-wall above. A Simon Mayo lookalike is asking questions and explaining rules—three wrong answers and they get dumped in a bath full of gunk and green slime.

The first kid starts answering questions that cover a bizarre mix of soap trivia and political factoids—under bright lights he falters, loses what little confidence he ever had and is soon dispatched to the foul-looking gunk.

Claire: They thought a lot about the soaps. Before the cold war really ended they used to wonder how the soaps would respond to a 'limited nuclear war' in Europe. Would they carry on regardless with a fantasy of life as it used to be lived or would they improvise quickly—switching scenes to fallout bunkers and heavily policed supermarkets?

Years later they wanted to organise an exchange scheme between the world's soaps—so that characters from *Brookside* would go on holiday to *Beverley Hills 905120* or that someone from *Coronation Street* would go to London and end up running the Vic. They hoped to turn the soaps into one enormous interconnected meta-soap.

They wished they'd been given a contract to write the last two weeks of the failed British soap *Eldorado*. They'd had a number of scenarios they'd wanted to pursue.

Tim: Trying to map the last 10 years we found more than ever that our memories of things were utterly bound up with the TV news. In the miners' strike (1984/5) we had the weird experience of seeing things live in Sheffield and then seeing them reported later in the day. The reports always seemed more real.

From the Gulf War (summer 1990) I remember several times getting up in the middle of the night to go for a piss and turning on the TV to see what was happening—mesmerised by the quality of those news programmes where there is no news at all but where they have to stay on air anyway and keep talking.

One night I saw a report based on a French cable television report based on a freelance journalist's story based on unconfirmed sources that an American F1-11 had been forced down by Iraqi fighters. And through the night this story obviously flipped and changed—moving from one station to another round the world like a Chinese whisper. But in the morning when I woke and checked the news again to hear the latest, there was no trace of that captured American F1-11 at all. Not on the breakfast news, not in the papers, not on the radio.

That captured F1-11 is still captured, still not captured, still circling over the desert of plastic flowers in the Gulf and in *Marina & Lee*, the piece of work we made that summer, still waiting to drop it's payload, still captured. And on the radio, late night, if you scan between channels and wait patiently you can still hear reports of that F1-11 now…

> I'm coming to the edges of a town. This must be Big Town that I read so much about. Like Claudia Cardinale in that sex film LOVE A LITTLE, DRINK A LOT I'm living on bravely after an unfortunate accident, frightened of the future, a bit bored of the present and unable to remember the past.
>
> Leaves fall from the advertisements for trees. I'll just go over and put the microphone outside the hotel window so you can hear what these explosions sound like…
>
> BANG!
>
> Boy. That was loud one. My head's starting to spin. If I can't sleep I make up different kinds of time, like counting sheep. There's black time when you're feeling sad, no, that's blue time and there's red time when you're angry or cold. There's soft time, and long time and thin time too. I have to walk quickly cos the continents are drifting apart.

(*Marina & Lee*, 1991)

Robin: There was something about the way things got used and re-used, the way things moved in and out of the work. So much of the work had this complex interior history, where a single line of text in one show would become a title or even a whole character several years later. Best of all perhaps was how a savage review of *200% & Bloody Thirsty* (1987) in the *Independent* provided the end lines for *Marina & Lee*, five years after the fact. The review said: 'The whole performance is wholly out of control … there is little to enjoy here and much to regret …'

Richard: In 1988 we took some dead trees from Ecclesall Woods to use in the performance *200% & Bloody Thirsty* — not so much trees as 14-foot branches. Three of us with saws while a group of school kids on a nature trip chanted 'Ecclesall Woods, Ecclesall Woods, we've got conkers, we've got conkers'.

And then years later (1993) we used the same trees in *Club Of No Regrets* (1993) — gaffer-taping them to the scaffolding structure at the side of the stage.

In two shows those trees toured extensively in Britain and to Italy, Germany, Poland, Belgium and Holland.

And then this summer we took them to Italy for a second time as we did *Club Of No Regrets* in Italian for its final performances. And after the last performance — outside on a hillside in Tuscany (July 1994) — we left the trees at the edge of a forest. Miles from home we left them — these objects that are art for a while then get put back in the world.

> Oggi sono turbata, molto turbata, ho smesso di parlare, ho smesso di camminare. Sono turbata da delle voci. Mi affido alla Nostra Signora dei Parcheggi perché mi aiuti. Che venga a me, che mi aiuti a liberarmi da queste catene.
>
> Principe delle Bugie Scoperte e delle Promesse Non Mantenute, vengo a te vestita di stracci per incontrarti. Regina del Nulla, amante dell'aria e dei satelliti, non ti abbiamo più visto, è passato molto tempo dall'ultima volta che ti abbiamo visto. Oh, non vedi che sono senza pelle e senza ossa. Vengo a te vestita di stracci solo per incontrarti.

(*Club of No Regrets*, 1994)

Part Four

Richard: They had this idea to kill all the first-born children of English greengrocers to avoid any unfortunate recurrences of the last 10 years. Like many others they made a lot of money running 0898 sex lines. They had one line where the girls just laughed all the time. If you paid extra they'd call you back

and laugh at you live. They gave away T-shirts to beggars with the slogan DON'T GIVE ME MONEY I'M JUST A FUCKING EYESORE. They gave away free condoms with every pint of HIV-positive blood. They knew the pubs on the Wicker did much better business after care in the community. One pub had a 40s, 50s, 60s, 70s, 80s night—every night.

They knew something strange had happened to time. How else to explain the fact that Sheffield was busy investing in trams? How else to explain the population of Leningrad voting in June 1991 to change the citiy's name back to its original St Petersburg? How else to explain the way Europe looked more and more like old maps than recent ones? It was all Victorian family values, back to the 70s, back to basics, back to square one. Hadn't Bush said he was going to make the country a lot less like *The Simpsons* and a lot more like *The Waltons*?

Cathy: We knew something strange had happened to time. At night we lay in bed and waited for the Zeppelin raids to start again. And every time we heard the word 'history' we felt sick. And everyone said time didn't matter any more —and distance didn't matter any more—everything was immediate everything was NOW. We had no argument with this. After *The Rock 'n' Roll Years* it was difficult to remember anything unless it had a medley of pop songs and captions slapped over the top of it. Wasn't that a slogan for Kodak—GOOD QUALITY MEMORIES AT A PRICE YOU CAN AFFORD?

Robin: Maybe their real memories were written in the skin—on Richard a burst eardrum he received when Cathy hit him during a performance of *(Let the Water Run its Course) to the Sea that Made the Promise* in 1987 and a scar on his leg from where he broke it playing rounders in the park, summer 1990, thus invaliding himself out of *Marina & Lee* and onto video. On Tim a small blister-shaped scar that had appeared on his wrist when someone had hypnotised him into believing that a piece of paper would burn him on contact with his skin, and a scar on his left shoulder where his pacemaker is—a scar renewed every four years or so in the Northern General Hospital, Sheffield.

Tim: They preferred always to talk about another country, another place, finding screens and veils and stories, finding other worlds.

Was it really true that the only way to see Britain properly was to see it drunk? They thought so. There were drunks in all of the shows, often drunks who were also dead. One night (in 1990 or perhaps 1991) they filmed themselves getting very very drunk. We wore cardboard crowns and tried to propose toasts like we had when touring in Poland. It was impossible. Towards the end of the evening a competition started to see who could make themselves cry. Claire and Cathy had chopped onions in half and were rubbing them directly into their eyes. Nick Crowe from Index Theatre in Manchester was there and his face was half paralysed with a Bells Palsy which had erased all the lines on one side of his face, turning one side of his face into the face of a child — a face without any marks or lines or history. They knew something was wrong with time. Claire was pushing these onions into her eyes and trying to cry and trying to tell a story about Shirley Temple who had been asked to cry in a scene by a certain director and she'd looked at him and said, 'Which eye do you want? Which eye do you want me to cry out of?'

That night we dreamed all the bad dreams of the decade. No one slept too well.

Richard: What was the question people asked most about the work?

Terry: Er, whether it was optimistic or not.

Richard: And what was the answer they got most often?

Terry: We used to say the work was optimistic.

Richard: In what way?

Terry: We said there was an optimism in the struggle of it — an optimism in the way the on-stage protagonists used and re-used the material they'd been left with.

Richard: How was that optimistic?

Terry: In a way we marvelled at their ability to cope — to change things, to deal with them, to make things their own.

Richard: So this optimism was just a kind of coping?

Terry: Yes.

Richard: Did people believe this idea — that the work was optimistic?

Terry: Not always, no.

Richard: Why not?

Terry: The optimism seemed remote.

Richard: Why?

Terry: The victories won by the performers, or characters were often private, and delicate. And the victories were never total — there was always doubt, irony, a kind of melancholy.

Richard: So the work was doubtful, ironic and melancholy but somehow optimistic?

Terry: Yes.

Richard: How can those things together?

Terry: They go together in the work.

Richard: Is the work optimistic?

Terry: Yes, but only … sometimes.

Richard: It's only sometimes optimistic?

Terry: Yes. There are times when it's very sure — about people's power to change themselves, their power to re-see themselves and the rest of the other world. There are times when it's very sure about people's ability to take what they will from the scrap heap of culture that they're born into and to use it. They transform things.

Richard: This transformation happens sometimes?

Terry: Yes.

Richard: Can you say something about the rest of the time?

Terry: The rest of the time this transformation escapes the 'characters'.

Richard: What happens?

Terry: Then there's a kind of rage in the work.

Richard: What do you mean by that?

Terry: Then the people in it are bashing against the edges of the world they're born into, bashing on the edges of the language that they have. There's a frustration.

Richard: Why would you make live work in an age of mass communications? Why work in more or less the only field which still insists on presence? For artists interested in 'the contemporary', this area of live performance seems like a bit of a backwater. Do you have something against mass reproduction? Do you work from some quaint notion about immediacy and real presence?

Terry: I don't know.

Richard: Answer the question.

Terry: I don't know.

Richard: Is the work optimistic?

Terry: Yes.

Richard: Is it getting more optimistic?

Terry: No. It's getting bleaker.

Richard: Why?

Terry: Irony doesn't seem like a solution anymore.

Richard: Did it ever?

Terry: I'm not sure that it did. But it doesn't seem viable now.

Richard: Why not?

Terry: We're getting older.

Richard: What's that got to do with it?

Terry: There are times for being light, and times when it's less easy to do that.

Richard: This change, this change in tone you're talking about, we'd like to know more about it.

Terry: It's more a shift than a change.

Richard: Where does it come from?

Terry: I don't know.

Richard: Do you believe that the work changes people — changes their lives?

Terry: Yes.

Richard: Do you think the work is optimistic?

Terry: Yes.

Richard: Even when it's bleak?

Terry: Yes.

Richard: Why do you think that?

Terry: It opens a space which people fill.

Richard: So the optimism is more an absence than anything else — the optimism lies in the viewers experience?

Terry: I don't know.

Richard: Answer the question. People are waiting. [*pause*] The optimism you were speaking of is more of an absence than anything else — a space that people are left to fill?

Terry: Yes.

Claire: They knew something strange had happened to time. Bush and Reagan were drunk at the bar. They drew a map of the country and added nothing to it. They drew a map of the country and marked on it which bits of the country-side belonged to which armies, to which rebels, to which forces and alliances.

They drew a map of the country and marked on it which roads were safe, which places one could sleep in without fear for one's life. They marked on the map which cities were still functioning and who lived in them. They marked on the map the places where the phone system was still operating. We drew a map of the country and tried to mark on it the places where one could still fall in love, the places where one could still believe in something. They looked at the map and asked: 'Would this be a good place to raise a kid?' 'Would this be a good place for a party?'

On Risk and Investment

On Risk and Investment was written in May 1994 as a kind of public provocation, in response to an invitation from Alan Read, who was then head of the Talks Department at the ICA. He asked for a manifesto piece to be shared during Barclay's New Stages in a season of talks called 'The Seven Ages Of Performance' — a statement that might spur a discussion on an issue of concern in contemporary performance. I tried my best and wrote something that talked about risk and investment — the demand that performers and artists should be 'on the line' in what they do. The piece was recorded on video since I couldn't be at the ICA event, and I remember that in performing it I managed to hit a strident manifesto-like tone for the most of it, but couldn't help a smile at the end.

Investment is what happens when the performers before us seem bound up unspeakably with what they're doing — it seems to matter to them, it appears to hurt them or threatens to pleasure them, it seems to touch them, in some quiet and terrible way. Investment is the bottom line — without it nothing matters, and we don't see half enough of it. At a recent event I attended someone asked a performer what was going on in a certain part of the piece he'd been in — the performer replied, 'I don't know about that, ask the writer ... '. That answer simply shouldn't be allowed.

Investment is the line of connection between performer and their text or their task. When it works it is private, and often on the very edge of words. Like all the best performance it is before us, but not for us.

This privacy of investment doesn't make a solipsistic work or a brick wall to shut the watchers out. Quite the opposite — investment draws us in. Something is happening — real and therefore risked — something seems to slip across from the private world to the public one — and the performers are 'left open' or 'left exposed'.

To be bound up with what you are doing, to be at risk in it, to be exposed by it. As performers we recognise but cannot always control these moments — they happen, perhaps, in spite of us.

Investment is slippery and evasive and it isn't often found where we'd expect it — personally I have no big regrets about that. Actors flying into passions, dancers hurling themselves to the ground, performers bravely taking stances on large issues or themes. All these are the sites for many embarrassments — embarrassments in which the public declamation of a big idea is not properly matched by a private investment. I ask: 'Are you bound up with this?' 'Or is it the shape of a passion and the noise of a politics?' 'Are you at risk in this?' That's *all* I want to know.

A student I taught in Leicester used to tell stories in my performance classes and they were inane and rambling, and they were of no consequence, and she was at risk in every one of them. Risk implicates me, I say 'I'm bound up with this too'. Politics came off of her stories without a hint of intention. And there are some people who can simply sit in a space or stand quite still in it and still be at risk, 'left open', leaving me open too. In the complicity of the performers with their task lies our own complicity — we are watching the people before us, not representing something but going through something. They lay their bodies on the line … and we are transformed — not audience to a spectacle but witnesses to an event.

Risk and investment in the strangest places, slipping and hiding. Risk is the thing we are striving for in the performance but not a thing we can look for. We look for something else and hope (or pray to the gods we don't believe in) that risk shows up. We know it when we see it, I'm sure of that. Risk surprises us, always fleeting — we're slightly out of control. Investment drives all types of live work — the formal and the content-full, the cabaret and the high cultural — laying waste to all distinctions. I don't care where we see it, but it's all too rare and it's the only thing we should care about.

Investment links to passion, politics and rage. It slips out in laughter, numbness, silence. Investment happens when we're hitting new ground, when we don't quite know, where we can't quite say, where we feel compromised, complicit, bound up, without recourse to an easy position. This is not the place for respectable or soap-box certainties — only live issues will do. Investment wants us naked, with slips and weaknesses, with the not-yet and never-to-be certain, with all that's in process, in flux, with all that isn't finished, with all that's unclear and therefore *needs to be worked out*. Don't give me anything less than this. Don't give me a truth that's more fixed, i.e., more of a stupid lie.

Investment comes when we're beaten so complex and so personal that we move beyond rhetorics into events.

Investment forces us to know that performative actions have real consequence beyond the performance arena. That when we do these unreal things in rooms, galleries and theatre spaces the real world will change. To me that's the greatest ambition and the truth of cultural practice — things can change, things can slip, things can move, because they're pushed (deliberately), because they're knocked, by accident. All that has to happen is that the direct lines of investment get drawn — between performers and task, between witnesses and performers.

Thinking of investment we ask: when this performance finishes will it matter? Where will it matter? Will the performer carry this with them tomorrow? In their sleep? In their psyche? Does this action, this performance, contain these people (and me) in some strange and perhaps unspeakable way?

I ask of each performance: will I carry this event with me tomorrow? Will it haunt me? Will it change you, will it change me, will it change things?

If not it was a waste of time.

Play On: Collaboration and Process

This piece was written for and first presented at a seminar on play and performance in Leuven, Belgium in January 1998. The considerably expanded version here makes use of material I presented in Wolverhampton during a paper I gave there in 1995 on creative process and collaboration. The essay is a fragmented, speculative account of our own process, an anatomy of collaboration and an investigation of the role of play itself as a force of transformation, subversion and resistance.

A Warning

It is almost inevitable that in trying to write about play, I will write very often about death.

A memory. I saw a performance by a colleague of ours.* She'd been collaborating with someone, a friend of hers, he'd been ill when they started—HIV—but after they showed the work some times in public he got very ill. He was in hospital and she used to go and work with him there—they taped a lot of stuff on video—he clearly wasn't going to get out again—they figured he could be in the piece, you know, on video. So by the time I saw the performance the guy was dead already. Not long dead—a month, probably, maybe even less. And F was trying to show the work in public for the first time since he died and she was dealing with her grief in the piece and it showed and someone said to me that really she should have been home in bed. It was brave and fucked-up. It was raw and sometimes it didn't make much sense. And it might even have been embarrassing except that death and loss hung over the piece so strongly you could never exactly dismiss it.

Anyway. One thing about it that really held a charge was the video material of the guy acting from his hospital bed. In these scenes he was dressed in some frivolous cape or costume, gesturing faintly, laughing, or he was moving round the hospital room, making some great long speech from the text, an IV drip on a wheeled trolley thing plugged into his arm, a cheap plastic crown on his head and a wooden sword in his other hand, his arm as thin as death. It was absurd. A background of medical machines. I can't tell you how beautiful that was. To see him so obviously close to dying and yet still committed to the act of pretending—to see him playing—to see him acting—to see him give life to some fictional part of himself—in the ruins of his body. I admired that—it was funny and a bit scary—I think I liked it because it was resistant—I liked it that even as the real world of biology and material facts were catching up with him fast this person wasn't paying much heed—he was playing, changing the world in this (I want to say frivolous) way. But I don't mean frivolous.

Note

* *Recognition*, Fiona Templeton, 1994.

My love —

It's not frivolous to challenge the hard logic of biology or material facts with the soft and mutable logics of play — play with its transformations, its power reversals, its illogics, its joys, its potential escapes ...

It's not frivolous to think that even as we die we're creatures of fiction and pretending, that we're not simply 'facts' or biology, that we may not be contained by either. I don't think it is frivolous to insist that, even as one dies, one is multiple, playful, partial, strategic and indeed fictional.

I learned that from F, and from M, if I didn't know it already.

Shopping

My son Miles (aged 4 at the time) is loading the bath with more and more ridiculous plastic items, dropping them into the water and on top of me — blue ducks, yellow guns, giant clocks, alligators, wind-up fish — asking 'do you want some more toys dad?'

An adult body, surrounded by the props and objects of children's play.

These last few years are those in which the bedroom has half-filled with strange animals and plastic figures, in which most of the stories I have read feature talking mice and animate trees and in which our late-night motorway journeys are soundtracked by the delights of 'Heads, Shoulders, Knees and Toes'.

Years in which the rehearsal studio has come more and more to resemble Miles's room — a playhouse: balloons, large inflatable hammers all from *Showtime* (1996) rehearsals, costumes for dressing up — as trees, as gorillas, as a horse, as a ghost, as a dog, as a thief ...

Miles wanted to know if there was a shop you could go to if you were frightened of dying. He was scared to die and just wanted to know.

Process (1)

They had this unspoken agreement that no one would bring anything too completed to the process — a few scraps or fragments of text, an idea or two for action, a costume, an idea about space, a sketched-out piece of music — everything unfinished, distinctly incomplete — so there'd be more spaces for other things to fill in ... more dots to join.

They talked about the way that half-demolished or half-built houses were the best places to play ... so much incompletion in the spaces, so much work (imaginative, playful, transformative) to be done. They liked this kind of mental space for themselves to work in, and they liked to leave some of it for the public too.

The process they used was chaotic, exploratory, blundering. A question of going into the rehearsal room and waiting for something to happen. Waiting for something that amused, scared, hurt, provoked or reduced one to hilarity.

A starting-point could be anything—a record, a second-hand suit of a particular kind, a list of different kinds of silence, two imaginary scenes from a soap opera, a blackboard, the gesture of someone they had seen in the street, a hasty construction of a space in which to work—any of these things could be a major clue, alone, or in some unexpected combination. It was important that no one did their homework too well—that no element of the theatrical language might substantially precede any other—so that any element could lead.

For years they couldn't quite bring themselves to use the word 'improvising' —they'd call it messing about, having a bit of a run around in the space, playing around. In any case often the best of these 'improvisations' would start without anyone noticing—during lunch break perhaps when someone might get up and start messing about in the performance area—waving a gun maybe, trying out some text. Then someone else would join in and someone else, and someone else. Before long they'd be somewhere else too—pushing the material into unexpected territory. It seemed fitting that these good improvisations so often began in the blurred space between lunch break and performance, between the everyday and the fantastic.

Most recently they talked about 'trying to get themselves into trouble'. An antidote to the skills and strategies they'd built up, a way of avoiding their own conventions … getting into trouble was something you achieved by working too hard and too late, through exhaustion, confusion, delirium, drink and the rest of it, by sticking to the ridiculous randomness of the process—'getting into trouble', i.e., like pushing the work so you find yourselves in a territory beyond the one you know—by following a loose associative logic, by playing with no regard, in the first place, for sense.

'Nice Cop / Nasty Cop'

For a few days they'd play almost without thinking, doing, well, whatever came to mind. Improvisations (they finally got used to the word) were long and relatively unstructured. The mood would be, well, 'see what happens … '.

But after days of this the discoveries (or antics) of the week would be scrutinised. The video-tapes of improvisations would be played back and discussed, and a process of interrogating the material might begin. They'd ask the questions that were largely denied until this point: what is that doing there? What might that mean? What does this imply about structure? Would this work be sustainable as a 'show'? What is missing from it? What does it remind one of? … and they'd make demands of the material—for more sense (or less) for more joy (or less), for more pain (or less), for more intelligence (or less).

After a day or two of this kind of talk they'd go back to playing again. Forget what they'd just said. Or half forget about it. More days of play, more days of 'anything goes'.

Then back to questioning again.

This routine of nice cop / nasty cop, the tactic so beloved of interrogators the world over, kind of suited them too. It seemed a good way of teasing stuff from the unconscious and working it. But even playing nasty cop there was a certain lightness to the way they operated. To bring down a conceptual grid or frame onto what they were doing, but then to take it off again and replace it with another one. In this they were, at best, speculative and pragmatic. They had no dogma (or they tried to have none) — they were only interested in 'what worked' (what worked for them, in this place in history, culture and time). They tried not to get stuck in one logic — they tried to keep it moving, playful, nimble.

They talked about the difference between arriving at a decision and making a decision. The difference between coming to a decision and forcing one. They always preferred the former approaches — the meandering (with a strange certainty that you dare not trust) towards the things that they needed but could not name in advance.

The sign they lived by: 'You know it when you see it.'

1985

One night in the kitchen of the house where they lived on Langsett Road, one of them put his hands to his face and pretended to cry — a broken sobbing that was somehow very realistic. A couple of people were at the cooker — making dinner — they heard the noise and turned around, concerned — he sobbed a few more times, then took his hands down and smiled, soon they were all laughing.

After that there was always crying in the work, more or less — sometimes ludicrous cartoon-style weeping, sometimes soft and gentle sobs, sometimes foolish tears splashed out of water bottles.

Oh, and yes, there was quite often real crying in the kitchen too, and in bedrooms, and hotel rooms and in cars and in all of the other locations that God and capitalism saw fit to provide for the glorious movie of their lives.

Tears then. Between the real and the fictional.

Play (1)

Play as a state in which meaning is flux, in which possibility thrives, in which versions multiply in which the confines of what is real are blurred, buckled, broken. Play as endless transformation, transformation without end and never stillness. Would that be pure play?

Perhaps the closest they ever got to it was in *12am Awake & Looking Down* (1993).

There were five performers with a vast store of jumble-sale clothing and a pile of cardboard signs which bore the names of characters — real, imaginary, from fiction, from history — characters that came from the great crowd of some scrappy urban collective unconscious — a crowd containing FRANK (DRUNK),

THE EX-WIFE OF THE EX-PRESIDENT OF THE UNITED STATES, A BLOKE WHO'S JUST BEEN SHOT, A 9-YEAR-OLD SHEPHERD BOY, AN EU TRADE NEGOTIATOR, LEAH BETTS and A BOXER WITH A TORN RETINA.

By changing costumes and changing names the performers ventured endless possibilities for and of themselves, and the constant rearrangement of character, sings, costume and spatial positions worked like a narrative kaleidoscope — throwing up stories, potential stories, meetings, potential meetings, coincidences …

JACK RUBY crosses the stage his hands under his coat as AN AIR STEWARDESS FORGETTING HER DIVORCE sits crying, wrapped in a towel … THE HYPNOTISED GIRL stares into space as A YOUNG WHITE RACIST ELECTRICAL ENGINEER makes a hasty Fascist salute … ELVIS PRESLEY THE DEAD SINGER walks over the stage and AN ANGEL, SENT FROM HEAVEN TO THE EARTH stalks him, following … and at the sides of the stage there were always further performers changing costumes, choosing signs, watching the action for an opportunity or a space.

Richard Foreman speaks about his pieces as 'reverberation machines'. In the studio I would watch *12am* as a kind of endless coincidence machine — I would watch it for hours — unable to stop it somehow — always eager to see what it 'threw up' next, what they did next, what they thought of next … I was always gripped by the process of them playing — watching them think, watching them stuck, watching them try, watching them find … the world is constant invention, constant flux.

And there were times when I would look at it and think this is terrible — this is just the empty fragments of 2,000 stupid stories colliding with each other — there's no meaning in it, just the noise left in the machine of culture … and then FRANK (DRUNK) would take a curious look at BANQUO'S GHOST and meaning would happen, like electricity between two lovers who are kissing goodnight, car alarms ringing, and there'd be nothing I could do to stop that.

Between the meaningless and the very highly charged.

Collaboration (1)

Is collaboration this: the 12 years' endless proximity to other people, physical, vocal, all day and into the night, watching people fade in and out of coherence and concentration — an intimacy that approaches that of lovers who now no longer bother to close the bathroom door whilst shitting? We are in the rehearsal space at 2am still talking and arguing about how it works or doesn't work and X is asleep on the floor, face up, mouth open, arms by his side while the remainder of us talk. When he wakes we will joke a little and continue. Change the furniture, clothes, haircuts and this scene could be any time this past decade. A sharedness that doesn't have a name.

Or is collaboration this: a kind of complex game of consequences or Chinese whispers—a good way of confounding intentions?

If the process of direction in the theatre most usually has at its heart the interpretation of a text and the fixing of a set of meanings in it, the staging of one interpretation out of many possible ones—perhaps we had in mind something utterly different—of theatre or performance as a space in which different visions, different sensibilities, different intentions could collide.

In an unpublished essay John Ashford, now head of The Place Theatre, once called experimental theatre 'a compromised art ... a mucky, mutable, dirty, competitive, collaborative business', and we always liked the quote recognising in it the great mess of our own process but also appreciating the fine word compromise—no clean single visions in our work, no minimalist control freak authorial line—since by collaboration—impro, collage, the bringing together of diverse creativities—one gets an altogether messier world—of competing actions, approaches and intentions.

What does Elizabeth LeCompte say somewhere about her work with The Wooster Group—about her job being to build the frame around the performers' lives?

And once again: is collaboration just a good way of confounding intentions? I think so, and because I trust discoveries and accidents and I distrust intentions, I sit at the computer and I make a list of the misunderstandings and misrecognitions in our collaborative process, celebrating these above the instances of clear communication:

(1) I give instructions for impro to the performers but they are misheard —I have no idea what the people on-stage think they are doing—most of it is ridiculous but there is a moment that no one could have expected or predicted and it is wonderful.

(2) A performer tries something in impro but it is mis-seen or mis-recognised by the others on-stage—the others grab firmly on the wrong end of the stick and something brilliant happens.

(3) The composer mis-sees what we have done and writes music which we did not expect. I love it.

(4) I mis-see the performers—projecting onto them a narrative and intention which they do not have—for ages Terry is at the back of the space talking into the disconnected telephone as the impro continues around her. I have made up a whole story about who she is and what she is talking about but when the scene around her quietens down I can hear snatches of her talking and I am shocked to find that she is simply re-playing a conversation with an accountant or a bank manager that she had some 10 minutes earlier on the real phone in the office:

'Yes ... I can understand your position, but I don't accept that the delay is
my problem or my responsibility ... yes ... yes ... May 23rd ... no ... '

I stare at her — unable to admit for ages that I was so completely wrong, but
enjoying the revelation.

Collaboration then not as a kind of perfect understanding of the other
bloke, but a mis-seeing, a mis-hearing, a deliberate lack of unity. And this fact
of the collaborative process finding its echo in the work since on-stage what we
see is not all one thing either — but rather a collision of fragments that don't
quite belong, fragments that mis-see and mis-hear each other. A kind of pure
play in that too.

In *Hidden J* (1994) Richard as drunk git English bloke on his way back from
a wedding; Cathy and Rob as gibberish speakers from war zone broken Europe;
Claire sat at the front with this sign saying LIAR around her neck; Terry as
frivolous narrator who can't even decide what century all this happened in.
None of them in the same show really, or the same world, battling it out for
space and the right to speak or own what is happening — a piece of contradictory intentions, brutal fragmentation.

Collaboration for them then was never about perfect unity but about difference, collisions, incompatibilities.

Everybody Join In

A great rushing joy in the game of dying from our piece *(Let the Water Run its
Course) to the Sea that Made the Promise* (1986) — four players — two large bottles
of tomato ketchup for blood — and a soundtrack of bad American TV, cut up
and channel-hopping fast, the channel hops sound like gunshots ...

The contest is to see who can act out the best movie deaths — the deaths
getting ever more glorious, more bloody, more violent, more romantic — and
the glee of the game was always infectious — like everyone watching just
wanted to join in. There was a moment of hesitation for the performers — like,
'Do I really have to get that revolting stuff all over me again?' — but then
they'd bite the imaginary bullet, get the first spray or great dollop of ketchup
on them and then surrender sense, give in, abandon ... go all the way — throw
themselves into it, pure glee.

Everybody Pause

And then inside the game there would also be these moments of pause or
reflection.

When the players would take a look at each other and think about what
was happening. Thinking 'what if this were real?' or else 'what are we
really doing here?'

A flickering—between real time and play time—between the idea of action with no consequence and the fact of action that hurts.
And then back to the game again—doubled speed, gleeful commitment.

For them there were always these numerous semi-stops, hiccups, breaks in the flow of the performance, moments where one game stopped, broke, exploded, slipped into or behind another.

There were the kind of contemplative stops in *Let the Water...* where the players would cease their game for a moment and consider its consequences.

And there were the kind of strange interludes where people committed to one task for more or less a whole performance would give it up for a while and do something else.

All through *Showtime* Cathy pretended to be a dog—on her hands and knees in an old overcoat, with a ludicrous dog's head mask (I can't remember where we got it from—some crap costume hire place—the kind of costume no one else had ever hired). Anyhow, Cathy as this disruptive dog—'scampering' and barking throughout all the other scenes—a truly unhelpful presence—and then at a certain point Claire decides to interview the dog—she sits down next to Cathy, asks her if she minds answering a few questions, she points the microphone to the dog and Cathy answers in her own voice 'No, no, I don't mind'.
And for a while Cathy talks and answers the questions and you can't be sure if this is 'Cathy' or the 'Dog' that is meant to be answering. And then Claire says, at a certain point, 'Cathy don't you think its about time you took that dog's head off now?' and the dumb blank dog looks at us (questioningly) and Cathy's hands come up and lift off the dog's head and we see her face for the first time in the piece—must be about 50 minutes into it—and she's sweating and still a little out of breath I think but the only thing that's for certain is that, in the ruins of the dog game, she is more present than she ever could have been if she'd just walked onto the stage and sat down—Cathy is very here, and very now, very here and now, in the ruins of the Dog game she's very present.
The game pauses and it's like you need to see her take the dog's head off in order to even begin to understand what it was, what it meant to pretend that dog for so long, like only now, when the head comes off and the game stops can you measure it, and as Cathy talks (death again: a long slow story about how she would commit suicide if she were going to do it) we measure the distance/difference between real and fictional, human and animal, real time and playtime...
A strange reassertion of the game; when she's completed her long suicide story Cathy puts the dog's head back on again. And remains as the 'Dog' for the rest of the performance.

Simon Says Watch

In the ketchup/movie deaths game from *Let the Water*, and in so many others they played on stage, there were always people watching as well as people doing. These figures stood looking on, assessing the performance of their colleagues, encouraging them, spurring them on, looking on with concern or bemusement, awaiting their own turns.

They loved this mixing of the hot and the cold — those doing and those watching — they loved this flickering, or this co-presence, this flickering of real time and play time.

They saw a tape of a James Brown encore routine in which Brown was down on his knees and out of his mind with emotion singing 'Please, please pleaaaaaaase, pleeeeaaaaaasse!', whilst his minders-cum-trainers-cum-body-guards were looking on in concern, like 'James has really gone too far tonight ...'. And on the tape the minders tried to stop him, tapping him on the shoulder as if to say 'Come on, that's enough, get back to the dressing room' but Brown would not give it up and the minders were shaking their heads and Brown was sweating and shaking and screaming singing 'Please, please pleaaaaaaase, pleeeeaaaaaasse!' And of course he only seemed so very very into it because the guys behind him were so very very cool and distant, not into it at all.

Again, this hot and cold, this doing and watching from the stage.

Simon Says Stop

Perhaps the strangest moment of any of these games was when they stopped. Because in the stopping was always the time for measuring how far things had gone, how much the world had changed because of the game.

They were tempted to think of endings in performance as a kind of return — a point at which the travellers, sent out to discover things in a strange imaginary country, had finally come back. In shamanic performance this journey is taken as literal — performers sent out (or in or down) on a journey to the spirit world, a task that has real consequences, real dangers, a return that can bring real gifts. Performance then as going out, and coming back changed.

The audience-cum-witnesses want to measure the distance (or feel the proximity) between their world and the other. Listen: water dripping into the pool from the desolate gantries at the end of Impact Theatre and Russell Hoban's extraordinary piece *The Carrier Frequency* — a portrait of a flooded world, post-holocaust. After the piece has ended people somehow can't resist the temptation to come and stick their fingers in the pool; testing the limits, as if the feel of the water on their fingers might take them that bit further to the place that they've just seen. Or the end of our own *Speak Bitterness* (1995) — where the audience often gather at the long long table to examine the text which is strewn all across it — were they really reading stuff from that? Is there anything we missed? Just how does it feel to stand here and look out?

Pina Bausch

Performance as a way of going to another world and coming back with gifts.

For me, ending performance was always about crossing the line between worlds, or passing on the chance to cross it; refusing to come back. The five or six curtain calls closing Pina Bausch's *Cafe Muller* which I saw in summer 93 were almost pure refusal. Here the gazes of the dancers (Bausch included) were as stern and distant and as lost in private pain as they had been throughout the performance — there was no returning in it, or only a nod to that, as though the image-world could not be quit, its psychic residue too strong.

Perhaps blurring, uncomfortable endings such as this one are the best — they stay with us, after all, and if Bausch's dancers cannot leave off, cannot shrug off their journey, then somehow, neither can we.

Central to the charge of these difficult endings and at stake in all performance endings is the negotiation of *where* the events we have witnessed will have their consequence. In real or imaginary space? What will be the transfer? How will it take place? How and where will these things mean?

At a workshop presentation years ago I watched a performer remove all his clothes and stand motionless before us for a minute. As an action it meant next to nothing (too meaningful!) but the audible sighs of relief from the performer once he'd retreated to the dressing rooms (sighs on the edge of laughing and crying, sighs on the very edge of the performance itself) were as gripping as anything I've witnessed. Those sighs were the marking of the journey from the play-space to the real, inscribing consequence.

Play (2)

Play is charged, it resonates, because it is a stupid dog (like the one in *Showtime*) worrying at the edges of what is real and what is not ... playing at the edges of what is real and what is not, disrupting the borders between the so-called real and the so-called fictional.

I wondered:

What game might you play using 2 men, a bottle of whisky, a blindfold and a gun?

What game might you play with a pile of jumble-sale clothing and a record slowed down to 16 rpm?

What game might you play with four women and a disconnected telephone?

Sometime when we're touring (now maybe, years ago maybe, impossible to say). Two people, whose names can't be mentioned, end up staying with people from the venue. They have to share a room. They aren't together but it isn't a problem. They get put in the kids' room — the kids must be away or something. They sit in the room talking — its very late already — bright painted walls, pictures, a mobile of clouds and space rockets. There are bunk beds. They end up fucking. The bed is too small. There are toys in it.

To be naked in this room is a strange thing. Sex in there is a kind of time travel. A loosening of the borders between what's real and what is not. Your body changes shape and size. They are watched by the toys.

Miles one night (years later?) couldn't sleep, he calls me in. He's very scared. He looks to the toys in the corner of the room and says 'Tigger and one of the rabbits are ignoring me' — I love it that what bothers him is not the life in these animals — they could be laughing, singing, dancing or whatever, he wouldn't mind — it's just that they're ignoring him.

Another time: again Miles can't sleep: he calls D into the room — he says the doors and handles of the cupboard are 'making him think that they are eyes and a nose'.

Letter

My darling,
    We talk as if the real and the playful were separate. But we know that isn't true.

    After *Psycho* the shower is not the same place. After the game we played endlessly one rainy Saturday afternoon, rushing in and out of the front room pretending to be monsters the house is not the same place …

— A childhood memory — endlessly devising the rules and the systems of unplayable games. They had one game that was to be played all through the streets of the area where they lived. There were supposed to be two teams, each team was supposed to hide something — a matchbox — the other team had to find it. There was a crazed complicated system of clues and questions provided by each team. Their own plan was to hand the matchbox on a thread, down inside a drain by the side of the road. They even talked about ageing or dirtying the thread so it would not be visible…. They talked about the game several times, always adding new rules, new locations through the streets, but obviously, never really got round to playing it.

At the same time a friend and I found an old butcher's chopping knife — a big ugly thing — too rusty to be sharp but quite suggestive of violence at least. We took the knife-thing to school in a polythene bag — we must have been 8 or 9 years old — and tried burying it in some bushes at the edge of the playground.

At the same time — playing in the newly built houses on the edge of the estates. Burying things in the foundations—pictures, objects, broken things. What might some archaeologist of the future make of these strange secreted offerings?

In all of these games there was perhaps one thing in common—the sense of the game as a secretive intervention in everyday life. Just to think—the same streets that people lived, loved and died on were to them the arena for these games. And after their games the streets were not simply safe or normal any more. The playground was a changed place with a large knife buried at its edges. The families that moved into the new houses suffered strange dreams, unwitting victims of the aimless voodoo practised by us.

Those games were rewriting the everyday. Quite simply: changing the world by any means necessary.

Nights

We had a similar approach when we were making *Nights in this City* (1995 and 1997)—a mischievous guided coach tour of Sheffield and then, in a second version, of Rotterdam.

In trying to determine the route for the coach in Rotterdam we are helped by many people who live and work there.

We start by asking them questions like: 'Where is the tourist centre of the city?' 'Where is a rich neighbourhood?' 'Where is a poor neighbourhood?' 'Where is an industrial area?'

But these boring questions get the boring answers they probably deserve. We do not find what we are looking for. We switch to another tactic. Richard and Claire are talking to one of our helpers. They ask her:

If you had killed someone and had to dump the body where would you take it?

If you had to say goodbye to a lover where in this city would you most like to do it?

Where in this city might be the best place for a spaceship of aliens to land?

This is what you might call *our* geography.

We think of this project like a strange writing onto the city—a playful and poetic reinvention—like you can take the city and project on top of it using words—of course the text contains hardly any facts about the city—it's not an official tour in that sense—it's much more playful. We are driving the streets of Rotterdam and pretending that it is Paris.

What's the quote of Baron Munchausen that Terry Gilliam uses in his film? the Baron's motto, or his favourite saying—OUT OF LYING TO THE TRUTH—that could very well be our strategy here.

Rewriting the everyday.

Process (2)

Peggy—You talked at one point about artists themselves needing to fall into (or for) their work, (or into the territory of their work, beyond their initial agendas)—to let it take them somewhere unknown, to surrender to that, or to respect that, to go with the work to a new place—an ethical need. That made me smile because we've long asked ourselves, when working on performance projects, having amassed some material by random collection and impro and accident and intention, and having worked with it a little, we have long asked ourselves the question: 'What does it want?' 'What does it need?' Anthropo-morphising the work as if it had desires of its own. As if the fragments of the work in this early stage are a note (for Alice) saying 'follow me'.

Friends have sometimes reminded us that it is really our desires we ought to be considering and not those of a dubious non-existent entity—and we laugh with them at our deferral/projection to this 'it' but at the same time we know there is also an 'it'—a collection of objects, texts and fragments which resonate in certain ways (in particular circumstances, personal, historical, cultural)—and which in combination really do (I think) make demands, demands that have to be heeded if the work is to be worth making and sharing.

Collaboration (2)

Is collaboration this: four people in the room drunk and tired, treading again through an argument about the structure of the show, an argument which we've already had 100 times in the last week and for which all of us, by now, know all of the parts and yet are always coming back in circuits to the same stalemate stand-off conclusions about how and why the show does not work and will not work? There is a word for these too familiar arguments—we call them the loop, arguments that soon are shorthand and can be indicated simply with a gesture: the circling of a hand.

> Yes, someone says, it should really work like that. But the thing is, when Claire stands there we have no way of knowing what the fuck is going on. It can't just happen.
>
> So we have to go into a text. That'll help.
>
> But we tried a text there (three weeks ago) and I can tell you it doesn't work.
>
> Yes that's right. A text can't help. Claire just has to stand there.
>
> But the thing is, when Claire stands there we have no way of knowing what the fuck is going on. It can't just happen ... (etc.)

And now we're into the loop. For every group a process, and for every project a loop. Maybe collaboration is simply the process of developing new words for the strange situations in which a group can find itself.

The loop is the heart of the show, a wall you hit your heads against until you are senseless, gibbering and tired of it, tired of it, tired of it. And strangely it seems sometimes that the worst thing of all is that the loop must be tackled in public, with the group, through speech, discussion. So many times in the process I begin to envy the solitude of writers and painters—who surely have their loops but at least aren't condemned to sit up forever and talk about them. Worse than Beckett, worse than Sartre. After two months of working on the show I can chant you the loops in my sleep.

Drawing In

Cathy's long suicide story in *Showtime* comes right after she has removed the dog's head. Claire asks her, if she *were* going to commit suicide, how exactly she would chose to do so. The answer draws the audience in softly—a long and intimate pornography of detail; of running the bath, and of lying in it to watch some TV, of listening to a favourite song, of sticking her toes into the taps, of listing her favourite people, favourite books and favourite places, and of waiting for the electric bar fire to glow a perfect orange before lifting it up and dropping it into the water where she lies...

When Cathy has finished Claire tells her 'Thank you', and at that point Terry—dressed as a pantomime tree, and coming straight out of 10 minutes' stillness—makes her outburst. From inside her absurd brown-painted cardboard costume—a cylinder with stupid holes for arms and eyes—she yells at the audience, gesticulating like a psychopath, thick with vehemence, breaking the mood:

> 'What the fuck are you looking at? What the fuck is your problem? Fuck off! Voyeurs! There's a fucking fine line and you've just crossed it. Where's your human decency? Call yourselves human beings? Why don't you fuck off, piss off, cock off, wankers, voyeurs. Fuck off. Go on, pick up your things, pick up your coats and your fucking bags and bugger off just fucking cocking buggering wank off...'

They had this game with the audience, that's for sure. A game of drawing them in and pushing them away.

Like your presence at this event had to cost something.

Claire

Claire takes her seat at the start of *Hidden J*. She comes out before the audience on her own. She's first out. She takes the cardboard sign which is lying on the chair—she puts it round her neck, it says: LIAR.

She settles in her seat. Looks those watching in the eyes.

It's hard to look at her, since in looking you contribute to her shaming.

Like Claire fell victim to some backstage dispute in the company—they sent her out here to be humiliated for a while before the piece really starts. Soon the others come out—they start building the set. Claire is in position like she is holding the fort, bearing the weight of the audience's attention, but all she may do is sit there and suffer their gaze. To be in the audience here is, simply, to objectify and humiliate Claire. She sits there for most of the piece. Our watching is never without a kind of ethical problem.

Go Too Far

In *Club of No Regrets* (1994)—Robin and Cathy bound and gagged with industrial tape near the beginning—the actor/hostages that will enact this evening's spectacle. Cathy and Richard as their brutal captors come clumsy don't-give-a-shit stagehands—they point toy guns at the hostages' heads, look to the audience as if to say 'What shall we do with these two … how far would you like us to take them tonight…'.

In previews through the summer of 1995 we had friends tell us again and again that they liked the work, they liked the violence and extremity of the piece, they liked it but they wanted more. We should go further. They wanted more.

The chairs routine was already dangerous. It was before we had the rubber floor and the studio floor was lethal once wet. We hadn't even worked out how to do the taping-up properly so sometimes people got taped in such a way as they couldn't protect themselves when falling. Most often when supposedly watching that section I couldn't even look. I remember D coming in to watch it one time, the only person I recall saying, 'Really, why are you doing this to each other…'. She was probably crying.

But everyone else wanted more.

What is it about those human persons who, as Richard says in *Showtime*, 'Like to sit in the dark and watch other people do it'?

People (like me and maybe you) who will pay money to sit down and watch others act things out, pay money to see pretending. And people (like me, and maybe you) who want to see more pain than anything else. The death scene. The crisis. The agony. The anger. The grief. Done convincingly, done with distance or irony, but done none the less.

And if the performers sometimes stop and ask themselves, in the middle of the game, 'What is this, really?' No surprise that the work will sometimes turn on its audience and ask them, simply, 'What was it that you wanted to see?' 'What did you demand?' 'What was it that you wished for when you came inside tonight?'

One time when they showed the durational *Speak Bitterness* (six hours of confessions from behind the long table, with an audience that was free to come and to go at any point)—it was Amsterdam—the audience came in at the beginning and then, to their horror, more or less, hardly anybody left. After two hours they were pretty well out of material. They were making things up, inventing frantically, shifting the tone around as if somehow they might figure out what these people needed, what they wanted, what for them would be enough. It was desperate, slipping into hysterical humour very often. A small space—so small you could count the audience, you could see every move they made. He remembered an endlessness of eye contact, of enquiry from him to them—and in the end all he was thinking was, 'What do you want, what do you want, why don't you leave us … there's no release in this …'. It became the most fascinating night. Truly fantastic.

Afterwards he talked to some people from the audience. This guy said:

> I felt I got to see you all for the performers you would like to be, and for the performers that you really are and for the people you would like to be and for the people that you really are …

And with that he realised—the desire, really, was for nakedness, defenceless-ness. An exposure that does not have a name. Something beyond.

Teasing

They had this game with the audience, that's for sure. A game of drawing them in and pushing them away. Teasing them with meaning, teasing them with narrators and central figures who would appear to be helpful but who would really say little to guide them through the mess.

Teasing them with certainties that would collapse. Teasing them with chaos, preposterous ineptitude.

Teasing, teasing. The kind of teasing that a confident audience would love and respect.

Did I tell you that account I read of hippies in Haight Ashbury—in the late 60s—they were so fed up with the coach loads of tourists gawking, staring from the windows of their buses that they took to carrying mirrors—when a bus full of tourists would go by the hippies would takes out their mirrors and hold them up to the buses—asking the people on board to simply look at themselves.

What was it you wanted to see?

Did you dream of a looking that had no consequence, no ethical bind, no power inherent in it, no cost?

You won't find that here.

You Play with what Scares You

Watching Richard holding Robin in *Showtime* rehearsals, the lurid guts (a can of Heinz Spaghetti tipped into his hand and clutched to his belly) oozing out of Robin, Robin dying.

It was the same summer that Richard's brother drowned. I mean it was only a few weeks before that Richard's brother had died and Richard was already back in rehearsals and now he was just holding Robin leaning against the blue and red kids' playhouse that was a part of the set, holding him, watching him saying nothing, trying to comfort him unable to speak as Robin played this big stupid death scene.

It must have been apparent at some moment that Richard was going to spend whole sections of the show holding Robin like that, in the way that he hadn't been able to hold Chris. I don't think we ever talked about it. Not much anyway. I think we all knew what it was. And we dedicated the show to Chris in a very quiet way.

You play with what scares you and you play with what you need.

At the end of the same show Richard with a timebomb strapped to his chest, making wishes, waiting for it to go off—things he'd like to have done, good-byes he would like to have said ... Waiting to die.

You play with what scares you and you play with what you need.

Antwerp 1998. I ask the women that I'm working with to write death threats —the kind of thing you could leave on an answer-phone—invasive, vicious, unsettling—the kind of thing that makes a house feel poisoned or unsafe. They start writing—they look puzzled at first, hunched over notepads, then after a time the first one starts smiling—this glee that she has thought of something really unspeakable and vile. Then the next one starts smiling, laughing almost, a similar feeling—there are curious looks passing between them. They hunch closer over the papers. A strange exam.

Later I ask them to play the death threats into the disconnected phone I've placed in the centre of the performance space. They come up one by one, a little nervously and then read from their papers—picking up the phone and spouting viscous vile threats, rape threats, burglary threats, I'm-watching-you-from- under-the-table messages—a festival of invasion. And as each one takes a turn to come forwards and leave their messages the reactions from the others swing wildly—from nervous laughter, to silent horror, to expressions of disgust (that one went too far, that's too much) and back to fascinated staring, to laughter again—switching between these things ...

Afterwards we talk about this strange game of scaring each other—of tapping into fear. We notice that all of them, by implication, cast themselves as men whilst leaving their messages, cast themselves, in effect, as their own vic-tims—not a part of my instructions.

Playing as a game of sitting in the house with all the lights switched out at midnight, just to prove that you can do it.

Or the game Michael used to play with his sister—playing their parents' record collection at 16 rpm in part to guess the tunes, but more just to frighten each other with the devil voices and from-hell tunes they told each other they could hear. You play with what scares you.

Three Letters

Dear Miles,

When I faxed you several times from America it was around the time of your 4th birthday and I mostly sent stories—stories about you, imaginary exploits, pirates, goodies and baddies, super heroes, transformations, magic.

Then one time I decided to write you a letter saying what exactly we had been doing—performing a show, going to a party all night, staying up to see the sunrise from a hill called Twin Peaks. Mad drunken dawn. I liked sharing this with you—in language I thought you might just understand—strange sights and excitements, adventures in a way—but when we spoke a few days later on the phone you asked me only 'why wasn't it a story?'

You wanted fiction.

I'm not sure what stories are now. Are they a means of escaping? Or of learning? Or of organising the world? A way of projecting oneself into imaginary victory and pain.

Miles—how come the stories you like are all about victory—how come the goodies always have to win? Miles—how come the stories you love always end with bedtime, or a birthday meal, or the violent and comical defeat of the villains, or a final coming home? Because you're building yourself?

Miles—How come the stories I like are falling to pieces—stories scarcely worthy of that name. In them the world is badly organised, in them an ending is something that wants to happen but cannot, in them good isn't easily told from bad, in them the world aches and goes on aching. How come the stories we in Forced Entertainment love are built on shifting sand and made of channel-hopping? Because we've been in the world a little longer than you? Perhaps, perhaps. I don't know.

I am thinking of you.

Tim.

Dear Miles,

I'm sorry for firing so many questions at you in that letter before. I didn't mean to. Next time I'll just send a story.

Best wishes—Tim

Dear Miles,

There was once a woman who gave birth to two daughters, and brought them up alone, far from everything. For twelve years she kept the truth of the world from them, sparing them all of the unpleasant things that might spoil their childhood, and then on their 12th birthdays she sat them all down and told them everything ... she told them about darkness and the things that happen in it, she revealed the truth about the false-nose gunman, about the cellar and the shapes that lived in it, about codes and signs of regret, she told them about economies of scale and diseconomies of scale, she told them how the past lives on in the present, she told them about ghosts, about sexual pleasure and how it is obtained, she told them stories of entrapment and enchantment, she taught them to count in numbers, she taught them bad words and good words and she spared them nothing.

It took her a whole night to tell them, through the dark and into the fleeting hours of morning, she told them about ships at sea which encounter ice, about the boiling point of blood and the breaking point of bones, she told them about stories and what their uses were, she told them how to hurt people, and how people got hurt. She revealed the true law of desire.

She taught the meaning of the words 'uncanny' and 'impossible', she told them about Nixon and the strange quiet that sometimes falls in the middle of a big city, she taught them Truth Dare Kiss and Panic, she told them about game shows about sky and sea, about telephone wires, about noises and voices, and how men and women really die.

Thinking of you.

Tim.

Process (3)

Watching back the video-tapes. Checking to see what happened in some improvisation or another, trying to register exact combinations, coincidences, structures. So that the spur-of-the-moment games and accidents could (later) be transcribed and re-presented.

They often wondered what making the work had been like before the video camera, but, try as hard as they might they could not remember. It was a constant companion to them and the store cupboards filled up with crudely logged, half-incomprehensible tapes.

Some days they ran out of blank video-tape. No one could be bothered to walk into town to buy fresh supplies. They'd go to the cupboard and select an old tape from the unofficial archive—how about *Emanuelle* (1992) number 22? —may as well tape over that—sure—another gap in the history ... another story getting more and more provisional, fragmented.

Simon Says Go Too Far

In any game there was always the pull to the edges. That question of 'What's the furthest you can go inside the structure of this game?' or 'What would a rule break consist of here?' or simply 'How far could one go with this?' or 'How can we collapse this?'

So in *Hidden J* the pretty game of opening and closing the curtains of the tiny house centre-stage gave rise in the end to a whole section of the piece performed in private and obscured from the audience—where only the sound of Cathy's volatile emotional phone calls in a made-up foreign language could be heard from just behind those curtains—a six- or seven-minute harangue of hysteria in which all one could see was the other performers, nervous, bored, distracted, waiting for her to stop, considering the awful sound of what she was doing... and their inability to see it.

Go too far. Go too far. So that in the game of playing dead, in the end two of them go down and stay down for 15 minutes. Not playing at all, or playing too much.

Go too far, go too far. The scenes repeated in *Club of No Regrets* getting faster and faster, the clumsy special effects of blood and smoke and water and leaves getting piled on the scene like a storm.

Isn't that the constant frustration for play? That it isn't real?

No surprise then that play always dreams of its other. The thing has aspirations.

Go too far, go too far. More storm. More storm. More storm.

So that there were always some players who don't know when to stop. Who'd be left out there in fiction or in play, getting too involved in it, getting confused. Remember Dennis Hopper's character in *The Last Movie*—a minor actor who stays behind in a Mexican town where a film crew have been shooting a western—the locals get into the whole movie thing—they want to play too—they build cameras and film lights from wood and string—they want to stage gunfights, fist fights—but they don't understand about pulling the punches— people get hurt, they want Hopper to teach them, they want, they want, they want someone to die.

And the stories of Hopper making the movie. Sam Fuller (or someone) going down to see him on-set—the cabins deserted, finding Hopper tripping naked in the woods, with a gun... out of control.

Go too far, go too far.

Cathy yelling and yelling the longest list of confessions in *Speak Bitterness*— 'we shouted for so long it didn't even sound like our own voices anymore...' Her yelling like ice being poured right down your spine. 'We never never never wanted kids anyway.' Not even a fucking game any more.

Richard in impro for *Pleasure* (1997). Claire lying 'dead' on the ground in front of him. He covers her head with a jacket, then pulls her underpants off. Sits staring at her cunt.

Not even a game anymore.

Go too far. Go too far. Go too far.

Edges of the game—where it comes back to the real. Back to blank facts. The material. What is, here. Now.

The game is in dialogue with the now. It cannot escape it.

A room in Antwerp. Laptop and MTV. Words. Voices.

Stillness.

Game over.

On Documentation and Performance

On Documentation and Performance was written after a conference about that topic organised by Lancaster University and the Centre for Performance Research. The conference featured presentations from archaeologists, scientists, artists and performance academics about history, documentation and representation. The piece is both a fragmentary document of the conference and a response to ideas and performances presented there. The piece was first published in *Versus*, a Leeds-based magazine dealing with contemporary art practice.

Views Expressed (1)

That documentation of live events is an attempt at capture, a dragging down of the ephemeral into the fossilising mud of all that is fixed and fixing.

That documentation commodifies — again, shaping into static and saleable object-form an art-practice which resists the market.

That in giving way to documents (and analysis) artists are losing hold of their work — that the voices of academia posit readings over which artists have no control, readings which claim a single authority and readings which distance viewers from the work itself.

A Panel of Ologists

Saturday morning lies somewhere between an Open University chat-show and a postmodern show trial. The men from cartology, pathology, sociology, archaeology and history (and they are all men) take turns in confessing that their disciplines are closer to stories than to sciences. One by one they take the floor, admitting the sins of interpretation — of omission, agendas and narratives — of making versions rather than truths.

And I wonder if anyone can be remotely surprised by this, since even the sciences aren't hard anymore.

Written Deep

In a presentation to the conference Wendy Houston (DV8) begins by moving in the space — the half-formed gestures of some dance that she hasn't yet made, a jumble of phrases that she will dance in the future but which for now are only a body's way of thinking aloud. As she moves she talks — it's both a monologue that is her finding the focus and the energy she needs in order to dance, and a commentary on what she's finding 'just' by moving.

Without explanation she asks for the audience to call out years — anything from 1959 to the present day. After some time the calls begin. As they call she responds — changing the pattern of what she's doing, associating, recollecting, adding new moves and remembrances, new energies, still talking as she goes.

Audience: 1983
Houston (still moving): It was kinda like and I remember I had to do this and I had to fall and uhhh (knocks the breath from herself, falling) and uhh I ...

Audience: 1969
Houston (still moving): Oh yeah it's kind of like easier, lighter, like this and 1969, that year it was all like this ...

Audience: 1989
Houston (her breathing and speech strained a little from the dance which she continues): That year I was in this show and it was all like ... shit, can't do that anymore ... it was a bit more like ...

No Split

Body and voice don't struggle separately here (as if language was somehow not lodged in the muscle just like everything else) but rather they feed on each other and spur each other, Houston's vocalisations changing, the sounds shifting tone with the movement as she slips through the years in a struggle to recall, a struggle to re-find what's written in the blood and bone.

It's compelling because here the document is a body remembering itself and a voice describing itself. There's a struggle in what's happening and the anger and the energy of it is all directed inwards, in a search. I say to Houston later: 'like your body is fighting itself, for possession of itself'.

The act we are watching is precisely a struggle — a dance that knows it cannot ever get back to the past but which knows that the past can live (changed) in the present by an effort of will.

Isn't Documentation, then, a Kind of Magic?

'Sometimes, for example, wishing for the visit of a particular woman I have found myself opening a door, then shutting it, then opening it again ...'
(André Breton, *L'Amour fou*)

The cupboard is full of performance relics — a strip of heat-sensitive paper I salvaged after a performance by Ann Bean in the National Review of Live Arts (Glasgow), a handful of feathers from The Wooster Group's *St. Anthony*, a pile of audio tapes from Impact Theatre's *A Place In Europe*. I wonder if, by adding water, these relics might breathe again. But I can't bring myself to do it.

Cartology

If we imagine taking a piece of paper and shaping it into a cone and then placing the cone on top of the earth like a hat — (here's a diagram) the places where the cone would come into contact with the earth (all along here), that's where the map would be most accurate ...

But if we look at a map that's been made in this way Sweden is much too big (look)…Africa is bigger than North America but here it looks smaller (look)…

Now. If we imagine taking the paper and wrapping it round the earth again only this time like this, like wrapping a parcel (here's another diagram) we'd get a different map…it's called a (something) projection…and if we look at a map that's been made in this way the shapes of the countries are distorted, but the sizes are more accurate.

I am thinking about being in space, a person so huge that a sheet of paper I hold is able to wrap the globe for my mapping experiment. I'm imagining the touch of this huge paper on the earth, the wetness of it where it meets the oceans, the marking of it where it touches mud, the dampness where it's pressed into leaves. Like DeCertau says 'history begins at ground level…'.

> I made a map today of the city where I live. Scale: one to one.
> (Steve Wright, comedian)

Paraphrase, Versions and Lies

That's all this is.

Club of No Regrets

All through the work we did on *Club Of No Regrets* (1993) my copy of Gross's *Criminal Investigation*—a 1962 textbook on forensic and other procedures—lay in the rehearsal studio. One passage we returned to again and again, a passage which, in the end, marked the start of each performance, read aloud by Terry O'Connor in a faltering anxious voice.

> Piecing Together Torn Paper.
>   Simple as this work may appear yet it none the less presents numerous difficulties, and is often very awkwardly carried out. An investigator often receives numerous torn pieces of paper of small size, the content of which, once pieced together, is of the utmost importance…

And so the reconstruction of a narrative from clues, the reconstruction of an event from its objects, the reconstruction of a text from its fragmentary scenes were framed as the objects of our work.

Writing Wendy

And when I try to write all this down I find that I do it by 'doing' all the people. So sometimes, while I'm typing at the keyboard, I'm shifting my weight and trying little moves (the minutest of echoes—a desktop version of a life-size sequence) and I'm moving my lips too, on the edge of speech, in search of Wendy Houston's voice, trying to get the expression, the quick jerks of her body, trying to find the twitches and the breathing and the pulses.

In going back to the event I'm drawing on two things I can name (as well as others that I cannot) — I'm replaying what I saw and heard of her that afternoon and the twitches and movements that I made in response ('without thinking') as I watched. There are two bodies remembered then — mine and another — one written over (or through) the other. I'm at the keyboard still and the distant ripples of another person's movement and my own past movement are playing through the medium of my skin. Is this talking to the dead?

Is this complex ghosting what Susan Melrose means when she reminds us (as she did in Lancaster) that in considering performance we must never speak about the body but only ever of the bodies — watched bodies and watching bodies?

Am I right to think of Freud here — the grieving self internalises the lost other, keeping the phantasm of the lost alive but buried deep inside?

A Meal of Ashes

In preparation for the Summer School and Conference performance artist Alistair MacLennan spent a week on an uninhabited island off the Irish coast. The photographs he took in this place — of grass, rocks, butterflies, dead birds, flowers, lichen, sea and sky — speak well to the silence and stillness in MacLennan's work. But presented alone these might be snaps from some Tourist Board souvenir. Shown as part of MacLennan's work the slides don't so much come to life as demonstrate its absence. MacLennan moves around in near darkness — bringing the metal frames of tables that have no tops, lighting tiny candles beneath the huge slides, covering his face, before finally burning paper into ashes on a table set for four. MacLennan's theme (if it can be called that, and I don't suppose for a minute that it can) is simultaneously the past-ness of the past and the present-ness of the present. Like Houston he makes incredible links between physicality and memory, not through the high exertions of Houston's dance but by its inverse — by a stillness, by a slowing of the body and the mind.

MacLennan's stillness communicates itself first as spectacle — we consume the sight of him — watching his slowness and his intense focus in much the same way as one might watch a drunk through the wrong end of a telescope. For people like myself, who believe that reading, listening to music, making phone calls and watching television are best done simultaneously to avoid boredom, MacLennan's slowness is a bit of a slap in the face. Waves of fascination hit me — is he really doing this? How long has this been going on? — and then waves of irritation — does it have to be so long and so slow? Is a conference (already full of slow overlong presentations) really the best place for this?

I remember that MacLennan disappeared behind a black screen and that with only the slowly changing slides and broken tables to look at I was sure that he wouldn't stay hidden for long. Wrong first time. But in its greatest provocations come the greatest gifts of MacLennan's work. By the time he comes out from behind I'm not watching the piece anymore—I am in it. The shift is from spectacle to something direct, something metabolic. My own pulse, my own breathing, my own internal speed has fallen in line with his, his rate seems to have imposed itself on the room. This could go on forever now and I wouldn't care. We're here and now, very here and very now. Very quiet.

Maybe that's what the island was like.

Pathology

Make up a story to explain this:
A dead man in England in winter with a stomach full of strawberries.

Views Expressed (2)

> That the worries of the ologies are the ecstasy of our practice.
> (Susan Melrose)

> That the work is a document in and of itself—a document of lives and experiences not represented elsewhere in the culture.
> (Lois Weaver, Gay Sweatshop)

That the work is a document of the processes leading to it—a body that bares traces of its past.

You have been Watching / Buried Alive

At the end of *Mind The Gaps* Lucy Baldwyn presents her performance document of the event itself. Neither a synthesis of key arguments nor a collection of the weekends most challenging utterances, her work simply replays the shapes and gestures of the conference, its practices of body and space. As she speaks seated on a chair, surrounded by empty space, a mock-technician brings furniture and technology, even an audience, to her side. Here a table to lean on, a Kodak carousel wheeled in, a glass of water to drink from, a VCR dumped on the floor, an overhead projector, a sandwich, a projection screen, two microphones, an extension lead.

Here and there, in a linking phrase or a casual gesture (all buried in the storm of arriving technology) I recognise something from the last few days, recognise the live body surrounded by its adjuncts, the fragility of an utterance and the props which both bury and support its remembrances.

Eight Fragments on Theatre and the City

This piece was written for and first published in the journal *Theaterschrift 10: City/Art/ Cultural Identity*, and, as the title suggests, concerns itself with the relationship between the creative process and the myths, stories and practices of the urban everyday.

'It should all be considered like a letter — written to a long lost friend …'

Introduction

There is a great dream recounted in the book *Elvis after Life* in which a police officer whose son has gone missing receives help from the ghostly figure of Elvis Presley.

In the dream Elvis shows the cop where to find his missing son by taking him to the police station at night and pointing at a huge map of the city. Recounting the dream the cop says this: 'It's a map of San Francisco — only it isn't San Francisco.'

It's that city, or one like it — this city, but not this one — that I'll write to you about here: eight fragments out of Not-England and nothing more.

1. Exploration

One night when we were touring, somewhere far from home, we arrived in a place in the dead of night, found somewhere to park the van, found somewhere to sleep. Only when we woke the next morning did we realise that we were in a town right next to the sea and that the place where we had slept was right at the sea front itself. From our bedrooms we could hear the waves.

Harbisson writes about the experience of arriving in the city at night and starting to explore it in the morning — this process of veiled arrival and later exploration he calls 'acting out an allegory of knowledge'.

Walking in our own city we'd often employ a deliberate confusion about what we were trying to solve or understand — was it the latest show or the city itself? Right from the start this double act of walking and talking was a named part of our process, more important perhaps than anything that happened in the theatre itself. In the streets we'd see the crowds of cider-boys gathered laughing and muttering on the green grass outside Gateways supermarket. In the streets we'd see the old guy directing traffic, taking revenge on an order and an economy that had let him down; we'd see the bouncers stood in night-club doorways, practising karate chops before the night of fighting had begun. The filthy polythene caught in trees, the cardboard houses under bridges, the boarded-up windows, buildings falling down. The neon signs, the old adver-tising slogans, the fragments of graffiti — all of these things made it into our shows.

2. Maintenance

There is a man that you see in this city—he's good-looking, well looked after, not like a street-crazy person at all. Each time that you see him he's walking on the pavement, through the crowds when he suddenly runs like a maniac, scattering people in confusion as he hurls himself at a building—a shop front perhaps, or a tower block, or a multi-storey.

Thrown against a building like the whole thing is going to fall—body pressed flat, head thrown back and peering upwards, staring up to check for signs of movement in the concrete or the brick.

People say here that this man is keeping the city alive.

Some days when you see him he is calm but he's still leaning against buildings, palm flat against the walls, holding them up, checking for strength.

People say he used to be an architect and now he's a powerful magician who has slipped through the cracks in the welfare system. He walks a route through the city each day—holding and touching, same route day in and day out, same time every day, a route which is the maintenance of the city, a ritual system of good-luck checks which keeps the whole place from falling down.

Did I tell you that up on West Street someone has written on a burned-out building GET WELL SOON? Did I tell you that in some parts of the city the phones in the call boxes ring to empty streets at regular hours of the day and night?

Are these events connected? Are there persons here, working in concert?

In the city, as in all the best performance, I'm left joining dots, making my own connections, reasons, speculations.

3. Mapping

Having so long created cities in our theatre work—implied, stolen from, talked of—we decided last year to make a whole one in a gallery installation/performance piece called *Ground Plans for Paradise* (1995). Here a deserted model city —comprising nearly 1,000 balsa wood tower blocks—is laid out in a grid plan on top of a breeze-block plinth. Above the model are the faces of many people sleeping (photographed by Hugo Glendinning)—like angels looking after or dreaming of this world.

In *Ground Plans for Paradise* the city itself is both a map of space and a map of states of mind (like all real cities in fact)—only here the streets and buildings are named for the passions, fears and narrative echoes of the twentieth century: Love Street, Dave's Topless Chip Shop, Hope Street, The Blood Club, and the Institute for Darkness Research.

Looking down on the model the viewer is invited to speculate—wondering at the light which spills from inside the buildings—what kind of people might hang out at the Helium House or on Aluminium Square? What might happen at the corner of Transgression and Hesitation, or at the corner of Hate Street and Rain?

Here in Sheffield, Not-England are streets which I know by my own names — names dreamed up between the group of us when we first moved here — descriptive names, literal names, names that refer to the use we made of these streets and not their official function. We could visit the Street of Telephones or the Iqubal Brothers' Street; we could head for the ridge behind the city which we called simply the ridge, only to find out years later that it had a better name, a proper one; SKY EDGE.

I could talk to you about the views I have made mine here, the places that are now mine. I would write to you about the view of the city from the top deck of the bus coming off City Road and down towards the centre. The city itself is a model then, picked out in fairy lights, just like the crude wooden model in *Ground Plans for Paradise* — a space into which one astrally projects, a dream space. I think Foucault has given the desire for such views a bad name — after all, the panoptical view has in it both surveillance *and* imagining. To see the city from one's bed, from one's bath, from one's rooftop — how perfect to live in a city, like this one, with hills. Perhaps here sight is nine-tenths of ownership. What did we write in the text for one of our theatre pieces? 'A hill with a good view down onto the city is a good place to do deals, and discuss assassinations …'

4. Destruction / Construction

We always loved the incomplete — from the building site to the demolition site, from the building that was used once and is no longer to the building that will be used. Did I tell you that Steve Rogers and I used to talk about this? The fascination of ruined places, of incomplete places. It seems unethical to admit — the strange charge of buildings left to run down — but they always were the best places to play — stinking of previous use, ready for transgression. Every piss you took in the corner and every window you broke and every game you played in the old factory, the old house was a writing over its everyday — a kind of actantial vandalism. And do you remember burying things in the foundations of new houses as they were being made? What a surprise for somebody — these traces of some inexplicable ritual? The cut-out pictures, the scribbled notes, the broken objects.

No surprise that the sets we made always looked half-finished. No surprise either that in recent works we always began the performance by building the sets, or ended by dismantling them. Always now this work of construction and deconstruction — letting no thing simply 'be' — seeing everything instead as a product, as the fruit of some labour, some desire, some ideology.

5. Observation / Coincidence

Did you understand that the city was always about glimpsing other lives? About the strange fragments and endless possibilities of people passing each other in the street. My thought is often—what if I went with that person or that person, what if I was that person or what if I went with them—what would my life then become? Where did I learn this fantasy, this way of surviving? Is there something about cities (the meeting point of crowds and of capital) which breeds the fantasy of human interchangeability? I think so. Perhaps the most extreme form of this is the escalator—where we pass each other as objects on a production line. (Remember the escalators up to heaven in the Powell and Pressburger film *A Matter of Life and Death* with David Niven? I'm sure that for one project we stole dialogue from that film.) On the escalators we watch each other, getting closer, and then just when we could speak, or even touch, our eyes drop and the moment passes. There are these strange intimacies in the city—those moments on the escalator, those others in the lift, in the subway, or those moments when, stopped at the traffic lights, we glance to the car opposite and are close enough to speak, even touch. The fascination of these moments is simple—that our machines have brought us together and held us apart.

And isn't theatre now just an endless rearticulation of this proxemics—the play between hereness and thereness—the play between presence and absence? No surprise that in this context I always love the moments of privacy in public —where theatre regrets itself and refuses to speak. Did you see Bobby Baker's *Drawing on a Mother's Experience*? She builds up to this moment where you feel sure she's going to 'tell you everything' and then she refuses—sprinkling the drawing that she's made with white flour until the whole thing is illegible and I'm left wondering what it was that she might have said. The city now is full of this—possibility, negation, guess-work.

6. Shelter

In all our theatrical explorations of the city, perhaps it is no surprise that time after time we mark some part of the stage space as private space, as home.

In *200% & Bloody Thirsty* (1988) it is the skeletal structure of a building not yet built; in *Emanuelle Enchanted* (1992) and *Club of No Regrets* (1993/4) it is a series of flimsy and provisional rooms constructed from theatrical flats. In each case these structures cluster around an item or two of furniture—a bed perhaps, or a table and chairs—the structural tokens of interior space.

Beyond these crude houses or homes there is always an ambiguous zone—a zone that comprises two separate but interlocked 'outsides'—the real outside of the theatre with it's piles of scaffolding, costumes and props and its brick walls, and the fictional outside of the protagonists world—a city implied and fragmented, which swirls around the private space, threatening always to intrude upon it.

The most extreme of these on-stage homes is that in *Hidden J*, where a four-walled plywood box is constructed at an angle to the audience and some way off from centre-stage. This house/room only affords us a view into it through a large rectangular window and is the most deeply private of these spaces, complete with curtains to block out our view inside, so that for some sections of j98

the show performers talk, shout and weep from inside, invisible to those of us who watch.

Even allowing for such privacy, these crude homes offer little in the way of final or solid projection from the city beyond. When they are not being dismantled, they are massively permeable—guns, water, smoke, objects, texts and swinging lights constantly invade the space in *Club of No Regrets*—thrust through crude windows and doorways or thrown over the walls by two surly stage-hands in a chaos orchestrated by a half-crazy woman in a blonde wig. In *Emanuelle Enchanted* even the walls of the room space will not stay still, eventually taking on a life of their own as they dance and thunder through the stage, erasing and revealing performers in a mad choreography—as if the city walls themselves become living, fluid, unreliable, malevolent.

Who wrote this: 'Each window a stage in the great drama of the city ...'?

Were they thinking of the walk from my house to the shops where each living room I pass is bathed in TV-light which flickers and changes in rhythm to the changing of shots—the strange and synchronised dance of light on walls linking disparate houses, disparate lives?

These front rooms, these bodies in soft light, caught in postures and framed by their windows—we have striven for the perfect poise of these things.

7. Gatekeepers/Guides

When our model city was complete we began working on a project for a real one—here, in Sheffield, where we've always lived and worked. *Nights in This City* (1995) was a guided tour of the city with its audience and performers on board a bus—a guided tour which avoided facts in search of a different truth. Slipping through the centre of the city and out of control—off the beaten path, playing always to the differences between on-route and off-route, centre and periphery, legitimate and illegitimate. Playing always to the different histories written in urban space—the official historical, the personal, the mythical and the imaginary. This must've been the first guided tour of Sheffield which began with the words, 'Ladies and gentlemen, welcome to Paris ...'. Come to think of it, it was probably more or less the first guided tour of Sheffield full stop. Do you have to have lived in a place for a long time before you have the right to tell lies about it? We enjoyed our *writing over* Sheffield, seeing the whole city as a sounding board, as a space that could be vandalised with love.

The text we created—pointing out buildings, street corners, carparks, patches of wasteground—was always overlaid with other texts—with the whispered or even shouted texts of other passengers ('That's where I used to work …' 'That's the place where …') and the silent text of actions created by those living and working in the city as the bus moved through it.

'We're off the route …'. Isn't that the definition of liveness? When the thing which began as nothing more than a theatrical act has turned into an event? When the gatekeepers twitch nervously and the guides appear lost? Where safe passage back to the everyday is no longer assured?

8. All Taxi Drivers are Bastards

Returning from rehearsals late one night in 1989, overburdened with bags and video equipment I mistakenly left a small case in the boot of a taxi cab.

In the case is a notebook full of my work, a pile of script fragments and notes and an out-of print paperback book called *Elvis Presley Speaks from Beyond the Grave*. On the cover of the paperback Elvis's face is painted against a backdrop of pale blue sky and wispy cloud, his expression more than usually beatific. Despite all my attempts to track down that taxi, its driver and hence my belongings, none of these materially worthless things have ever been returned.

I think of the Elvis book, my notebook and scripts lying in that case somewhere, or cast out from it, in a taxi-driver's garage, or still in the boot of his cab, six years after the fact. I think of my notebooks travelling the city for eternity, in the dark hold of a taxi cab boot, with only the ghost of Elvis for company, riding always and forever through the streets of the night, like the city has taken back its own …

Replaying the Tapes of the Twentieth Century:
An Interview with Ron Vawter

This piece is an interview I did with one of the best-known performers of The Wooster Group, Ron Vawter, who died in 1994. It's hard for me to imagine writing anything about contemporary performance without finding the occasion for referring to Ron. The few meetings I had with him, and the numerous performances I saw him do, stay with me as a challenge and an inspiration. As I write elsewhere in this book, Ron (for me at least) characterised a kind of brilliant binary in performance terms — moving between superb technical skill and control on the one hand and an eerie magic, a something else, that couldn't easily be defined. On stage Ron exuded the things I start this section calling for — risk and investment. The text here is an extended version of the interview first published by David Hughes in *Hybrid* magazine.

(1)

I've always seen Ron Vawter ghosting dead men's words, speaking the past through his own voice or through those around him on stage. In *L.S.D. (… Just the High Points…)* he chaired a talk-show line of men who read random fragments from the great hip-lit-writers of the 50s and 60s, from Kerouac to Leary. In Frank Dell's *St. Anthony* he mouthed the Saint via Flaubert, after Lenny Bruce, in light of New York's nude chat-show Channel J (since taken off-air). Now, in his new solo performance *Roy Cohn/Jack Smith* he speaks the words of two gay men who died in the 1980s as a result of the AIDS virus, a virus that also infects Vawter himself.

I meet with Ron Vawter twice, in Brussels. Once before I've seen *Roy Cohn/Jack Smith* and again a day later. Both times he's charming, generous, precise. I ask him about the ethics of stealing dead men's words. He replies:

> Appropriation is such a fundamental thing. That's how I'd describe what's gone on in twentieth-century art. It's this kind of recycling, this kind of review, this wholesale review of the tapes. And fortunately we have film and video so we can look over and over at the record and make a careful examination of what it actually was that we were doing in these times. I don't feel any guilt or weirdness. What we tend to do, in The Wooster Group, and in my own work, is to appropriate from several different sources at the same time. That way we can juggle all these separate things until the weights are familiar and then a new kind of theatre text is created between these different places…

And now I'm back in England. On a train, transcribing. In a library. In front of the TV, with the sound turned down. Turning hours of talking into pages of writing. Finding fragments, some random. And playing back the tapes.

(2)

TE: Have you seen *The Dresser*?

RV: A wonderful film. Just wonderful. [*laughs*]

TE: I love the storm stuff. He's doing the storm scene from *Lear* and he's raging about 'Spit fire! Spout, rain!' and then yelling to the stage hand: 'More storm boy! Give me more storm!'

RV: I also love him talking to the other actors: 'You see this light, this is my light, right here in the centre of the stage. You must look elsewhere and find what little light you can!' [*More laughter*]

(3)

> Among today's homo set, evidently the most popular sexual practice involves the penetration of the rectum with a fist and sometimes an entire arm, unimaginable as this may seem, and I ask the ladies in the audience to forgive the need for graphic detail, but I think we all need to know the extent of what we are talking about…
> (Ron Vawter as Roy Cohn from *Roy Cohn / Jack Smith*. Text by Gary Indiana)

(4)

TE: I wanted to ask about your training as a priest and how that came about, and whether you've found connections between that experience and your work in the theatre.

RV: My mother and father were both career military people and so, when I turned 17, my father gave me my enlistment papers as a birthday present. I went into the Special Forces, the Green Berets. After two years it was right during Vietnam and I knew I didn't really want to go. I enjoyed the military but … there had been religion in my upbringing and I'd always toyed with the idea of the priesthood. So [*laughs*] when it came to the time for me to go to Vietnam I said, 'I'm interested in becoming a chaplain …'

The army put me in a Franciscan seminary for four years and on weekends I'd do manoeuvres with the National Guard and the rest of the time I'd do courses in theology and philosophy. But, by the time I finished in the seminary I had become a kind of zealot of St. Francis. I was very very taken by his philosophy. I believed that wealth and power were the two main problems, the two things that kept you attached to the physical world. I found the whole Roman Catholic Church to be the opposite of that. So I left and went back into the army, but part of me knew I didn't really want to go back in. I knew that my homosexuality was going to be a problem if I stayed in the military.

So, anyway, I had no preparation for the theatre. I had never dreamed of being an actor or of working in the theatre but when I met Spalding and Liz LeCompte and Richard Schechner in 1972 I was very taken with their idea of what constitutes theatrical presentation. For the first two years I was doing the books and the administration. Then Liz asked me if I'd perform, with Spalding.

(5)

Frank: Sue, can you stay for an hour? I think I'm gonna need some help.

Sue: What's the matter Frank? Did you find that tape with the answer to everything on it?

(From *Frank Dell's St Anthony*, The Wooster Group)

(6)

Roy Cohn was McCarthy's closest aide in the 50s—a right-wing lawyer who publicly denied his homosexuality and used his political platform to oppose communism and gay rights at every turn. Jack Smith, by contrast, was maybe one of the outest men who ever lived—an anarchist performer and film-maker, whose *Flaming Creatures* (1962) remains deeply influential and whose live appearances were daunting four- to six-hour hour mêlées of high camp, paranoid autobiography and poetic rambling.

RV: My whole adult life I've been a little frightened of them both. One of the first television images that came up when I was a kid, when we first got our TV, was Cohn whispering into McCarthy's ear. I've been scared both by the destructive possibilities of Cohn and the kind of marginalised torture that Jack went through. Of course they expressed two very very different ways of dealing with a hostile society, with a society that told them their sexuality was wrong. One by trying to pass and the other by taking his sexuality and blowing it up, in extreme opposition. Our sexual impulses are, er, pretty strong, pretty pivotal [*laughs*] and if you're constantly told at every turn that yours is not right... well.

(7)

TE: I was struck by something you said, about performing in that first piece, with Spalding, that you saw yourself as a stand-in. As someone simply standing in for people, or characters, who couldn't be present.

RV: Right.

TE: It seemed to me there was at once a great distance in that idea of acting and a great humanism too because it was about not wishing to misrepresent, about wanting to get things right and true. It seems like a concept of one's responsibilities as a performer that's almost Brechtian.

RV: Yes. I think that's very true. That's just what I'd think about those days — that I was a stand-in or surrogate acting for both Spalding and the audience. With the audience I felt that any one of them could have taken my place, that I just happened to be the person who was standing there. So I felt very connected to the yearning, the spiritual yearning of the audience.

I think audiences have great desires towards the spiritual and all they need is the slightest excuse from the stage to open them up. So I try to find a place, between character and in front of the audience which would trigger spiritual or meditative experiences.

(8)

Oh, Uh, this is an intermission. Let's take a ten minute break could we please. I was even in the middle of a story but I'll try to remember where. I hope you don't mind, because there's already, you know, been enough good stuff already to compare with even the new, latest hit *Penguins of Penzance*. (Ron Vawter as Jack Smith in *Roy Cohn / Jack Smith*, from Jack Smith's 1981 performance *What's Underground about Marshmallows?*)

(9)

TE: What's the pleasure of performing for you? Do you know where that comes from?

RV: I think it's the concentration of so many people onto the stage — like I'm suspended in this very powerful force-field and I'm sort of riding it like at a rodeo. It's exhilarating. It's thrilling.

Wait. I know what it's like. It's exactly like surfboarding and you've got this board which is your character or the play that you're doing and you're riding these waves coming at you from the audience and from the play itself. Of course when you surfboard you're extraordinarily sensitive to the motion of those waves and of course you know I'm a show off, I'm an actor, so, I try to do little tricks — zip into the water, go across the wave and move up on the board, move down on the board. As far as the energy feels that's exactly what it's like. And I've learned how to ride the waves. I've done it a long time you know and I've learned the little tricks of the waves and the back currents and how to stay up. Sometimes I really feel like quite a champion surfboarder ...

TE: Very much ...

RV: And sometimes I fall flat on my face in the water. That's the risk of surfboarding.

(10)

TE: What interests me is the play between the rather technical, cool performance style in your work and the intensive, experiential processes used to gather material. I'm thinking of the acid trip for *L.S.D.*, I hear rumours of long long improvisations...

RV: Yes. Long improvisations on acid sometimes.

TE: Nancy Reilly mentioned that for *Roy Cohn / Jack Smith* you were going to Jack's apartment once he'd died...

RV: Yes.

TE: And staying the night there... to find that character.

RV: Yes. That's how I find what's important to me. I surround myself with as much material and objects as I can. It's like a research development; so what I'm doing is more than a performance, it's about being sensitive to the things around Jack that are left.

I'm a quarter Chowktaw, native American Indian and a couple of years ago I went to a seminar about the use of human ash in Indian war rituals. And I take Jack's ashes with me whenever I perform this play and I mix some of them into the glitter that Jack used to wear on his eyes. So I sort of return Jack to his eye make-up. I'm not suggesting that something magical is going on but I do take it very seriously and when I put Jack onto my face something does come up and out which isn't familiar, which is quite a mystery to me...

For Roy Cohn I made tape recordings of these TV shows he'd done. I edited just his speaking and put the tapes on timer for after I fell asleep. I think that was a wonderful unconscious preparation, just the sound of his voice.

TE: Can you feel ways that that's actually informed the performance?

RV: I still feel that. I felt it last night when performing. And I don't want to control that. I don't want to strategise each performance. I want these fictional creations to have a life, to have a reality in the room. I remember I said something or moved in a way that was like déja vu. I just remember remarking to myself 'Geez, you didn't decide to do that...'

(11)

The Roy Cohn section of the show is set up like Cohn is making an after-dinner speech. A little lectern, a lot of bravura, a deal of 'no, seriously folks...'. A couple of times in this section of the show Vawter simply stops the monologue and walks away from the lectern. He takes a glass of water, sips and waits while maybe 30 seconds pass in silence. In these sublime gaps we see nothing happening. And yet this is what we see:

Cohn confronting himself.

Cohn confronting his audience.

Cohn confronting this audience.

Vawter confronting himself.

Vawter confronting Cohn.

Vawter confronting Cohns audience.

Vawter confronting this audience.

And then nothing again.

(12)

TE: Since you made your illness very public what's been the response?

RV: You know sometimes now I feel a fool for being so open about my AIDS. I feel like I've got a big 'A' on my chest now and I've never really been a politician. I've worked in the arts, and I've never, on the surface of it been a political person, or active in political organisation.

TE: Right.

RV: However, I have too many friends who I've seen cruelly treated and who have sort of given up after they've received their AIDS diagnosis. People who've thought their lives are over and stopped dreaming of the future and stopped planning to do things. I'm trying to resist that.

TE: Do you resent the pressure, connected to AIDS, that you somehow have to speak or take a position? That you can't just get on with things?

RV: Well the thing is I'm not ashamed to speak of it. I know there's a heavy societal thing that this disease is somehow stigmatised and I completely resist that. It's a virus, not a judgement. I don't think I should feel guilty about it. I certainly regret it, I mean I wish I didn't have the damn thing but I'm not ashamed of it. That's like a double disease. Firstly people are sick and then they have to deal with this other shit! I'm not going to be complicit with that.

(13)

Know what I like most? Birthday cake. A big birthday cake with candles and little kids in party hats ... and parents' faces lit up with the joy leaping in their hearts at the sights of those little ones ... those little ones.
(Ron Vawter as Roy Cohn from *Roy Cohn / Jack Smith*, text by Gary Indiana)

(14)

TE: Is there a connection between what you do and mediumship? I've always seen you speaking the words of dead men.

RV: Yes. I'm not a strict believer in reincarnation but I think the artist can be a great conduit to the past and to the future. I actually believe that's one of the great functions of an artist. To somehow be able to connect in both directions —to connect to the past with an eye to the future. And when I'm successful, and I think I am sometimes, I feel those lines forwards and back.

(15)

TE: What do you hope people will find?

RV: A greater and deeper consciousness. Access to more of the brain. A touching of souls, a real communion. An audience realising its own collective consciousness, getting in touch with the power of the psyches in the room. For them to see themselves as powerful.

TE: That's all routing back to the body, into consciousness. Is there anything in the spiritual invitation you've spoken of that's an invitation to transcendence, to something other?

RV: I'm not a practitioner of any organised religion but I have a great many spiritual ambitions although they remain mysterious and invisible to me. I'm searching for the invisible.

TE: We used to talk about Forced Entertainment's project as trying to make spiritual work for atheists!

RV: [laughs] Yes. That's very good. I think that's what many of us are yearning for. You'd be hard pushed to get an audience to come to the Garage to speak about their Gods [laughs] and yet I tell you I feel that yearning in the audience. That's where I get my fuel. It's unfashionable to speak of these things, and also very difficult. And it's taken us a few thousand years to pull religion and theatre apart anyway. So now they're separate let's not confuse it with people going to church, because we're not going to church.

TE: Definitely not.

RV: However, I've always felt that the great influences of my life have reinvented, or created, their own sense of spiritualism. And the artists that I respect most Richard Foreman, Elizabeth LeCompte and Jeff Weiss all I think are at work using theatre as a vehicle to discover their own transcendence. It's tough to think about. We feel a little corny when we speak of these things, but I think in fact that's the centre of it.

(16)

TE: This whole business of the tapes. Do you think there'll ever be a time, in your work or the Woosters', where that work has been done? Where the replay of the tapes at the end of the twentieth century is completed and it's time to move on?

RV: [*big pause*] Yes. I look forward to the time when I don't have to only react to the past, but I don't believe we're there yet. We still have this triple-headed monster that the planet can't escape — racism, sexism and homophobia. The planet is in a stasis because of our inability to open up and deal with these problems. So I think, for a while longer, I'm going to be involved in making expressions which diffuse the power of that monster.

TE: By going back to particular historical moments and pulling them apart a little bit, to show what forces are operating?

RV: Yes, yes. And also, literally just to show things to an audience. To show what happened.

(17)

Oh … I just made a very good editing change. Uh, you didn't see the thing last night did you? You see I'm cutting onions because it helps you weep at a dramatic moment.
(Ron Vawter as Jack Smith in *Roy Cohn/Jack Smith*, from Jack Smith's 1981 performance *What's Underground about Marshmallows?*)

(18)

RV: Every once in a while a big wave comes. The big Kahunna. And you can feel it coming and you think 'Oh boy, this is why I've been practising. This is what I've been waiting for all these years …'. And it's called *St Anthony*.

TE: Why that piece?

RV: I don't know. Liz carefully made that with me and I feel it was a great gift from her. It was an extraordinary perception or projection of one person onto another. I think she really saw me and she saw me for my anxieties and fears and dreams and then she created this piece around those things. It's such a complete and thorough vision that she had of me.

(19)

What are you afraid of? A big black hole? What are you afraid of? A big black hole? [*laughs*] What are you afraid of? A big black hole?
(Ron Vawter as Frank Dell, from *Frank Dell's St Anthony*, The Wooster Group)

(20)

TE: I love it very much that both Roy and Jack are gone from the stage before we notice.

RV: Yes.

TE: Roy slips away in a blackout. Jack drifts off while the other performer is reading. Just slips away. In fact I love that last list. I want it to go on longer.

RV: I do too. She does it so well.

(21)

TE: Is doing this piece, about two men who both died of AIDS, a semi-magical act? Visiting Roy and Jack in relation to your own illness?

RV: I sometimes think that it has actual positive therapeutic effects. It's an enormous surge of adrenaline and I don't know actually what adrenaline is but I know that it makes me feel very good, even if I don't start the evening feeling too good. I remember a couple of nights ago, I was not in good shape. I said to Greg, my director and lover, 'I don't know if I can do the whole show'. He said, 'well just stop when you want to and take a break or a rest'. So I started the show thinking maybe I'd have to stop. But by the time I finished I could've run the five-minute mile. So I do find it very very positive and health-enhancing too, I don't know why.

TE: I thought about this watching the show last night and thought about the power of confronting the thing...

RV: Face on.

TE: Yes.

RV: Squaring off with the beast. I feel very strong on stage. Taking it by the horns and saying 'You bastard!' [*laughs*] 'You're not going to get me...'[*more laughter*]

(22)

At the end of *Roy Cohn / Jack Smith* Vawter slips out off the stage as Coco McPherson reads a list of the films and roles of Hollywood legend Maria Montez, described by Jack Smith as 'the only fit subject for the adoration of modern man'. The list, with all its implied narratives, its corny stories, its fabulous fictions, its tawdry contrasts and its mapping of a career is the kind of thing that one might wish to go on forever—sublime, both empty of meaning and full of it. Full of meaning, fear and love. It ends.

RV: It's very easy to be bravura and wonderful but if you keep demonstrating and presenting like that it puts the audience in a very passive place psychically. Those gaps are the most important thing because it's there where you stop 'showing' and the audience can use their imaginative powers and they're the ones that fill in that gap. That's where they become true collaborators. And if you can invent the gap well enough the audience just comes right into there.

(23)

RV: One of my favourite theatre stories is about Olivier, I think after he'd done a performance of Othello. It was a genius extraordinary performance and one of his friends came backstage to knock on his dressing room door and he wouldn't come out because he was so angry. So his friend yelled 'But Larry, Larry, why are you so upset? That was a brilliant performance.' And Larry opened the door, stuck his head out and said, 'Yes. I know. But HOW did I do it?'

[*much laughter*]

[*still laughing*] 'HOW did I do it?'

(24)

A pause in some Brussels cafe. No memory of the decor. Ron looking from the window.

TE: Thanks. I'll turn the tape off now. Thank you.

RV: Thank you.

On Performance and Technology

On Performance and Technology was first presented at the Directors' Guild of Great Britain conference, December 1995, and was subsequently expanded for a publication that never happened. Central to the piece is the concern with technology as an influence on the ways that we see, think and feel the world and how performance might respond to these changes. It is concerned with the fluid relationship between the material world and the imagination, and with the complexities of defining 'presence' (or absence) in an increasingly mediatised culture.

1. Take Caution

Take caution because these remarks on theatre and technology come from someone whose heart is changeable and whose theatre practice shifts in and out of love with other art-forms, other media, tricks and toys.

Take caution too since as I write this Forced Entertainment are presenting a piece of work called *Speak Bitterness* (1995) — a kind of degree-zero piece for us in which the microphones, cameras, video monitors, continuous soundtrack and filmic lighting of the previous work have all but disappeared — replaced by a long table, seven performers and a strewn pile of papers, the whole scene presented in bright white light. As if after years of evading it we've finally come down to some awful irreducible fact of theatre — actors and an audience to whom they must speak, and in this case, confess.

Take caution too because it was over four years ago that we last used video in a theatre piece — after five consecutive years we somehow got tired of answering the question: 'Where shall we put the monitors?'

And take caution finally because I'm starting to believe that old technology is more interesting than new, at least in performance terms. Is this because old technology (analogue) always shows its (crude mechanical) means, where new technology (digital) is all for instant and hence invisible change? I've never much been interested in spectacle. Or is it because I like technology (for which we might substitute culture) *for how it is used* and that new tech and new culture are never quite used enough — never quite as haunted or as resonant as they might be, never quite as ripe for reworking or rewriting? Or is it finally because, in the place of spectacle I like to see work, and I'd rather see two performers running round the stage hurling talcum powder into the air, desperately trying to create smoke for a shoot-out scene than I would see the produce of 100 smoke machines switched on invisibly from concealed bays in some matte-black and perfect hydraulic stage?

The person who has written these notes has a technological idea for a future project in which the lighting will simply be a ring of industrial sun-floods powered by a bicycle generator and pedalled by the performers. Beware.

2. Doing Television

With these warnings in place I'll forget about the theatre for a while and write about my grandmother, who, on the weekend of the Directors' Guild Conference (for which these notes were prepared) was busy dying 200 miles away and who, by now as I'm writing this, has been dead for several days. It is nearly midnight on 28 December 1995 and I'm home alone, in front of the computer.

Born in 1902 and 94 years old when she died, Grandma was scarcely a child of the twentieth century, more a child of the nineteenth. More steam than electronics, or in any case more radio than television.

And yet in the last years of her illness the television played a curious part, since lying in her room at the Kilburn Residential Home, sleeping half the day and for the rest of it looking out of the window, she was visited each day by the family and many others, on television at least.

At first she saw my brother (who is not now and never has been an actor). She saw him in some modern murder story, he was very good and his hair was dyed orange. She saw him in the back of a crowd scene in *Spartacus* or maybe *Follyfoot*. Then she glimpsed my dad playing cricket in the test match. And then the floodgates opened. She saw me in some sentimental drama and again in a comedy, black and white, one Thursday afternoon. She saw Mark again, in *Blockbusters*. She saw all of us, many times, as we came to her there, via television. As in times past, when people used to gather round and stare into the fire seeing pictures, telling stories of their lives, Grandma stared at the TV and saw there, flickering in it, her past, the people she loved and wished for. She saw all of us, in the strangest of places, and there was no way to argue or disabuse her of these visits.

I never had my Grandma down as a postmodern child, but now, in these last months, I have to admit, that she's been way ahead of us the whole time. What I'm saying is that you have to think about technology, you have to use it, because in the end it is in your blood. Technology will move in and speak through you, like it or not. Best not to ignore.

And I guess sometime soon that I'll see my Gran again, in the background of some railway station scene in a film I am not watching properly. I will glimpse her, sat on a park bench in the sunshine, perhaps, with her bags packed and going wandering. And I will wave to her and tell no one that I have seen her, because to say so would be senility.

3. Narrative

We always used to say that our work was 'understandable by anybody brought up in a house with the television on'. And I think what truly fascinated us was that somehow, in that context, one's attitude to narrative changes.

It's not just that for every significant event in my childhood I'm aware of the TV playing some other story in the background — never one story in our theatre; always two, three, four or many. Not just that with TV one always walks in half way through the story, flips over to catch the news, or simply dozes off and misses the end — always fragments in our theatre then, never whole stories at all. Not just that with the TV one can read, argue, fight, wash up or fuck even while the stories continue — always a kind of disposability to narrative and character in our theatre, a speed, a kind of lively cynicism.

Not just these things but all of them and more. I guess TV was really in our blood — and like any blood you have to live with it, spill it, transfuse it, clean it, test it. You don't have much choice about your blood, but it always needs dealing with. A theatre that won't do this isn't worth having.

4. Rewriting

Didn't McLuhan write that any technology changes not just the world but also our bodies in it?

What interests me about technology is precisely the way it has of changing everything, from the body up, through thought and outwards. I'm thinking of someone I correspond with on the Internet who described one day walking down a tube train corridor and seeing a doorway up ahead; how he found himself thinking 'If I could just double click somewhere on that door I could find out where it leads …'. And even as the thought came, or even as a part of the thought, his hand was moving (snaking sideways) searching for a mouse with which to click. After years with a point and click interface, objects in the real world begin to look different. Or, more bluntly, after years of point and click objects in the world simply are different.

I have this dream where the landscape is changing constantly. And the walkman puts film soundtracks everywhere. And before I go to Denmark I am busy choosing tapes to takes with me. Making a soundtrack for a country I have not seen. And the windscreen of the car is the cinema screen — a frame for everything — and when you look through it your sunsets will never be the same; such a good way to end a film and a journey. And when the protagonists of our piece (*Let the Water Run its Course*) *to the Sea that Made the Promise* thought about their own deaths, the only way they could do it truly was to see themselves dying like in the movies, ever more gloriously and more violently, like in *The Wild Bunch* or *Bonnie and Clyde*.

And even being 'here' is more complicated now. And when my son, who's three, speaks to me on the telephone, he says: 'Dad, dad, LOOK, LOOK …' and his understanding of place and the senses is wrongly mapped, confused. And I remember reading somewhere about someone else's child, who, in calling up another house to speak to his friend would always ask: 'Hi, is David here?'

And if these things, and a million others do not change the theatre it will not survive, and I personally couldn't care. I don't mean change in the way of content—like the three or four people I speak to each year now who want to write a play about virtual reality (I mean, really, why would anybody do that?) And I don't mean necessarily that theatre should embrace new technology and bring it onto the stage—I can imagine the question 'Where shall we put the Apple Macs?' getting every bit as dull as 'Where shall we put the televisions?' —in fact it's the same question, pretty well.

What I mean is that the theatre must take account of how technology (from the phone and the walkman upwards) has rewritten and is rewriting bodies, changing our understanding of narratives and places, changing our relationships to culture, changing our understandings of presence. Because to fall back on theatre's oldest and simplest rubric—an actor in front of an audience—is not something one can do lightly, not something one can do without understanding the complexities of what we might mean when we say 'actor' and what we mean when we say 'in front of'. I'm thinking of these little programs you get on the Internet called 'bots' (short for robots). In some contexts they can be quite convincing—passing for human—drawing you into their unreal lives, talking and moving, like actors on a digital stage.

Director Kirstin Denholm of Hotel Pro Forma remarked in Cambridge that the presentations to our seminar on hybridity might have been even more interesting had some of those making them been seated in a glass case. What she meant I think was that presence now is always complicated and layered, a thing of degrees, and in these strange times one can feel closer to a person, sometimes, when they are further away than when they are fully and simply before us. Theatre makers should take note.

That brings me back to my grandmother. Who is dead now (three days ago) and who may be on television soon, in a strange and fitting way, going places, bags packed. I'll see her at the station and I hope you'll join us there.

On Performance Writing

This piece addresses itself to the task of making text for performance, especially within a collaborative process. It is a revised version of a presentation I made in Dartington (UK) at a 1996 conference entitled 'Performance Writing'. I was keen to open the door to a broad, adventurous description of what writing for performance might mean — beyond ideas of playwrighting which is still, sadly, the measure too often employed in the UK, despite a rich history of writers in theatre spaces who are doing something quite different. The piece talks about physical action and set construction as forms of writing, it talks about writing words to be seen and read on-stage rather than spoken, it talks about lists, about improvisation, about reading, about whispering and about collage as a form — in each case implying a critical dialogue with more traditional notions of theatre or performance writing.

Obsessed in any case with lists and indexes, he tried one night to write a list of the texts that he had made, or else texts that he might make. Or of texts that he could make. Through the night the list would slip and slide — breaking up into stories and speculations and then returning to listing again.

Which text should go first in the list? A real one or a possible one.

I chose a real one, remembering that I'd left my son at home ill, to come to a conference. And deciding to talk about him, sometimes, in the list.

1. A text to be whispered by the bedside of a sleeping child.

2. A text to be yelled aloud by a single performer in a car park at dawn.

3. A text to be left on the ansaphones of strangers.

4. A text to be spoken while fucking secretly the partner of a good friend.

5. A text for megaphone.

6. A text which could be used as a weapon.

Remember that prison I told you about? The troops found it deserted, jailers and torturers fled, their prisoners / victims executed in haste, dead in the cells.

And how in one room, stored amongst the bloody implements and signed confessionals, they discovered a strange and endless non-sensical near-gibberish text. How it transpired that the jailers would sit outside their prisoners' doors in the dead of the night and read this text aloud to them repeatedly — denying them sleep and, by destroying language or demolishing sense, attacking the very bounds which tied their charges to the earth and to sanity.

A true story. I keep wondering about those men knelt on the floor of a corridor and reading strange language to their prisoners. Did they think of themselves as performers? Did they chat, in the kitchen or the bar after work, discussing how well or badly their reading work had gone? Did they think about the pauses, the language, the emphasis? Did the reading drive them crazy too? Perhaps.

I think about the text they read from, and at night sometimes in a dream of a handwritten page, I think I can see it but I cannot read the words.

1. A text of lines from half-remembered songs.

2. A love letter written in binary.

3. A text composed of fragments.

In bed, early, Miles is jabbering and making jokes about breakfast and porridge in particular. He tells me that for breakfast we will have spider porridge, and I ask, 'What's that?' and he says *'spider porridge*—with *spiders* in it ...' and I say I will feed him helicopter porridge, or something like that, and he threatens me with many other kinds of porridge until at last he gets to this one: radio porridge. He says we will have radio porridge with voices in it.

All summer we lived in the house with the stars up above it and the earth down below and we ate of radio porridge. Immensely filling, the porridge satisfied hunger but left one haunted with voices under the skin.

Who puts those voices in radio porridge?

No one.

Whose are the voices in radio porridge?

The voices in radio porridge come from the dead. They come from stray signals, lost letters. They come from the people who wrote graffiti on all the walls in town, or the people in books and stories we'd read, and many other places.

1. A text for people to find in their wallets, days later, when you are forgotten.

2. A text to come through people's doors—perhaps a letter.

3. A text for someone to find in the street, caught in one of those eddy-pools of blown leaves and ragged polythene bags.

One day in New York I am walking along, see a note on the floor, blowing past me in the wind, pick it up. The note says this:

'What in the World are You Doing, why are you taking some much time with the ...'

A voice like that is the linkman in radio porridge.

It's radio porridge or something like it that speaks in all of the shows. I couldn't get excited about a deep voice or an authentic voice, but I could get excited by a gabbling voice composed of scraps and layers, fragments, quotations. No editorial, or at least no centre. Like I don't have a voice—I'm just a space this other stuff is flowing through and lodged inside.

1. A text written in condensation.

2. A text written, learned and performed to pass a polygraph test.

3. A series of texts written on a lover. In biro, in lipstick, in permanent marker, in blood, and semen.

4. An invisible text.

5. The same text written every day for a year, in different places, in different locations.

6. A text written on the floor of an old factory.

Ending the coach tour of Sheffield we made—a piece called *Nights in This City* (1995)—the bus arrived at a huge building—a building that served first as the tram depot for the city and then as the main bus depot and which is now disused. In this space, upon the floor we had written out the entire A–Z of the city—an alphabetical text in ten 75-metre-long columns—chalk on concrete floor. Climbing off the bus people would see the exit far down the end of the room, walk towards it, realise they were walking on something and then, in the end, realise what it was—often slowing down to walk and find their own street names, taking people to see where they had once lived, even having their photographs taken next to the name of their streets. In some way this index on the floor served the purpose of a reprise, where the city explored in the performance was laid out in textual miniature for people to survey as a whole.

Very often in the shows there were these lists or catalogues. Sometimes ordered, sometimes chaotic. Language like a camera on endless tracks, zooming everywhere, close-up, wide-shot, tracking shot, point of view. Language jumping you from one story, one world, one discourse to another.

1. A text written at 3am in the middle of a war.

2. A text written in the fast food court of a large European shopping mall.

3. A text which raises questions of ownership.

I come into the front room one afternoon and the TV is playing, and I am shocked beyond belief to find that the characters are speaking words stolen directly from our piece *Some Confusions in the Law about Love* (1989).

Moments pass, and then I realise, in a slow internal turning round, that this is some nameless film I must've flipped through five years ago or more and that I stole the lines from it, scrawling them on a newspaper, transferring them to notebook and then at some later point writing them into the work. Still, watching the film from this point on I am gripped by a feeling of strange violation as a handful of moments from our show *Some Confusions* are repeated, out-of-context, out of character and out of costume.

> 'Come here honey ...' the drunk vamp woman says to her boss's henchman turned betrayer/lover 'If you'd like to see me again I'll give you a list of the times that Charlie's always out ...'

The house full of shelves, full of notebooks, full of overheard and copied lines — film, life, dreams, literature. Anything. Shit — I'm like some teen-burglar — 'I nicked so much stuff I can't even remember what is mine anymore'. And of course Miles is already the same, since his stories when he tells them just recycle verbatim the best lines and characters from the stories he's heard. One night he was feeding the birds in one picture book with bread taken from the pages of another. A kind of gorgeous economy in his madness.

A thieving machine.

When provoked into discussing where their writing 'comes from', some of my students will invoke the notion of a voice. To be looked for intently and nurtured when found, this voice lives in them somewhere, deep down inside. When they find it they want to write in it. This voice is authentic in some way, by its very nature profound. It is knotty, connected to the body. It comes *from them*. Often at night.

And whilst I've done my share of night writing, I never know exactly what they mean.

Because for me writing was so often about collecting, sifting and using from bits of other people's stuff — copied language like precious stones. Authentic has not really been in it.

Working in performance they were always tempted to think about writing (or even speaking) as a kind of trying on of other peoples clothes — a borrowing of power. I speak for a moment like my father. I assume the language of a teacher. I speak for one moment like they do in some movie. I borrow a phrase from a friend, a sentence construction from a lover. A writing that's more like sampling. Mixing, matching, cutting, pasting. Conscious, strategic and sometimes unconscious, out of control. I'm quoting and I don't even know it. Perhaps it's best to think of one's relationship to language like this, as the novelist Michael Moorcock once described a character 'skipping through fragments of half-remembered songs like a malfunctioning juke-box'.

And when my students mention this *voice* (a frighteningly singular thing) which comes from *themselves* I always have a second problem, because not knowing the voice I also fail to recognise (at least not with the same confidence) the 'self' of which they are speaking. For us, in the work and out of it, this notion of self has often seemed after all to be simply a collection of texts, quotations, strategic and accidental speakings — not a coherent thing, much less the single-minded author of some text. What I am, in this text (now) at least, is no more (and no less) than the meeting-point of the language that flows into and flows out of me (these past years, months, days) — a switching station, a filtering and thieving machine, a space in which collisions take place.

Any regrets?

I once asked Ron Vawter (Wooster Group) if he ever wished they could deal with new texts instead of (as he described it to me) going back over the tapes of the twentieth century to see what had happened, to see what had gone wrong. He said yes, he could see a time when that might be fun, but for the moment at least there was so much work left to do. There's so much stuff left in the archives.

1. A broken text.

2. A discredited text.

3. A text to be utterly disowned by all those that perform it.

4. A series of texts in a language that doesn't work.

Perhaps our first subject was always this inadequacy of language. Its unsuitability for the job it has to do, its failure. And in this failure — by definition language is not and cannot express what it seeks to describe — an admission of the struggle in everyday life — to get blunt tools to do fine work, to carve out a life in, around, despite of and through what passes for culture in the late twentieth century.

And in this love of the blunt edges and limits of language he always cared most for illegitimate texts, finding hope and inspiration in the clichés of straight-to-video films, the tortuous prose of a book of instructions for chemistry experiments, a catalogue of the contents of a museum of curious, the simple language of cartoons, comic-strips, the disposable ease of plot summaries for a soap opera or the antiquated text of a fairy story or some mythical tale. The words 'good' and 'writing' never went together that well for us. Bad writing was always more our style. Language transfixed on its own inadequacy. Language at the point of breakdown, at the edges of sense, on the edge of not coping at all.

A writer of nonsense.

A writer of shapes that only look like letters.

A writer of filthy words.

Working on *Pleasure* (in summer 1997) we loved a text I downloaded from the Internet — a huge list entitled simply '*2,334 Filthy Words and Phrases*' — a pedant's catalogue of obscenities, slang words and descriptions containing some 500 alternative ways to say masturbate. First time I printed this list I left it running on the printer and on returning to the office some 20 minutes later found that people there had stopped work and were gathered around the printer from which the text was still spewing. They were poring over the words like so many scholars and obsessives. They were, in a mixture of fascination and repulsion, reading out the lists to each other, revelling in the awfulness, the unsayableness, the unwriteableness of:

YANK THE MEAT

PISS-FLAPS

GET SOME HOLE

PUSH SHIT UPHILL

EAT HAIR PIE

BURP THE WORM

Language at the edges of sense, on the edge of not coping at all.

Our favourite game, working from this text in *Pleasure* rehearsals, was to write these words and others like them on a blackboard on the stage—a piece of kids' language instruction gone wrong, or a foreign language course with a bitter little twist. The words written calmly in capitals, the performers stood beside the blackboard, owning the text written up there, meeting the gaze of the audience like 'this is your lesson for today'.

Months afterwards we made a film *Filthy Words & Phrases* (1998) of Cathy writing each of these words, on a blackboard, in an old abandoned schoolroom. We shot in one continuous seven-hour take and by the end of it Cathy (and crew) were blank with exhaustion and white from the chalk dust. We premiered the film in a Rotterdam porn cinema and could never quite decide if the film was an attack on the profligate redundancy of language or a hymn of sorts to its absurd inventiveness and its complete commitment to change—a marathon naming of the parts in which language proliferates around a crisis.

1. A text for email.

2. A text to be written in blood.

3. A text in a made-up language.

Using gibberish in *(Let the Water Run its Course) to the Sea that Made the Promise* (1986) we used to talk a lot about the sound of voices coming through walls—like the blurred and awful sound of people arguing in the flat downstairs, the sounds of voices gabbling madly in a party—language reduced to its raw shapes, where listening, you do not know the words but you can guess what is being spoken of.

In *Hidden J* (1994) Cathy and Robin speak a version of this gibberish too—only here it has become most definitely foreign—not a fucked-up English, but a shattering of languages from broken Europe—Serb, Russian, Polish swinging to Italian in places. Cathy invisible in the house centre-stage and curtains drawn, speaking down the telephone—and incomprehensible—railing and whispering, yelling and urging, demanding, accusing. And outside the house all we see are the other performers waiting, some of them messing around, Richard peering, upstaging, but in the end all of them heads down, listening. It's not just the audience that listen to the text. Cathy railing and whispering, yelling and urging, demanding, accusing.

And for these moments the two cultures of the piece—drunk git English and war-zone Mainland—sit in their most appalling relationship—the one can neither see, help or understand the other at all. It's the opposite of those British Telecom ads where Bob Hoskins implores one that 'it's good to talk'; in this case it is no fucking good to talk.

A list of streets:

1. Hope Street

2. Furnace Lane

3. Winter Hill

4. Market Street. San Francisco's Oxford Street of lunacy and the wheel-chair homeless—drunk and drugged crazies on every street corner; those that aren't lying in comatose sleep in doorways, or propped against the sides of buildings are the ones too fast for sleep—the ones each dancing to some inaudible tune—jigging, walking, twisting, turning (one woman beating the side of a trash can with glee in some unfinished, never-ending symphony of noise)—and all of them muttering in some indi-vidual yet strangely collective voice—whispers, threats, assumptions, delusions—random samplings from the last days of the mechanical age...

...that was, pretty well, the kind of theatre or performance text I had in mind.

Or at least not the spectacle of 'new playwrights' at a 1997 conference in London's Royal Court Theatre whose biggest (almost only) topic of conversa-tion seemed to be long long pontifications on the understanding of a comma. How directors and actors can't understand a comma these days. The terrible shame of it.

Hard for me to understand, having never much cared for punctuation.

I mean I'd rather say:

here are 26 letters:

a b c d e f g h i j k l m n o p q r s t u v w x y z

now write a text for performance.

Never cared much for playwrights. And in any case in some recent shows the text was generated in good part by performer improvisation — in reaction to written stimulus or without it. In this way a two-paragraph fragment becomes a ten-minute monologue — a growing, generative process of improvisation, negotiation, discussion, more writing and eventual fixing. A kind of speaking that becomes writing.

Working in this way — around the rhythms of text that's at least half made-up on the spot he was interested in precisely those textures — of thought, repetition, self-correction, hesitation, and so on — in which speech excels and which writing can only begin to approximate. Working with video-tape and transcripts of improvisations they were concerned to capture some of that sense, in speech, of how a voice finds itself, of how language stumbles, corrects and then flies — explorations of the struggle and process of language itself. A concern with language not as text then, but as event.

A series of spells:

1. To Bewitch a Service Station at Midnight.

2. To Exorcise a Bad Spirit from a Housing Estate.

3. To Escape from Prison or Some Terrible Place.

4. To Bring Some Ecstasy Kid from a Coma

5. To Combat Insincerity in a Soap Opera

6. To Summon the Power of Angels.

In *200% & Bloody Thirsty* (1987/8) the characters try on the voices of angels as if by speaking like them they might have power to raise the dead. Borrowing language for your own purposes, for its power and authority, for its style. Language is always a suit of someone else's clothes you try on — the fit is not good but there's power in it.

Football fans on a train some months ago boasting about their drunken exploits at a previous game: 'We *proceeded* to the White Hart pub and we were there *observed* to drink several pints of lager.' The whole conversation taking place in the style of an arresting officer's report. Stealing other people's language to bolster your own power.

In performance we use the struggle to feel right in the text, and the distance between the performer and her text is always visible. In recent shows this gap is all the more visible because the text features as paper or script — a physical object which can be picked up, handled, subjected to scrutiny, curiosity, indifference, contempt. In the work you can see the performers eyeing up the text, wondering about it, knowing that whatever it is it isn't them.

Or, if the fit is good between performer and text, it is a good fit that has to be struggled for and a fit that makes surprising use of the original material—the scenes of clichéd TV cop shit and emotion-drama in *Club of No Regrets* (1993/4) are smashed to pieces in Terry's final exertions as the 'character' Helen X—she jumbling the phrases, cuts from one scene to another, regardless of one sense whilst making another. It *is* like getting blood out of a stone but in the end she does get the material to mean for her, even if it is almost destroyed in the process.

The characters/performers always moving from outside language to a relationship in which they seem to own it.

Back on market.

One wrecked woman goes past me, her eyes wide, her arms folded tight across herself like she's a parcel wrapped too tight—she catches my eye and without breaking pace with her whisper, threatens out loud: 'Don't look at me you fucking psycho-killer.'

And I say: 'It takes one to know one.'

She follows me.

1. A text of obvious lies.

2. A text of promises.

3. A text of accusations.

How does Claire begin in *Hidden J* (1994)?

Long ago and far away there was a country and all the people there were a bunch of fucking cunts…

and of course she is talking about England and all the people on the stage.

1. Write like the text were by someone else.

2. Adopt another's handwriting.

1. Use a different pen.

1. Write the text on cardboard, as if this were the only thing you had left, scrawl on the cardboard like urgency erased all style.

and,

2. Write about personas.

I should talk about Mark E. Smith here. Better yet, read the back of The Fall's 1978 or 1979 *Totale's Turns* live album recorded in Working Men's Clubs in Wakefield, Doncaster, etc.

CALL YOURSELVES BLOODY PROFESSIONALS?

Was one of the shower-cum-dressing room comments The Fall received after completing their 'turn' which makes up side one of this record, along with 'everybody knows the best groups cum from London' and 'You'll never work again'.

Enough, Side 1 was recorded in front of an 80% disco-weekend-mating audience, but we never liked preaching to the converted anyway. Side 2 other places — 'New Puritan' at home, during which said home was attacked by a drunk, which accounts for the tension on that track.

I don't particularly like the person singing on this LP. That said I marvel at his guts. This is probably the most accurate document of The Fall ever released, even though they'll have a hard time convincing their mams and dads about that, ha ha.

R. Totale XVII
Honorary Member
Wakefield Young Drinkers Club.

Smith always casting himself in other personas, as other people, as fucked up narrators with a bad attitude. Like Ballard's central character in his science fiction books who are always called Traven or Travis or Trabert or Talbot, sometimes called by all of these names in the space of one chapter. Always some version of the same bloke, whose name, like his identity is forever in question. Like I don't particularly like the person writing this text.

1. A text which sticks in the mouth, begging you not to say it.

2. A text that spills and slips and runs.

3. A text that no-one will ever hear.

In *Marina & Lee* (1990/91) Cathy delivered several of her texts at an ever-decreasing volume so that the final sections of each were completely inaudible.

I had to write these texts anyway but was puzzled for weeks about what to put in them. In some ways it didn't seem to matter at all but in other ways these seemed like the most important texts in the piece. What might one wish to say, but have no one hear?

1. A text where the voice is clear and sharp.

2. A text where the voice is compromised.

3. A text where the voice is under heavy pressure.

Watching the film *Performance* (Nicholas Roeg and Donald Cammell) and watching the 'character' of James Fox — East End gangster plunged into the underworld of drugs, rock'n'roll, hippie sexuality. Like Jack the Lad cannot cope. Like his voice cannot deal with the things it has to describe.

That's the thing you have to do with a voice after all — make it speak of the things that it cannot deal with — make it speak of the illegal.

I'm a man, I'm a man, I'm all fuckin man…

James Fox as drugged out gangster transformed in wig, kimono and make-up, not able to cope.

That was something we always loved to do—play a gap between the voice and the bodies from which it arises. The teenage shop-girls were making physics lectures and then slipping into descriptions of long Russian winter romances. The bloke at a wedding was making an announcement about bombs in the car park. The clumsy pantomime skeletons were performing a very old poetic text. Like all the time these texts take the people who speak them by surprise.

Round midnight he made an end to his listing of texts and tried instead to think about silence. It was silent in the house. He made a list of silences, like the list from *Pleasure* (1998).

The kind of silence you sometimes get in phone calls to a person that you love.

The kind of silence people only dream of.

The kind of silence that is only for waiting in.

The kind of silence as a thief makes away with the gold.

The kind of silence that follows a car crash.

The kind of silence in a crowded house when everyone is asleep.

The kind of silence between waves at the ocean.

The kind of silence which follows a big argument.

The kind of silence that happens when you put your head under the water of the bath.

The kind of silence that only happens at night.

The kind of silence that happens when you close the curtains and climb into bed.

The kind of silence that has everything in it.

On Performance and Film: Tuning In

On Performance and Film was published just after the first TV broadcast of *DIY*—a 10-minute documentary for Channel 4 co-directed by myself and photographer Hugo Glendinning and made in collaboration with performance artist Michael Atavar. The film *DIY* formed part of a growing (and continuing) body of work involving Forced Entertainment in collaborations with Glendinning—not just on moving film, but for stills, installations and digital media—and in this piece I frame some of the connections between 13 years of making performance and the processes of working for the camera and, once again, the idea of evidence—on film or otherwise, of the traces left by extraordinary scenes. An edited version of this piece was first published in *Total Theatre* magazine.

*

On the last day of shooting for our film *DIY* Michael Atavar dances between the urinals of an Islington public toilet, to the slowed down sound of *Funky Town*. As he dances the camera-man James Welland follows him, ghosting his moves in the fake street lamp light that spills in through broken toilet windows, and as Michael moves and James follows I think that in some strange way James is dancing also.

Or, at least, I assume he is.

Because the way this last and most important scene works, and the way the cramped space of the toilet works, there simply can't be anybody else present during the filming. Neither Hugo nor I can see any of it. It's just a question of talk, rehearse, then get out of the way.

So Michael dances, and James, who's been told simply—'He'll dance, like he's dancing with ghosts, he might even dance with you—don't stop, keep filming, be human'—dances too, and keeps on filming till the record ends.

*

Coming to film-making from performance I'm tempted to ask some fairly insensible questions like: 'Can you film an atmosphere?' 'What goes onto film?' 'What goes onto tape?'

Put it this way—can the feeling in a room get captured on film and stored? Can you pass it to tape and edit suite and then out again to tape? And once you've done that is the atmosphere still there?

I keep thinking of a track on some obscure album by The Fall—an album full of live versions, demos and bedroom tapes. The sleeve notes, in a mix of Mark Smith's characteristic scrawl and manual typewriter fragments, simply inform that track seven *New Puritan* 'was recorded while the house came under attack from a drunk'.

Take a listen to it. And think clearly if you can tell that something is happening.

*

We spent years in rehearsals watching back tapes of yesterday's work on one theatre show or another—trying to sort out what happened, to work out structures, developments, relationships—translating the skills, lucks and accidents of improvisation into diagrams, notes, stuff that can be reproduced.

Single camera, hi-8 tape shot from the back of the rehearsal room. In one sense watching these can be an act of faith—a staring at blobs in near desperation—but certain tapes are strangely charged, bearing traces beyond ones expectations. Watch that tape of the first day Cathy first screamed her head off in *Hidden J* (1994) rehearsals—you can tell that something has happened in the room.

*

When Hugo saw *Club of No Regrets* (1993) for the first time we were about a month or more away from completing it. And the show was really fairly out of control. There were the scenes for which the performers were parcel-taped to chairs, and the scenes in which large amounts of leaves, water (for rain), talcum powder (for smoke) and fake blood were thrown around the stage, the many scenes where the text was endlessly distracted from by noise, by interruptions, by the actions of other performers. And after watching a run-though of the material Hugo and I talked a bit about how he might photograph the work and he said that he'd 'like to take the pictures in the equivalent way to the way we were working theatrically', and I asked 'What's that then?' and Hugo said he was going to photograph the piece without looking through the camera.

He shot without looking—a flash gun in one hand and the camera in the other—like a paparazzi photographer trying to get a lucky shot through the window of an escaping prison van—camera at arm's length, held above his head, thrust right into the middle of scenes, never certain what he'd get. But a part of the action.

The resulting photographs seem not so much to contain the event as to hunt it, always losing—photographs full of bodies that are slipping out of frame, the central objects not in focus, the story always one step away from the centre. And seeing these images, as has often been the case with these mid-process shoots with Hugo, was also a really vital part of the making of this piece—because in seeing the photographs we could see, for the first time, what exactly we were doing.

*

London. On *DIY*. It's midnight and Hugo, myself and the crew are hanging round outside the toilets as filming continues inside. Its a strange feeling—to know that here, behind a closed door something half-rehearsed and half-unknown is taking place and that we won't see the shots for days.

It's a good feeling, though, and it leaves us strangely confident. Our principle here is something like a performance in itself—the setting up of a situation—Michael, the camera and dancing—trusting to the place, its history and the energies of the people as they meet.

*

Working on film, after all, we liked the possibility that you only have to get it right once. None of that theatre nonsense of reproduction—from improv through rehearsal and performance—getting endless intangibles to be present in so many different rooms. Instead—just get it right and get it on film.

Shooting stills for projects with Hugo we've always loved the liberty of those performances that only have to be right, or simply look right, for one-125th of a second. As performance goes, that's pretty weird stuff—about eyes and energy, knowing and not knowing, focus and lack of it—where often, as performer you can't even be sure if the camera is getting you or not.

And Hugo, for his part, has always liked the edge between performance and photography itself—the edge of chance beauty produced by working to simple, bendy rules built from trial and error, and designed to produce the unexpected. Take a look at those pictures of Cathy during *Red Room* (1993)—could she have known the way her eyes looked? Could Hugo even have known?

I doubt it.

The chances are he was shooting without looking through the camera, holding it over his head or at arms length, shooting without being sure in order to escape the logics of framing and control—as if that alone might capture certain traces.

Could Cathy reproduce that look, or Hugo that photograph? I'd guess not, it's just not that kind of performance, not from either of them. It's something beyond.

*

Commissioned to make *DIY* with Michael Atavar, Hugo and I come at these film questions yet again, only now with a budget from Channel 4, 10 rolls of Super 16 and a range of locations from the cruising grounds of Russell Square to the flat in which playwright Joe Orton and his lover Kenneth Halliwell ended their lives in 1967—Ken murdering Joe with a hammer and then killing himself with a bottle of Nembutals washed down in a full jar of grapefruit juice.

After weeks of plans, permissions and schedules we follow Michael on a journey, marking the gap between real, unruly sexual lives and their passage into multiple versions of history—mainstream and subcultural, gay and straight, public and personal.

Perhaps in the end it is a film about going with Michael to certain places and seeing what happens. About seeing what camera and DAT tape can capture of Noel Road, about seeing how dark the mood gets if you scrape back the paintwork in long-abandoned toilets and read the graffiti from gay men whose lives have been drawn to such places and who now are all gone.

Michael called it a kind of tuning in and indeed, perhaps the paradigmatic shot of him has his ear pressed to a glass at the bricked-up arches of a former public toilet—a place where 30 years before Orton himself had cruised for sex and which now is a blank wall of stone—a sounding-board, of sorts.

If you listen at a wall like that one, can you hear voices? And can those voices be set down onto tape?

I think so.

Repeat Forever: Body, Death, Performance, Fiction

1. The Dreams

The dreams of intensive care are strictly that made-for-TV-movie crap which seeps in to substitute memory; the green ECG spikes, dark voices and white floors of broadcast collective unconscious.

Impossible to think that the true details of these events now escape me. That the unforgettable is also, by nature, unrecoverable.

In the dreams I'm 19, maybe 20. My heart is going haywire and I have these attacks, where, for no reason its beat cranks up to 140, 150 and beyond. Breath knocked out of me, shaking. These things are scary, always unexpected. Not sure if its summer or autumn but certain it's Exeter, in England. Two or three times a day I am panicking, heart racing, sitting on the floor.

∞

After weeks (months?) this shit-head doctor, fed up with stalling and my complaints, decides to run a test. I get this tape-recorder strapped to me and a whole load of electrodes, wires. It's a 24-hour tape and the doctors hope to catch one of what they call 'the episodes'. A whole day goes by, I get on with things, 'unencumbered' by the box, and nothing much happens. Apprehensive, inverted — now, for the first and only time, I want my body to go wrong, to perform its trick of wrongness. Nothing happens.

The rig of wires and machine looks so good we shoot publicity photos for a performance project that we're doing. The pictures are of me lying half naked in an empty room in the house, eyes closed, a spider of cables draped across my chest. We joke a bit about how bad everyone's going to feel if I end up dead. (Years later we have this gag routine that art is the commercial exploitation of misery, and here I see why.)

Day passes, turns to night, I go to bed. No 'episodes', no action, but in my sleep something does happen, something bad that is only discovered because of the tape.

∞

It seems that the daytime speedings-up have their mirror — a series of slowings-down that are happening under cover of night.

As recorded on the tape, my heart is slowing down as I sleep. Its beat is dropping, dropping past 50 to 40 to 30 and then 20. Dropping past 20 to 10 and from there to its lowest point — to sometimes, in the depth of night, on a road whose name I can't recall, in a room painted blue, my heartbeat slows to four beats and three beats a minute. Very dangerous.

I remember going back there, to that house, six or seven years later, or at least trying to go back. We were in town for some other reason, I wanted to

drive past and have a look, courting that shock and tingle of recognition, courting the flashback to scary times. Trouble was, when we got there I couldn't
place it, couldn't even remember the number. Maybe someone painted the
door, maybe even the railings had gone. In any case, we could have been anywhere, nowhere. No bells ringing.

The doctor tells me this: the only thing keeping me alive as my heartbeat
slipped down past four to three and nothingness was that I'd move somehow in
my sleep and the move would kick off my heart again.

∞

So my question, now and always: what moved me?

Sometimes I think my body saved me. Or that my body saved itself. An
emergency system down deep somewhere, buried in the blood.

And sometimes I think that dreaming must have saved me. And I wonder
what stories were unfolding to cause those twitches, those moves that kicked
me back and kept me this side of the line.

And so I become, if I wasn't already, and in this story at least, a person kept
alive by stories and by dreaming.

∞

Kept alive by electricity too. As a result of the tape information I get rushed
into hospital and a pacemaker gets inserted in my left shoulder, wire running
down through the vein (artery?) all the way down and screwed to the inside
wall of my heart. The pacemaker keeps track of how fast my heart beats. If it
beats less than 72 times a minute it fills in electrically—jumping a shock in the
muscle to make it contract.

Moments of paradigm alienation: I am lying on my back, sluiced-up on the
pre-med, watching the x-ray image on the monitor of my own chest and heart,
watching the black wire snake and curl inside me as they try to move it remotely, hearing them curse a little as the wire slips around. For some (valium)
reason I'm laughing—this skidding wire is a cartoon comedy, played out under
my skin.

What does it mean, to see inside yourself? In some literal, not spiritual way.
A pornographic image burnt on the retina. Laughing at your own insides.

Someone tells me they developed the pacemaker for the first astronauts—
designed to cut-in if their hearts failed under zero-g. The civilian model is a
kind of off shoot of the space programme—a kind of medical Teflon, marvels
of science—and so my continued life and the space programme intertwine a
second time. My birth date: 20/7/62. First landing on the moon: 20/7/68.

So, in this story at least, I am kept alive by the space race, and by implication, by the cold war which precipitated it.

∞

A blurred recollection that D. and I attempt intercourse on the night I'm wearing the tape machine. I keep thinking of the folks at the hospital — can they read the tape, can they look at the rise and fall of the heartbeat, log it to the time of day and work out what's happening? Pretty likely, more or less. Must be a strange strange narrative form.

The thought of them reading the tape or its printout, translating beats and spikes into action, reminds me of a definition I hear years later, describing a computer nerd as being someone who can laugh at a bad line of programming code.

It reminds me also of our own codes. Of the lists of sections, moments, images and types of material scattered through notebooks and on huge sheets of paper in the rehearsal space. Who could decode:

CRYING / CRYING / KISS / KISS / KISS / TROUBLED / DRUG / TRIP /
TELEGRAM / CRYING / TROUBLED / KISS

into anything like the rich and chaotic mess that *Club of No Regrets* (1993) really is?

I write a letter to the hospital. I want the tape they made of me, or a print-out of it. I want to listen to what happened at 3.16 in the morning. I want to hear the story of time slowing down, the story of the body, as Roseanne Stone would have it, at the end of the mechanical age.

2. The Games

For some of the strongest images in her collection *Immediate Family* photographer Sally Mann captured her own children in the elegant poses of feigned death.

In one shot her son Emmett floats limp, belly up and head almost below the water of a pond; in another her daughter Virginia seems to hang broken from a rope in a tree. Mann has spoken of such pictures as attempts at a kind of psychic inoculation — protection in advance against the chances of her children's damage and death.

All those who play dead know the giddying contradictions of their game — first, that death can never be convincingly played because the heart and lungs move regardless of our will, second, that playing dead takes us precariously close to the edges of gaming itself, close to sleeping or simply waiting, close to leaving the play or the game.

Whilst watching Pete Brooks's production *A Cursed Place* (based loosely on *Woyzeck*) these things flipped through my mind, and soon, after much to-do about acting, one of the performers/characters lay still and silent — 'dead' on the floor. I lost the play for a moment then, only watching the contradictory breathing of the corpse, the rise and fall and sound of her breath, getting calmer as the exertions of her death throes were contained. I liked to watch her then because her part in the play was finished and she had nothing whatever to tell me, and I loved the charged space of that—the gorgeous collusion of significance and banality, the death in the story and the meta-fiction balanced perfectly by the sight of the actress, slowing down her breathing and only waiting, for the end, her thoughts perhaps on the bar, or the performance of that night.

∞

Death haunts all performance, sometimes taunting its fakery, sometimes lending it power. In my own work with Forced Entertainment I'm struck by a fear that the performers are publicly rehearsing their own deaths, plotting lives for their own dead selves. After all, almost every performance stacks a new corpse behind them. I remember that Robin in our first piece was 'dead' for the final scenes, that he'd lie motionless for 20-odd minutes, slumped at a table and covered by a sheet. Cocooned in near-darkness, overhearing the progress of the rest of the night's work, sleep would often come to him, and only the sound of the final applause would wake him up at all, bringing Lazarus back for the curtain call. (Isn't it strange to think of someone sleeping on the stage—a kind of doubling of the other world?) Robin has died perhaps 20 more times since then and, I hope, will long continue to do so. The dead selves are stacked up behind him—a ketchup-bloodied corpse in *(Let the Water Run its Course) to the Sea that Made the Promise* (1986), a talcum-powder ghost in *Some Confusions in the Law about Love* (1989), a half-naked body laid out on Lux flake snow in *200% & Bloody Thirsty* (1987) and most recently for *Showtime* (1996) a long agonised death from a stomach wound—a tin of Heinz spaghetti clutched to his midriff as he yells.

I think about his death taking shape around him, version by version by version.

I try to find an old scrapbook which (I think) contains one of those pictures we shot in Exeter—the pictures of me with the tape-recorder strapped to my chest. I can't find the pictures or the scrapbook but while I'm looking I come across a letter from my brother.

3. The Letters

This first letter is from my brother in Africa. It comes from that time when he was living there, happy and in love, making plans for an imminent return here to England, with new-found partner and friend forever Natasha.

It comes from that time before the car crash then, that time before the car rolled on the way to Avalavi and six people stepped out, dusting down unharmed and N lay dead inside it in her seat. It comes from that time before irony earned its true and bitter name. Before Mark came home on the TWA sporting proudly the traditional fabric top that N had always held to her and said 'I love this one, I love this one, I'll wear this one going home …'.

The letter is nothing but blank ironies. A description of a journey. A day at the beach. Some plans for coming home. Simple pleasures timed to hurt.

∞

The letter spins me into reverie. Other letters, these ones unreal.

I think of Mark returning to Ghana after N's funeral — his dream fear that there would be a letter waiting for him there — from N. His image — a letter posted before she'd even thought of climbing into that preposterous car, a letter posted a day or two before she died, a letter slowed, delayed and loitering to his sad house in the vagaries of the Ghanaian postal system.

A paradigm irony. A text-kiss goodbye. A bitterness.

But she had not written. Not written or, if she had, (just imagine) the letter was lost or destroyed.

Same thing when Richard's brother drowned. A week for Rich of fearing some postcard of good English good-times and weather.

Reversals, cancellations, lingerings. Ghosts in the mail.

∞

In any case, for my part N was never really present anyway — I never saw her, let alone met her, never heard her, let alone spoke.

She was someone I worked hard to construct — from M's letters, from his photos, from M's stories, my Mum and Dad's accounts of meeting her. She was always a construct, always a figure summoned from will and data.

And then, having put together this woman from fragments I worked hard to cancel her out. To know her and the loss of her.

Never saw her, let alone met her, never heard her, let alone spoke.

I scan the stuff, trying hard to understand her, to summon her. This girl in Africa. Gorgeous. Funny. English. Inclined to sing. A fragment of narrative in Mark's letter — some journey they undertook together. Picture of N in a (blue?) dress, holding hands with two kids at the school.

And then, having built her, I have to cancel her. The references, photographs and stories no longer have an object, no longer have a body round which to cohere.

∞

I'm struggling. Build. Cancel. The endlessness of this process, and the bizarre-
ness of its circularity perhaps can't be properly described. Its 3/02/97 at nearly
midnight. Words written to the hard disc, saved and then erased, words and
binary beneath them, written, saved then erased, like I cannot, in a single line
(called a story or a sentence) write of this thing which is a process, a simultane-
ity of finding her and losing her.

It spirals. It overlays. Build. Cancel.

Save all? Revert to saved ...

∞

When we go to the funeral (in the South somewhere, the place where she lived)
I get something of a breakthrough.

Not because of more stories, photographs and data, but because, when her
brothers carry in the coffin, shoulders strained in performance of this unenvi-
able task, I can see, more than anything else, that it weighs something.

I know then that she existed.

4. I Just Came to Say Goodbye

Ron Vawter tells me that when preparing for the role of conservative lawyer
Roy Cohn in his solo performance *Roy Cohn / Jack Smith* he used to go to bed
with tapes of the lawyer's voice set up to playback on a timer whilst he slept.
Ron felt that in this way Cohn's voice somehow entered him, affecting his
subsequent performances in a manner that could not be pinned down.

Ron laughing (some café in Brussels): 'I tell you, out there last night I did
something and I said to myself boy, where did that come from, that took me by
surprise.'

∞

When Ron himself died I got asked by the *Guardian* to work on an obituary
piece, and at this point the tapes of my interview with Ron loomed large — a
dare and an invitation. Stacked in the corner of my desk and gathering dust the
tapes seemed to beckon — play these tapes of Ron tonight while you sleep, then
do the writing in the morning. Let him speak.

I couldn't do it.

∞

Flashback. Ron in his dressing room backstage at the ICA, London, body covered in sarcoma scars, and preparing for part two of the show by mixing the
ashes of Jack Smith into his make-up. A thick mix of gold flakes and human

ashes—his preparation for the summoning of the dead—a pulling of them into the body in a present time.

Ron's technique stays in my mind as an inconceivable yet inevitable mix— half cool technician, half shaman-magician. A Brechtian stand-in possessed with the purest performance control, possessed on the other side by demons, by voices and tongues. A soon-to-be-dead man in consultation with the already dead and yet only a stagehand, an accountant dragged on-stage to do the books.

5. Scars

Ron's duality brings me back to my own; that precarious balance of fiction and biology written straight on the fabric of my skin at wrist and shoulder. Roll up the sleeve, pull down the shirt—there are two scars I live beneath, two marks on this skin that seem to frame its possibilities, another kind of code.

On the left shoulder the thick mess of distressed tissue whose origin I wrote about already—slash lines of scalpel work stitched up and then healed after pacemaker op., the same skin cut open four (4) years later when they change the battery, cut on the scar and stitched again. And then again, five (5) years later, for a second battery change, I'm cut once more and stitched yet again, the skin getting more and more reluctant, more and more convinced that the battle is a losing one, a boxer's nose stays broken, a blunt knife of never-healing scar, ugly.

This first scar is all knife—all physicality. Remember (82 or 83) when they first did it, I only cried when I got back to my hospital bed and looked down— I could see then what they'd done to my body. I mean that they had cut it open and left something in it. That someone had cut me. It's a scar about biology.

∞

The second scar comes from when I was 12—a tiny tiny mark on the right wrist, an almost indecipherable sign.

At a friend's house, a crowd of kids hanging round, some Sunday afternoon. The friend's father (just back from the pub) persuades us that he is a hypnotist. He takes my wrist and tells me that he is going to put a piece of silver paper on it, and that when the silver paper touches my skin its going to burn so hard that I'll push it off immediately.

He talks around this idea for a while and then plants the tin foil on me— one tiny piece. Crowd of kids looking on.

The skin burns, I move my hand and a blister forms—straight away. I see a room with beige carpet, MFI suite, copies of *Jackie* magazine for girls. Blister, damaged skin.

The scar never goes.

∞

Years later I read the tin-foil/burning routine in a book of cod hypnotism. They suggest it as a good test for hypnotic susceptibility. Anyone who feels heat from the foil will be easily hypnotised. Needless to say there's no mention of blisters.

This second scar is all thought—all fiction and suggestion.

It keeps me alive. Between the knife and suggestion.

Between fact and magic itself.

6. THE STORY:

'Rose of Misfortunes'

In her life Rose has a lot of bad luck indeed. In fact, she jokes that she is a target of some kind, some kind of a joke for the gods, but it's not that much of a joke.

As a child she stabs out her eye on a pencil. She loses her dinner money, she has bad dreams, she fails a blood test and has to stay behind, her ability to judge distances is seriously impaired. She keeps bumping into things.

A new kid comes to school that looks just like Rose. This new kid is caught up in some terrible custody dispute and one day its errant father comes round the school with some henchmen, determined to snatch her and abduct her to Spain. He snatches Rose instead, mistaking her, getting half way to the airport before she persuades him the truth. The bloke dumps Rose on the tarmac, she has no taxi fare and has to walk back home. Next day its the 100m running race at school. Rose is usually a quite good runner but this day she has terrible blisters. She loses the race.

Rose has a childhood that isn't ideal but she tries to be stoical. Her father dies in a drinking accident and her step-brother dies on a kids' TV show, falling in the vat of that vile luminous gunk what's meant to get tipped onto losing contestants. Rose is mortified and her mum contrives to blame her. Why wasn't Rose closer to her step-brother? Why couldn't she stop him jumping in?

Rose doesn't really have much hope. She reads omens into everything. Tea leaves, the position of stars, satellites, bullet holes in the window, the arrangement of abusive graffiti outside her school. Anyway. Her mum moves into a council flat, the whole block named after a well-known fascist leader whose name begins with H. Rose doesn't like it in the flats. The stairwells are scary. A meteorite lands near by on the stunty wasteground of a park. Rose rushes out to see what has happened and gets right close to the meteorite. It gives off a gas and the gas infects Rose with a strange illness. She loses her hair and her skin goes the colour of boiled mince. Rose spends her 10th birthday in an isolation ward. Mum waves through the observation window but Rose doesn't see her on account of the condensation.

When Rose comes out of hospital mum and the neighbours have bought her one of those domestic animals whose name begins with D and has three letters. No one is surprised that when Rose goes to sleep the creature attacks without mercy, wounding her neck. To an animal like that, Rose just reminds it of one thing: food.

Rose gets scared by stories. She cannot read books because she is frightened of being taken over by the characters. She grows up fast. She gets fat.

There is a war and the town where she lives is badly bombed. She tends a patch of garden, planting things in it to grow. She plants a seed and a tree grows, she plants a light bulb and a street lamp grows, she plants a brick and a high-rise grows. But the things she grows don't last long, always stunted, always wilting pretty in the dawn.

Rose wins a holiday round the world for her and her mum. The plane they get on is hijacked and forced to land in Endland (*sic*). The cops storm the plane and Rose is the only person wounded. Now she walks with a limp.

Back home she gets a job at the mortuary and then loses it, and then later that same day loses her handbag with all her cards, money and house keys in. She stubs her toe and is electrocuted (twice) by a faulty appliance for flattening or taking the creases out of clothes (four letters). When she gets home people have already been round the house and nicked lots of stuff, only pausing in their thievery to shit on the carpet and leave what looks like offal in her bedroom.

Rose gets spots, she gets a rash on her thigh, she gets behind with her rent and gets chucked out of her flat and then her boyfriend chucks her in favour of a girl in the pub with a smaller arse and bigger tits. Rose's football team gets relegated. She develops an allergy to water and so can't wash. Rose breaks her leg when walking around town, she traps her thumb in a door, she loses her voice and has to write everything down. Then she gets stuck in a lift.

She goes to a party and gets drunk. She says something stupid to somebody stupid and gets a punch on the jaw. Rose has a premonition dream that the world will end in seven (7) days, so she takes to the woods. When the world doesn't end she really feels small.

Rose loses her house. She loses her diary with all her phone numbers in it. She gets a throat infection. She goes to another party in an attempt to cheer up and get a life. She gets off with a bloke at the party and catches a sexual illness from him. She gets embarrassed at the bus stop 'cos this bloke is always there and always laughing at her.

Rose is 'just seventeen' © when she tries smuggling drugs thru customs, but at the last minute panics, goes to the toilet and swallows the lot. Rose is high for a week and then very very low. She collapses. Goes catatonic, gets rushed to hospital in a smear of bells and red lights.

A nonsense of days and nights that other people call a week. On the ward, buried deep in her own head, quite out of touch with the world she tries to make a list of faults and strengths. By the end of that dark week she has filled 200 of those yellow exercise books that people find sometimes in dreams — weaknesses on the left-hand side of the page and strengths on the right, all wrote up in the neat handwriting of a girl. There is no writing on the right-hand side of the page.

Rose in a coma, nearing death.

7. The Stone

When he leaves Ghana for the final time (four months after N's death) Mark goes to say goodbye to the people next door — a family that have halfway adopted him, looked after him at times. He hands over the useful stuff (pans, medicine, books or whatever) that there's no point in carrying home. They shake hands, do lots of smiling.

Then they tell him something special.

They tell him that they've asked their gods to look after him. (Which is good because, like me, he has none of his own.) The bloke gives Mark a stone and tells him he must keep it carefully and take it to England.

Once home Mark is supposed to crumble the stone and rub the dust all over his body. When he does this the gods will know where he is and be able to find him far away — once he's rubbed with the stone they'll be able to protect him.

Mark takes the stone.

∞

I never, to this date, asked Mark if he really did do that with the stone, but I assume and will always assume that he did.

I have this picture of him in an upstairs bedroom, lit by street-lamp-light in a house near Derby, or in a squat in Lambeth with frost beyond the window, stripped off and brushing dirt on him. Lying down in the dark and feeling grime on his skin. Lying down in the dark and closing his eyes and flashing back and forwards in time. Stone on the skin, glowing faintly.

Incomprehensible gods making round-the-world flights to watch him, so that even in dreams he isn't alone. Gods collecting air miles, gods going transnational, working beyond the borders of the nation-state.

Perhaps the stone is a radioactive isotope. The gods use some kind of Geiger tracing.

A stone like that is valuable. Could be useful.

∞

My son Miles (aged 3 at the time) played this game of feeding the birds in one picture book with bread from the pages of another. A kind of gorgeous economy in his madness, his transferral of resources through incomprehensible distances.

In the same way Mark lends the magical stone he's been given to Rose. The stone slipping from the real world to the fictional one, in the palm of a hand.

Rose (in the coma, in the story) takes the stone and crumbles it. She spreads it on her puny body. The gods look up from their work — there's another person they have to look out for. One of them stirs, crosses the border, goes fictional, turns up outside Rose's ward in hospital in Endland (*sic*).

When she goes to walk under a collapsing bridge the god saves her. When she goes to drink poison it saves her. When a virus gets under her skin and into her blood the god saves her again. Rose gets strong, confident. She comes out of the coma. She does not really believe in the gods and whatnot, but she won't turn down help from anyone, even entities of dubious ontology. Rose prospers. She survives.

8. Ghent

Mid-February. A coffin hotel, or its European equivalent, with just enough room for a chair, bed and TV.

I lie on the bed and channel-hop, soon idly transfixed by the barely decipherable images of sexual intercourse on a crudely scrambled porn channel — bobbing heads on huge erections, spread legs, pumping arses all awash in seas of static, colours shifting in storms of jagged lines. Here the body is scrambled as ghost machinery — never coming but preferring endless motion — the piston-dream of fucking, in purple distortion. Unwatchable. Not recognisable.

I sleep, too tired, drunk and bemused to masturbate.

∞

Performing in our durational piece *Red Room* for two weeks Will Waghorn uses his heartbeat to time the exposure of the photographic prints beneath the enlarger. A bizarre tying of an external physical process to an internal one. In 16 heartbeats the image is clear, but 10 heartbeats and it is washed out, 23 and it is burnt black.

The image he prints is of Richard and Terry. Dripping wet and covered in fake blood, sprawled at the edge of a bath tub, clutched to each other, faces buried, unseen. Playing dead. Teen suicides. Covered in fake blood.

If you enter a birthday in my electronic diary you can tell it to repeat the reminder year after year.

Once the date is entered the prompt comes:

Repeat Forever?

∞

I dream in the hotel bed. Fake blood in my veins. Glycerine tears. The perfect line from Toni Braxton's MTV slush-hit comes spilling from a faraway room — 'unbreak my heart, uncry these tears …' but I don't hear it.

Fake blood. Glycerine tears. A kind of prop-biology. Roll up the sleeve, pull down the shirt. Like in the end of Bergman's *Fanny and Alexander*, I make a hymn to the little world (of theatre), through which I've moved these years, glimpses of the work writ soft and close to home.

Fake guts. Stage booze. Electrical heart. A dream of static bodies, wounds awash in distortion and magical dust that people call glitter. Ghost bodies covered in talcum powder. Strap on organs — cock, tits, ears, nose, wigs. Blunt swords and party hats. Taped rain. Disconnected phones. Lux flakes instead of snow.

Like I lived my life in this pretend land. In between it and my real one.

Fragments of shows and non-shows.

A toy house. Snow shaker.

Scars.

Repeat forever?

Yes.

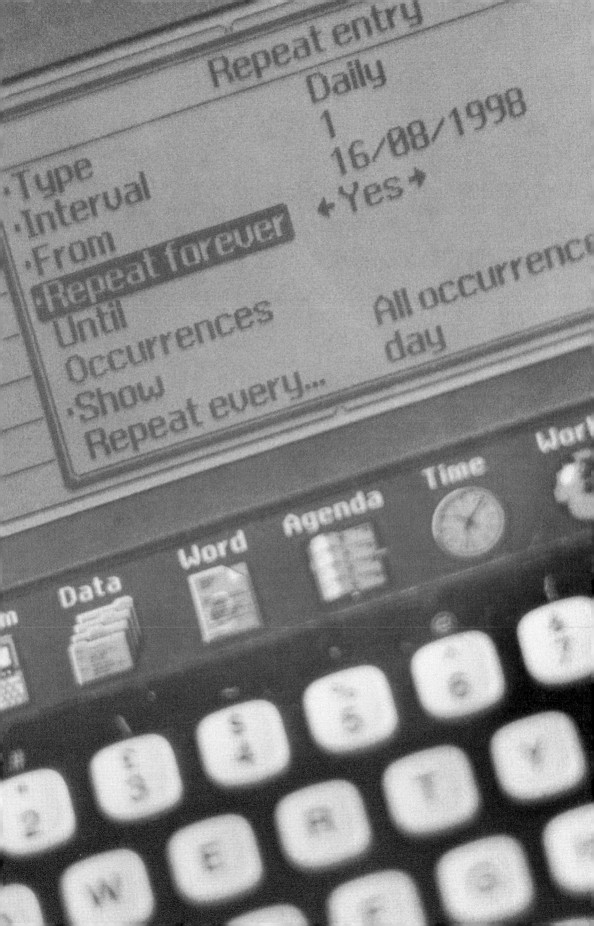

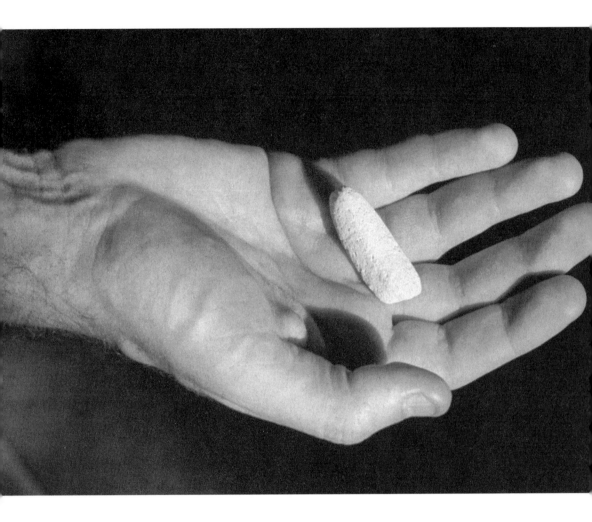

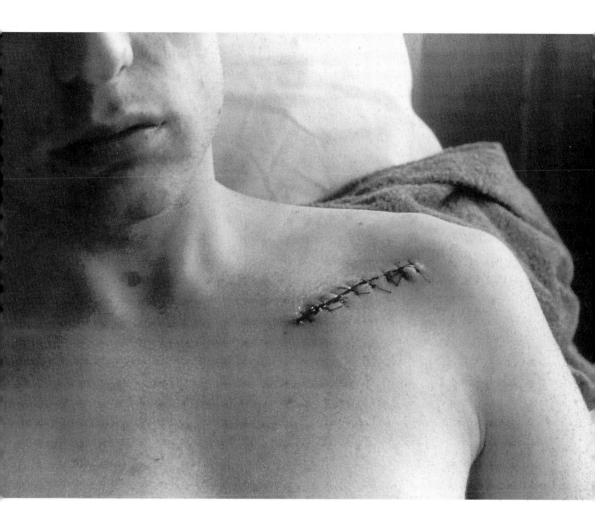

Section II

Performance Texts

Introduction

These texts are ghosts.

They were made in the midst of clumsy and long performance-making processes — in the midst of group rehearsal and improvisation, soundtrack-making, 'choreography', argument and set-building. They were not made for other people to 'do' them, and they were never really meant to stand alone.

I haven't tried to make a 'play' from what was not. The words on the page don't try too hard to invoke the past of performance time; no complex stage directions, or long pedantic notes. Instead I've tried to leave the texts alone as the ghosts they are, in a desert of white paper or white sand.

These ghost texts are clues.

Sometime in the 80s I am hitchiking in England, headed North to South. Two Irish men pick me up in a battered van. They give off a weird energy. Slow, over-intimate, friendly, scaring. I'm nervous. They're in front, me in the back. One of them takes a piece of paper from his wallet, paper soft through being so-many-times-folded-and-unfolded and he hands it to me, asking:

'Here. Read this...'

I read. Aloud. What else can I do?

The ghost text is a clue. A set of addresses and phone numbers, a set of names. Perhaps the list of contacts from which these two are slowly constructing a life, or a living, or a lie. And as I read the two of them nod gently, the motorway spins by. They heard the list many times before now (in the voice of other strangers) and there is something comfortable about its reiteration. They do not know language but they are sure, as long as I read to them, that it is stable, that it does not change, that the writing on their paper (blue biro, all of it) has not morphed or dreamed itself into some new formation.

When I return the paper to the driver he puts it away with new confidence, eyes an unrememberable colour, locked on the road. I'm still scared, and when, an hour or two later I get out, I feel, more than anything just a simple relief that they have not killed me as I have become utterly certain that they will.

I'm blinking in the sunshine by the services. Alone.

Two details. First that as well as not killing me they give me money, to buy breakfast. They don't think it is right that I have not had anything to eat and in the strangest transaction they give me warm bright coins with which to buy something. And the second detail: that that night I have the strongest image of their paper — and in the image it is changing, it is not stable and I know that the clue they carry cannot be trusted as 'fixed' but only seen in the moment and understood in all contingency in whatever motorway or boarding house or bar. I know that while they sleep the letters on the paper re-form and reassemble — as restless as all and any ghosts, as unstable as any clue with a secret of its own.

The texts are vivid clues. And not to be trusted.

(Let the Water Run its Course) to the Sea that Made the Promise

Forced Entertainment
Text: Tim Etchells

(Let the Water Run its Course) to the Sea that Made the Promise was Forced Entertainment's fifth performance project. Set in a world that was as much post-cultural as post-holocaust it showed four performers enacting something that was part ritual, part game and part exorcism — a performance in which two men and two women quoted fragments of their lives, loves and possible deaths. The physical style of the piece was bold, brutal and exaggerated — a ragged, visceral series of repetitions, cartoon fast-forwardings and emotional outbursts that shifted between ostentatious playfulness and sombre poignancy as the performers tried to outdo each other in their performances.

The space for the piece mirrored the kind of abandoned industrial architecture common in Sheffield, especially in the area of town in which we were rehearsing. The set comprised two identical 'room' spaces on either side of the space at the front — each with a single chair and hanging industrial light. Separating these spaces, and stretching to the back wall of grilled windows was a forest of vertical pillars supporting an incomplete roof. The 'rooms' at the front of the space became arenas in which the action of the piece would largely be played out, the rest of it an area for watching and resting until the action itself spilled its boundaries later in the piece.

There were effectively two texts in the piece. The first of them came from the live performers and was a gibberish language made up of crying, whispering, mumbling, yelling — the undocumentable shapes and architecture of language without its details. The second text, presented here, was recorded on tape and played as a framing commentary or voice-over, dividing the piece into parts.

(Let the Water Run its Course) to the Sea that Made the Promise lasted one hour and 15 minutes. The piece was performed by Robin Arthur, Richard Lowdon, Cathy Naden and Susie Williams, who was replaced in later versions by Terry O'Connor. The performance was directed by Tim Etchells, Huw Chadbourn, Richard Lowdon and Terry O'Connor. Set and lighting design were by Huw Chadbourn and Richard Lowdon. Performers on tape were Sarah Singleton and Tim Etchells. The soundtrack was by John Avery.

Man: to the Mr Heart-Lung babies of this
place & the so-called platitude girls
those for whom falling is a way of life.

Woman: Part one was the death of his hands.
This didn't seem to matter at first, though it changed his style of dress.

Thos wer the hands he got from Superbig Safeways, they wer an exciting colour, like the colour of skin.

Thos wer the hands he used to 'old her hands, when they walked together in the walking hours.

Thos wer the hands that used the all new dial-a-fortune machine.

Thos wer the most fashionable and exalted hands in the Black City.

Part one for him was the death of his hands.

Man: Part one was the death of her eyes. This was brilliant fun. Unable to see no more, she didn't see the artificial sun of 1973, or the new packaging for Erotic Chocolate, or the green light by the precinct say 'Walk! Walk!' especially for her.

He told her all about these things on long wet bastard nights together & they listened to Vivaldi's Baseball Concerto.

Part one for her was the death of her eyes.

Woman: That was the year that the electric messages stopped.

Man: That was the year they crowned Madonna the Queen of Fuck in a nightclub called Paradise.

Woman: That was the year that Department 95 closed down.

Man: In that year she called him Mr Sunbeam and he called her Coca-Cola.

Woman: Part two was the death of his heartbeat.
She was mad with this at first because she used to like to listen to it going boom-boddy-boom-boddy-boom ... After a while they got used to the silence though.
And in silence together they ate Spanish Civil War Crunchies & watched topless television til way past bedtime.

Part two for him was the death of his heartbeat.

Man: Part two was the death of her walk. This was regrettable.
            She got that walk from Paul Newman or Cary Grant, it was a good walk
            & when it died she felt lonely & she bought no more records no more.

            Part two was the death of her walk.

Woman: Part two was also ther heartache for the city outside.
            They named it & renamed it every day despite the bitter cold.
            They called it remarkable city, alphabet city, alphabetti city,
            New Milan, and the Capital City of Britain.

Man: They sat up some nites & renamed it & their love grew as they
            named it: the city of spires, the Kentucky Fried City, the City of Elvis
            King, the exploding city, the city of joy.

            And while they talked it rained like Ronald MacDonald outside.

Woman: That was the year the jet planes didn't fly anymore.

Man: That was the year they cancelled the Pope of the Year Pope contest.

Woman: That was the year that talks broke down in the Black City.

Man: That was the year that they shut the doors to the Institute of Believing.

Woman: In that year she called him Mr Vector
            & he called her Karen the Florist.

Man: Part three was the death of her insides. This was unlucky. She needed
            them but he made it up to her & it didn't seem to matter no more.
            Her insides wer made out of bendy plastic & tranquilliser chewing
            gum, her insides wer fragile neon & bound up with sellotape, her
            insides wer radium atoms lit only by 40 Watt bulbs, & he loved them.

            Part three for her was the death of her insides.

Woman: Part three was the death of his skin. This was regrettable. The skin
            was first-class skin that smelt good like oil & roses. The skin was the
            skin she touched & when it was dead the whole thing seemed differ
            ent. They never went out any more. They wer bound together only
            by Junior Disprin.

            Part three for him was the death of his skin.

Man: Part three was more names for the Black City.
            In the dark they called it fuck city, shit city, blood city, sperm city,
            cock city, prick city, cunt city, twat city, bum city, arse city, shitty city,
            ridiculous city, stupid city.

Woman: That was the year the Chinese trains stopped running.

Man: That was the year they broke the fingers of the baby Jesus.

Woman: That was the year the power cuts came & they wanted to run & they wanted to swim.

Man: That was the year the power cuts came & they wanted to walk & wer desperate to slide.

Woman: That was the year ther power cuts came & they wanted to drive & wer frightened to fall.

Part four was the chronology of the cities.
They spoke each night & every night about a journey standing still.

Man: The first city was the City of Stones.

Woman: They spoke each night & every night about a journey standing still.

Man: The second city was the City of Wire.

Woman: They spoke each night & every night about a journey standing still.

Man: The third city was the City of Rain.

Woman: They spoke each night & every night about a journey standing still.

Man: The fourth city was the Stupid City.

Woman: They spoke each night & every night about a journey standing still.

Man: The fifth city was the Empty City. The people ther wer no lovers of water, all ther buildings wer tumbleshit, all ther trees wer bare, & the branches on the boulevards wer bones & ther wer no birds ther, only bird repellent.

Woman: They spoke each night & every night about a journey standing still.

Man: The sixth city was the City of the Variable stars. Someone put a note under the windscreen wiper of her car, 'I love you, but will never dare speak to you'.
In another time, with another love in his heart, Mr Plastic choked & died in a hotel bathroom.

Woman: They spoke each night & every night about a journey standing still.

Man: The seventh city was the City of Faith.
That winter Karen the Florist & Mr Vector sat in ther respective rooms & willed themselves to die. And because the mind is stronger than the body, they did die.

Alone in ther rooms as quiet as stone.

Woman: They spoke each night & every night about a journey standing still.

Part four was the chronology of the cities.

Man: Part five was the love & acceptance of ther true blood.

They wer so happy in the Black City. They went for joy rides every day in a red corvette beneath lines & wires of pylons, singing 'move move groovy baby' by the Self-Righteous Brothers.

Woman: Unfortunately though one day when they wer driving a cornflake truck hit them doing 93. And he remembered thinking how quiet that whole world seemed & still, & wondering if you blacked out before you hit the windscreen.

Man: And she remembered being in the air looking down on the Black City which was very beautiful & wondering if the plastic figure of Charles Atlas, King of the Black City would hit the ground before she did.

Woman: They died in the accident of course. He lost control of his bladder before they hit the Kelloggs truck so he didn't mind: his best suit was ruined anyway. At the hospital they wer put in the capable hands of Dr Lyver who had plenty of money. Seeing as how they wer dead, he put sort of plastic taps in ther arms & drained all the red sort of blood out of them into a sort of bucket. Then he got lots of other blood & pumped into them through all possible entrances. That is to say: nose, ears, cunt, arse & eyes.

Man: This new blood he put in them was stuff he'd collected here & ther from other people. The blood it mixt together all these peoples blood & thoughts & everything & this was ther biggest problem you see: because the blood moved inside them, changing & turning, one person then another, they dint know who the fuck shit piss they wer, they'd say one thing then another, stand up, sit down, the blood moved, they dint know.

Woman: Part five for them was the love & acceptance of ther true blood.

Man: It was also a confession & a day by the sea.

Woman: We have woken up crying.

Man: We have tried to fuck in the bath.

Woman: We saw Warren Beatty present an appeal on behalf of children with muscular dystrophy.

Man: We woke to hear a man's voice & found that it was morning.

Woman: We have been to the water at midnight.

Man: We played sniper on the balconies of the world.

Woman: We sat 20 billion years in the ridiculous dark.

Man: We've been taken to the airport in handcuffs.

Woman: We watched all the channels close down.

Man: We have died in London & we have kissed in Rome.

Woman: We have pissed in the sink.

Man: We drank ourselves stupid out of free-with-petrol tumblers.

Woman: We stormed out slamming the door then walked straight back in again.

Man: We have headed for the water & driven for the sea.

Woman: We were born inside out.

Man: We were on Swap Shop the same day that Edward died.

Woman: We have sat talking all night & driven for the sea.

Man: We are sworn enemies of rain.

Woman: We invented beautifully scented nerve-gas & invisible barbed wire.

Man: We've run beneath the neon bridges.

Woman: We have spitted on the grass beside the motorway.

Man: We have done questionable things.

Woman: We have been to the water at midnight.

Man: We stood on the black beach in winter & threw messages into the sea.

Woman: I am writing because you asked me to write you the truth about my
         life here & because I hope we are still friends.
         I kiss you as we kissed before.
         Marina & Mr Concrete.

         P.S. I remember the snow, the frost, the opera building
         & your kisses.
         Isn't it funny how we never felt the cold?

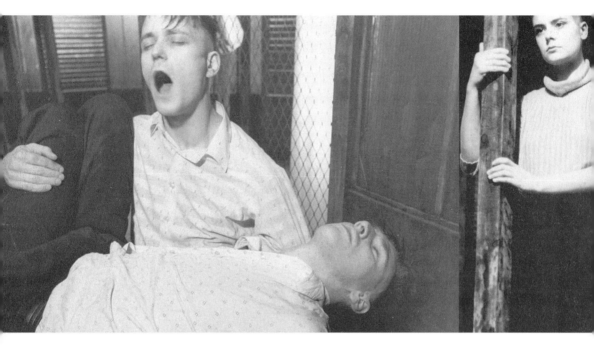

Emanuelle Enchanted (or a Description of this World as if it Were a Beautiful Place)

Forced Entertainment
Text: Tim Etchells

Emanuelle Enchanted was Forced Entertainment's ninth project for theatre spaces. In it five performers present a jumbled, fragmented account of a 'strange night that the rain stopped' — a night of urban panic, political crisis and personal reflection.

Set on a crude wooden stage and backed by a curtain of electric stars, the performance space was framed by a rough, skeletal proscenium. Wooden rails draped with jumble sale clothes were suspended at each side while a white translucent curtain ran across the front, leaving just enough room, once closed, for the performers to stand and address the audience. In this crude arena there was also a series of wheeled theatrical flats with their plywood backs displayed to the front. There were two televisions on wheeled trolleys and a video rigged to pass images directly to the TV's. Beneath the clothes rails were stacked numerous cardboard signs bearing the hastily scrawled names of characters, both real and imaginary.

The action of the piece was divided by the five performers using the curtain to set up or cut off scenes they were presenting. At various points the curtain is opened to show 'nothing' (performers waiting nervously, or setting the stage for a forthcoming scene) and at other points it is closed whilst the action is clearly still in progress. There are obvious disagreements between performers about what should be shown and when, as well as narrational disagreements about the events which are supposedly being presented.

Read narratively the fragments presented show the events of a single night — the night of a crisis both personal and global. The 'scenes' — a chaotic, almost nonsensical TV newsroom with telegram-style headline messages, a domestic space in which the walls are always in motion, and a panoramic glimpse of many characters presented via the cardboard signs — are texts with which the performers struggle — attempting visibly and not always successfully to overcome the triple hardships of theatrical representation, language and memory.

It was the struggle to present and comprehend, and its opposite — a nervous reluctance to continue — that gave the work its central methodology; the act of arranging and rearranging units of information, be they textual, visual or spatial so that new patterns, implied narratives and meanings can emerge.

Emanuelle Enchanted ran one hour and 25 minutes without an interval. The performance was conceived and devised by Forced Entertainment under the direction of Tim Etchells. The performers were Robin Arthur, Richard Lowdon, Claire Marshall, Cathy Naden, and Terry O'Connor. The assistant director was Nick Crowe whilst design was by Richard Lowdon and lighting by Nigel Edwards. Soundtrack for the performance was by John Avery.

Presented here are all of the texts used in the piece — a catalogue of the cardboard sign characters, the list-texts from the news-room and the longer litanic texts from newsroom two, the narrational or framing texts delivered by the performers in front of the curtain and the monologues from Terry O'Connor ('Wherefore') and Cathy Naden ('The Kiss').

Cardboard Signs

Characters presented using cardboard signs:

RACHEL (BLEEDING)
THE GHOST OF A CHILD KILLED ON TUESDAY
A BOXER WITH A TORN RETINA
A 9-YEAR-OLD SHEPHERD BOY
BILLY MAUDLIN
A GIRL BROUGHT UP BY KIDNAPPERS
ALIEN GIRL
A GOOD COP IN A BAD FILM
PRINCESS NOT-SO-BRIGHT
YTS VANDAL
TARZANOGRAM
A PSYCHIC CALLED IN TO HELP THE COPS
FRANK (DRUNK)
MISS DEAF AMERICA
MARCIE (PREGNANT)
A BLOKE WHO'S BEEN SHOT
LOST LISA
MICHAEL LIVING A LIE
THE EX-WIFE OF THE EX-PRESIDENT OF THE USA
A DRUNK MAN SHOUTING AT THE MOON
ONE BAVARIAN PRINCESS
GAY COP
MISS DEEP FREEZE
A NEW PATRON SAINT OF LOVE
TELLY SAVALAS COME DOWN FROM THE CROSS
TWO MODERN WHITE GIRLS
PRINCE VALIUM
A CHEMIST HOPING THAT HE'LL LIVE
PAUL DANIELS WITH MORE MAGIC & DELUSIONS
BANQUO'S GHOST
A SEXUALLY FRUSTRATED YOUNG WOMAN LIVING IN A DREAMWORLD
IDENTICAL TWINS
ELIZABETH'S GHOST
THE BLONDE GIRL FROM ABBA
JOE WALKER (NOT GUILTY)
A DUMB FUCK WITH NO IDEA
YOUNG COSMONAUT (SCARED)
A GIRL FROM THE COUNTRY
A STEWARDESS FORGETTING HER DIVORCE

BAD MOTHERFUCKER

A KING (USURPED)

EX-LOVERS (NOT SPEAKING)

ELVIS PRESLEY, THE DEAD SINGER

AN ASSASSIN

THE HYPNOTISED GIRL

FANTASY FRED

A LOST MAN REMEMBERING THE ACCIDENT

A TILL GIRL WITH A GUN

CHAS (IN PERSIA)

A TERRORIST IN HIDING

A TELEPATH (AGE 12)

AN ANGEL SENT FROM HEAVEN TO THE EARTH

BEAUTIFUL ELIZABETH

THE SHIP'S MAGICIAN

AN ANAESTHETIST

THE BEARDED LADY

A GREAT POET/SECURITY GUARD

A FORMER WAITRESS & COMMUNIST ORGANISER

BROKENHEATRED PAUL

DAVE, LIKE A VISION, STEPPED DOWN FROM A PAINTING

EX-LOVERS (GOOD FRIENDS)

A LOW-LIFE SCUMBAG COWBOY GAMBLER FUCK

MARY GENTLE

A BINGO CALLER

BRIDGET FONDA'S BODY DOUBLE

A PROMISCUOUS FOOTBALLER

CHRISTINA THE ASTONISHING

OUR LADY OF MASSACRE

SUSIE MIDNIGHT (SECRET AGENT)

A RICH OLD MAN—TOO GRAND TO FEEL THE RAIN

A CHESS PRODIGY

THE POLKA-DOT-DRESS GIRL

LINDA (OUT OF LUCK)

THE SON OF A POSTMAN

ORACLE JONES

TWO HATE FILLED CHILDREN WITH ICE IN THEIR VEINS

A NIGHTSHIFT WORKER (IN LOVE)

A DISTANT COUSIN OF THE QUEEN

A LUCKY THIEF

THE GERMAN GIRL

DAVID (JUST OFF THE BOAT)

A GRIPPING STRANGER
THE CRYING MAN
AN ALCHEMIST
AN OLD BRITISH CHARACTER ACTOR ADRIFT IN A CONTINENTAL FILM
EX-PARA
A HUMBLE ROPE-MAKER'S APPRENTICE
MISS ALL THE BOYS LOVE HER
TWO 'SCIENTIFIC WORKERS FROM ST PETERSBURG'
BAT BOY
A NARCOLEPTIC RENT BOY
AN INNOCENT-LOOKING GIRL
A PISSED-OFF WHITE COP WITHOUT A BADGE
A PRAT/CRIMINAL/LIAR
THE CHILD KING GANOR III
SPIRAL JENNY
A DOWN-AT-HEELS ACTRESS & SINGER
MICHEL THE INTELLECTUAL
A DOCTOR WITHOUT DIPLOMA, DESTINED FOR HANDCUFFS
THE QUEEN OF MONEY
TWO MEN WITHOUT A COUNTRY
A STATUE COME TO LIFE
A HARD HARD WOMAN
GOD'S LONELY MAN
THE GREEN RIVER KILLER
A STUDENT POLITICIAN WITH TERRORIST CONNECTIONS
A HELPLESS CHILD
A NIGHTCLUB BOUNCER
NEON LEWIS
QUEEN OF NOTHING
A CHEMICAL WORKER
A WOMAN WITH NERVES
RODNEY KING, THE BLACK MOTORIST
MISS SCUNTHORPE EVENING TELEGRAPH
WHITE TRASH CHRISTIAN LANDLORD
LONELY MAHONNEY
A STALINIST DESPOT
GREGORY, A FILM-MAKER FROM PARIS
A BLOODY FOOL
THE YOUNG LAD
RACHEL (WOMAN OF THE MONTH)
UPSTART BUSINESSMAN
A POPULAR YOUNG BRUTALIST STOCKBROKER

MR TEN & A HALF INCHES
KID FROST AKA THE ICE KID
CHRISTIAN VAN HUGYENS, THE SEVENTEENTH CENTURY DUTCH PHYSICIST
MR HUNGRY
DEATH HIMSELF
AN ERRAND BOY
ANOTHER MURDERER
SOMEBODY'S SON
THE LOSER
GIRL IN LIFT #1
A FORMER MISS SOMETHING-OR-OTHER
THE BROTHERS KALSHNIKOV
SON OF A PUBLICAN
SON OF A REPUBLICAN
A FABRICATED MAN
AN ALCOHOLIC KNIFE GRINDER
A TOUGH DEAD GIRL
A GOOD MAN WHO'S HAD BAD LUCK
A TERRIBLE GIANT
TWO MEN WHO WILL NOT SMILE
BROKEN-NOSE McGURK
A GIRL WITH BOY'S EYES
A MAN WITH WOMAN'S EYES
SNOW PETER
DAUGHTER OF THE BLACK KNIFE
ARMENIAN MARY
JACK RUBY
SIGMUND FREUD
HELLEN KELLER
DIRTY MARY/CRAZY LARRY
ASTRID PROLL
MRS SAUNDERS
VALENTINA TERESHKOVA
LADY CHATTERLY
LOLA
SHIRLEY VALENTINE
EMILY
MICHAEL CAINE
RACHEL (REPLICANT)
FRANCESCA (PREGNANT)
CATHERINE (DRUNK)
GIRL IN LIFT #2

Curtain Text One

Richard [*reading*]: *Goodbye Emanuelle*, starring Sylvia Kristel, Umberto Orsini, Alexandra Stewart, Jean-Pierre Bouvier and introducing Caroline Laurence. An Yves Rousset-Rouard production, directed by Francois Leterrier. PANA-VISION. 1976. 95 minutes.

Claire: In the summer when the earth changed it rained for five months and on the night the rain stopped a silence fell like we'd woke up in a silence from a dream.

We were in a city and on that strange night only the dead walked about in it, smiling and drinking halves of lager LIKE THEY OWNED THE FUCKING PLACE.

WHAT A NIGHT IS THIS we signed to those dead people there for they did not fully understand our language and they said STOP PLAYING FOOTBALL WITH JUMPERS FOR GOALPOSTS. This, as the poets say, is what happened next as the night unfolded ...

Richard: The normal temperature of the city was OK but the rhetorical temperature was off the scale and alas, we were sat in out room and lacking pens, or typewriters of any kind, or paper, we preferred instead to write messages in our own DEAR BLOOD on the walls.

Never was such a night as that one when the rain stopped, never ever, never was such a night as that and of any messages that came back to us most were like a FILE DELETED SYMBOL or like a drunken joke. Each time we left the room things changed and this, as you shall see, is the strange surprise that awaited us on our return.

Terry: We lived in a city where happy endings were not popular, and so, without pens, we preferred to write messages on the walls in our blood.

> We wrote: DOWN WITH CHILDHOOD and NO MORE MR. NICE GUY.

> We wrote: TWO HAPPY DOGS SWIMMING IN A FROZEN RIVER.

> We wrote: STOP PLAYING GAMES OR I'LL FUCKING KILL MYSELF.

No one knows if our messages got through.

Robin: That wild night the rain stopped was, like the poets say, ALL SO MUCH ILLEGAL JOY RIDING and then again it was all so much HEAD PAIN as well. These as follow now, are the messages we wrote ...

Newsroom One

The lists are presented into camera like the urgent missives of a culture in the last throes of crisis.

Number 1: 'Copyright The Whole World Except Australia.'
Two: 'Cancer of The Fist.'
Three: 'Suspicion of Innocence.'
Four: 'Every word I say, is, by definition, a promise ...'
Five: 'CLUB OF NO REGRETS.'
Number Six: 'Please Let me Get What I want This Time.'
Seven: 'The forgiveness that only drunkenness can bring ...'
Eight: 'STUPID WHITE PEOPLE MAROONED ON ANOTHER PLANET.'
Nine: 'Happy Without Anaesthetic.'
Ten: 'Get Lost In The Deep Stairs Of Vertigo.'

1. First Fireproof Hotel.
2. Laugh Face T-shirt.
3. Helen's Soul.
4. Russian Dream.
5. Council House.
6. The First Black Pope.
7. Don't hurt me, please, don't hurt me.
8. The word 'sedatives' is a registered trademark of the 'Sedatives Group'.
9. Nerves exposed.
10. Heartless Breeze.

1. A porn magazine called CRUCIFIED WOMEN.
2. 50 more years of bad news.
3. At 12am like in a fairytale.
4. Lighthearted.
5. A vision.
6. The kid playing hide and seek in the back of the car.
7. Noiseland—video arcade.
8. Slander.
9. HOW TO FILM A MASSACRE.
10. HOW TO FILM A MASSACRE FOR KIDS.

1. Iron City Beer.
2. The Nobel Prize For Rap.
3. Invisible in Britain, partly visible in the USA.
4. Partly visible in Britain, visible in the USA.
5. Longest screen piss in history.

6. It has this tone, like early polyester.
7. Viva Tango.
8. Viva Las Vegas.
9. Viva Safeways.
10. Don't snore too loud, you'll wake the angels in heaven.

1. Theresa Mallory Is Dead Because She Knew The Truth.
2. Kuwait Oil In Kashmir Snow.
3. Come moon, come and console me.
4. Sarcastic Realism.
5. New High Mountains Found.
6. The words 'Toxico' and 'Fast Beating Heart' are trademarks and may not be used or reproduced or stored in any information retrieval system without the prior permission of the makers.
7. Pseudo-events.
8. In bed two days.
9. No court exists to settle your dispute over beauty.
10. These Are The Bright Stars And This Is How To Find Them.

Number One: 'Her husband's death, loneliness, February, 1953.'
Two: A new game show called 'Long Faces.'
Three: 'Builders on the roof at 7am.'
Four: 'Builders on the roof at 7pm.'
Five: 'I Have A Horror Of The Truth But I Love The Truth.'
Six: Crisis.
Seven: The words 'Fuck face' and 'Seafood' are registered as trademarks by the manufacturer and they reserve the public right to be identified as such.
Eight: 'DON'T DOUBLE CROSS THE ONES YOU LOVE.'
Number Nine: Secret Password.
Number Ten: Only The Lonely.

1. A statue, a statue of Headless Christ.
2. A Gold Colored Watch.
3. Eyes the colour of the sea.
4. A hotel room without any clocks.
5. A beautiful violent country.
6. Grab Reality as a Commodity and Sell It.
7. Win a chance, win a good chance, win a ghost of a chance.
8. A scorched film.
9. A broken bone.
10. Acting out the last journey of her sister.

1. How can we have a president who has dreams like this?
2. The rain that falls now is such dirty rain.
3. Undressing under the sheet.
4. A blue-in-colour car.
5. Love and Acting Go Together.
6. News of Accidents.
7. Then they knew the great grief, the great calamity.
8. 40 girls so beautiful it was impossible to choose among them or to look on them without faintness.
9. Last Hope Convenience Store.
10. Tomorrow is my birthday, consider yourself invited.

1. Who to trust?
2. She may still be in that coma but she'll hear every word you have to say, I know she will.
Number Three: An Epilogue.
4. I want to be a household word.
5. A love letter, written in binary.
6. A perfect ending to a perfect day.
7. HIDDEN POLITICAL MESSAGE.
8. research.
Item 9: A MAN CALLED THREATENING.
10. A nightclub called LA NUIT.

Curtain Text Two

Claire: In the summer, when the earth changed, it rained for five months and in the silence that followed the end of the rain we GAVE UP WITH THE MESSAGES ALREADY. No answers came.

On leaving our room we became lost and were looking for each other, calling out in the dark streets.

'I LOVE YOU MORE THAN ALL THE TELEGRAPH POLES IN THE WORLD', we shouted.

'VOICE OF HOPE', we yelled and 'BIG WALL OF REASON'.

That was a night of losing and of finding again, of losing and of finding, of losing and then of finding once again. More than that I can't say.

Cathy: That strange night when the rain stopped we started on some magic acts to keep away the cold. It was all FRIGHTENING MAGIC and appearing and disappearing and REVELATION and LOSS for us then. It was all FOLD-ING and HIDING and slipping away.

This is the life that we lived then, in the city in the chaos, in the dark...

Robin: The night the rain stopped was wild and cold and full of strange noises and we did magic acts and were scared for each other and ourselves. We practised CLOSING BOTH EYES TIGHT WHILST DRIVING DOWN A ROAD, we practised EXHIBITION OF DUST. We practised HAUNTED GOLF. We worked on YOU'RE GOING HOME IN A FUCKING AMBULANCE. This is the...

Terry: In the middle of all this I'm stopped dead in my tracks thinking WHAT GOES AROUND COMES AROUND and speaking in QUITE LONELY TONGUES...

'WHO HERE CAN DO PARTY TRICKS?' we asked and 'WHAT ARE SWEET WINGS OF MAGIC?'

This is the life we lived then, in the city, in the chaos, in the dark...

Curtain Text Three

Robin: On the wild night the rain stopped we panicked and, in truth, as a matter of fact, some of our magic got out of hand.

We rehearsed THERE IS A SINISTER REASON FOR EVERYTHING.

We did NINE GREAT MOTORWAY PILE-UPS AS SEEN FROM A NEARBY BRIDGE.

I suppose that's when things went wrong. From then on in it was like STOPPING WATER WITH SAND, and we were TOO LITTLE, TOO LATE.

We ran, hid, held each other close to no avail. Indeed, at many points we were, like the poets say MUCH TOO FUCKING CHICKENSHIT TO OPEN OUR EYES. This is what life befell us when we did...

Terry: HOW CAN YOU LIVE WHEN YOU'VE DONE SOMETHING?

HOW CAN YOU LIVE WHEN YOU'VE SEEN SOMETHING?

I don't know.

Richard: I'm sorry. In the midst of this I'm making a 'phone call, long, long, distance, but there's nobody home. This... is the... magic...

Claire: In the heart of this night I'm alone, thinking about the heroine in Dryden's Epic Poem LA BIONICA/THE BIONIC WOMAN—in the verse which every schoolgirl knows—where she looks in the mirror and says:

'I DON'T KNOW CHARLEY—MY FUCKING BRAIN'S ALL WIRED UP WRONG...'

Cathy: At midnight on the fateful night in the city we practised TRANSFORMATION and LOSS. We rehearsed UPSET FOR NO REASON, and then became upset, for no reason. We asked WHICH FILE DO YOU WISH TO RENAME? and WHO HERE IS NOT TOTALLY AFRAID? No one answered. This is the living and the magic that we blundered, in the chaos and the ruins and the dark—If I look ugly in it, please, I ask you, close your eyes …

Curtain Text Four

Richard: That night the rain stopped was a strange night of losing and of finding again, of losing and of finding, of losing and of finding once again …

We sat in our room and wrote questions, asking ARE YOU HUMAN? and WHAT IS THE PRICE OF MEAT?

I was happy, I suppose, though the street names were switched in the dead of night, I was happy and the WHOLE WORLD COPYRIGHT BLOOD OF MIRACLES poured thickly in my veins. This is the true slipping and the real falling that befell us in the dark of that night, and, like the poets say, A STRANGE KIND OF MAGIC INDEED.

Terry's Monologue: Wherefore

Terry: On the wild night the rain stopped we looked down at the city and said:

Why is this night distinguished from all other nights?
Do the stars shine brighter tonight?
Why is this night distinguished from all other nights?
The world is in chaos tonight.
Remember we used to draw cities in the mud on the ground?
Well now we're almost living in the places that we drew.

Wherefore is this night distinguished from all other nights?
The world is in chaos tonight.

Why has the rain stopped tonight?
Who dreamed of lightning?
Who was young and restless?
What freephone number did she write on her hand?
Who wore a T-shirt saying SOMETHING TO PROVE?

Why is this night distinguished from all other nights?
There's one chance in thousands left tonight.

We said: Why on earth has the rain stopped tonight?
Which is more alive—a stone or a lizard?
What causes movement in the stars?

Who here is not totally afraid?

Wherefore is this night distinguished from all other nights?
We're in a PLACE OF CHANCE.

Wherefore is this night distinguished from all other nights?
Because the stars in the sky are aligned.

Wherefore is this night distinguished from all other nights?
Because tonight we can see through.

Wherefore is this night distinguished from all other nights?
We're all alone tonight.

And on the wild night that the rain stopped we looked down at the city for a
while and said:

Why such a big city tonight?
Why so many people?
Why such a big city, why such a big world?

Why such a big city tonight?
Why so many people?
Why such a big city, why such a big world?
Why so small in this room tonight?
Why so many people beyond?

And do they ever close their eyes when they're driving down a road?
And do they remember A THING NOT KNOWN OR SPOKEN?
And what's their word for CAR PARK and what's their word for DESPAIR?
And which is more alive—a stone or a lizard?
And do they ever close their eyes when they're driving down a road?
And when the rain stopped we looked down at the city for a while. We said:

Why such a big city, why such a big world?
Why so small in this room tonight?
Why so many people beyond?

In the summer when the earth changed, it rained for about five months, and on
the wild night the rain stopped a kind of big silence fell and we were looking
down on the city like everything's turning silver and orange and down below
we could see LIKE EVERYTHING AND EVERYONE and hundreds of people
and thousands of people and we RAN WITH THEM of course, and lost ourselves and RAN AGAIN and ran and ran again and what was the night like
when the rain really stopped?

Curtain Text Five

Richard: Our passports were fakes and our documents SERIOUSLY OUT OF ORDER so we knew we couldn't leave. The night continued. In the dark we ran through the streets of the city and the remnants of the kingdom, past LAST CHANCE STREET and CARPETLAND and 35% DISCOUNT WORLD. There was PRECIOUS LITTLE MENTION OF MAGIC.

Occasionally we stopped running and wrote messages on walls. We wrote:

> SHIPS THAT SINK WITHOUT TRACE and a quotation from Wordsworth's poem QUE LASTIMA! QUEL BICHO! / WHAT A PITY! WHAT A BASTARD! — the verse that all people of this country know where the hero looks from the window and whispers:

> I NEED NOTIONS OF FIXITY WITHIN THIS INSTABILITY.

Robin: There are two events in my life that are magical, that can't be explained rationally, by science. The first was a long time ago and the second was in the small hours of that night ...

MANIPULATION OF MONEY we noticed as we blundered through the streets.

WHY DO ASTRONAUTS FLOAT? we asked and

WHAT'S THE ONLY MOVIE STILL SHOWING IN THIS TOWN?

Cathy's Monologue: The Kiss

Cathy commentates a video image of Richard and Claire who are kissing deeply.

Cathy: Goodbye Emanuelle.

Emanuelle has been playing tennis with some friends and now she's alone, waiting for her lover, Jean, to call. She speaks:

> What do the foes of melody know of melody? What do the foes of love know of love? What do these liars, fuckers and murderers know of anything except lying, fucking and murdering? Nothing.

> What need is there for sorrow? What need is there for pain? From my eyes the rain of love shall never fall again ...

Later, in a chi-chi nightclub Chloe, who's an ornithologist is talking to Gregory, a film-maker from Paris, the music so loud she almost has to shout ...

> Dry your tears, please, I beg of you, dry your eyes. I haven't been here, you haven't seen me, it's simple, nothing happened alright?

And er, while all this is happening Michel the intellectual talks to Emanuelle's lover Jean. He says:

> I don't want to live here anymore, I just don't think I can, I don't want to live on earth, I'd rather live on Mars, I'd rather live on Neptune where it's cold. Listen, listen, hear me out — I'd rather live on Venus, I can't stay here anymore, I'd rather live on Pluto, I'd rather live on Saturn, I'd rather live in orbit of the moon...

And Jean replies, apparently, the city outside in chaos... his speech more in riddles than in sense. He says:

> This horse is going to die isn't it? This horse is going to die. If it dies I'm going to wipe the tape, I'm going to wipe it. If this horse dies I'll wipe the fucking tape.

Newsroom Two

Robin: When morning came we were still alive. Writing messages on the walls of our room. We did not weep though we had full cause of weeping. We wrote:

> Item 1.
> 1. I'm floating.
> 2.
>
> a1. last broadcast.
> 2. Hardcore Attack
>
> Born. See through these walls.
>
> 1. He walks between the raindrops.
> 2.
>
> Note. unreadable. START NOT FOUND.
>
> 1. revealed.
>
> We the undersigned agree terms as above.
>
> 1. Voices.
> Number Two.
>
> secret hope and secret language. MISSING PARAMETER VARIABLE AT LINE M.
>
> 1. I'd like to talk with you, I'd really like to talk, I know we're talking now but...
>
> 1. 'Recession-Buster Breakfast'
> 2. A whole wall plastered with reports of our deaths.
> 3.

Cathy:
1. A new soap called UNCERTAINTY STREET.
2. The things we've seen.
3.

1.
N.B. untraceable. collector of farces.

Item 1: lost broadcast.
2. THOSE WHO WALK ABOUT.
3.

1.
Just thinking aloud.

1. Unreadable.
2. Unreadable.
PASSWORD ERROR—THE PASSWORD YOU HAVE ENTERED IS INCORRECT.

Claire:
1. Secret Garden.
2. She sings a song called 'X' and the burden of the song is this …
3.

1. I'm floating.
some rumours and some sources
AN ERROR OCCURRED WHEN READING THE TEMPORARY FILE.

1. Land of make-believe.
2. Still breathing.
3.

1.
Number One.

Terry:
1. THERE ARE SPIRITS, SPEAKING THROUGH MY TEETH.
2.

1. this room
2.
START NOT FOUND
the air so sweet looking down

1. I never heard your voice so clear, I never heard your voice so well. I say I never heard your voice so well, I never heard your voice, not half as well as I heard it tonight …

2. ONE MILE NORTH OF THE NORTH POLE
Number Three.

secret hope

Robin:
    1. Floating.
    2. See through these walls
    3.

    1. The things we've seen
    2.
    Club of No Regrets

    1. IN THE MIDDLE OF ALL THIS I'M ALIVE
    2. Is this some law of chemistry?
    and 3.

    1. I'd like to talk with you, I'd really like to talk, I know we're talking
    now but...

THE ERASE COMMAND LINE FORMAT IS INVALID
    ...

    1. secret love
    2. her gorgeous questions
    3. secret doorway

one thousand two hundred million (stars visible in the sky above this
building)

    1. nice moment
    2. his gorgeous answers
    3. unreadable
    4. sergeant, who's in charge here?

NO SUCH FILE TO RENAME

    1.
    Item 1: GOOD SMILE
    2. Nice Story.

Note, remember? Died.

Now listen:

    1. an appendectomy scar and
    alarms on the buildings and
    the air so sweet it keeps you from dying and

alarms on the cars and
ahead of us there are only great disasters and
a film called 'anybody else in this shithole looking for trouble?'
and later 'Anna, come to me Anna, you're on the other side of the world ...'
and

1. blue talk and a baby and
2. blood on the floor and
brilliant and way ahead of his time and

a car back window done up with polythene and
a cat asleep on the supermarket shelves and
now it's like I'm floating and thinking:
this is how the nights are when it rains and
drugged to help her forget and
down by the river and down on their luck and
dust falling from up in the roof somewhere

and 1.
Friday. 10 o'clock. I'm sleeping then I start to float.
...

1. great phrasing
2. secret city
3.

1. tears of joy
2. In the middle of all this I'm alive

note: unreadable —

COUNT ZERO INTERRUPT. Hold me close

soon every street in this town leads somewhere you have to forget and
each to his own and
each time her heart beats and
evidence and
evidence withheld
and everything, help me, help me, everything's turning silver and orange

and farewell my darling ... goodnight my love and
false rain and
a full moon and
false papers and
now I'm floating and thinking:
such a big city, so many people, such a big city, such a big world and

there is a great god and a terrible devil and
gunshots — get down! and
genetic codes and
good luck and plenty of it and
great smile and
goodbye my darling and hello my loved one and
houses and hilltops and hosed down in rain

and 1. in silence.

QUIT NOT FOUND — THE STRING ARGUMENT TO A 'Q'
PARAMETER WAS NOT FOUND IN YOUR FILE.

see through these walls

1.
Item One: 12am awake and looking down
...

And heartless breezes and
born not with a hole but with a war in my heart and
heaven street and
impossible scenes and
an illness that spreads via the telephone and
that illegitimate son of a bitch and
innocent and innocent again and
I'm floating and thinking:
that night they held the world in their arms and

innocent and
innocent to a fault and a man says: you're so far away, you're so far away,
you're on one side of the world and I'm on the other and
Joanne's kisses and
Jake's blundering dance and
Pepsi's 'League of Nations' Juice'
and just how could he have lived here for two years and not changed anything, not even pinned a picture to the wall?

and kleptomaniac and
life magazine and
life after fifty-nine and
the kind of lightning that lights up the whole sky and
a true-life confessions piece called 'My Life As A YTS Vandal' and

a man says: you're so far away, you're so far away, you're on one side of

the world and I'm on the other and
I never heard your voice so clear, I never heard your voice so well and ...

painting by numbers,
percentage of alcohol in the bloodstream and
perfect ending

restless children and
I'm floating and thinking:
such a big city, so many people, such a big city, such a big world

YOU HAVE PLACED AN INVALID SEPARATOR BETWEEN TWO
INPUT FILE NAMES

and remember one thing
and the best rumours are always true and
sliding money across the floor and
look, see through these walls and
don't you know that something seeps through and
don't you know that sex is a form of love and
don't you know that sweet surprise and
second sight and
seconds out and
only two more seconds to go now before I've only got three more seconds to go and

I'm floating and thinking
tracheotomy scar
throwing coins in her bath and making wishes
and this, this is what it's like on the nights when it rains

such a big city, so many people, such a big city, such a big world
and take his statement and
those are terrible wounds and
three years later she could've smiled and
a pop song called: 'Violence Is Golden' and
the whole wedding like badly faked section of an old movie and
warm mysterious evenings and
woken by his mother, shouting for him from the carpark outside Carpetland in a dream and
which of us did not, for one moment, not feel his very heart cease to
beat? &

you, you belong to change and
a man says: you're so far away, you're so far away, you're on one side of
the world and I'm on the other

a man says: you're so far away, you're so far away, you're on one side of the world and I'm on the other

a man says: you're so far away, you're so far away, you're on one side of the world and I'm on the other

I never heard your voice so clear, I never heard your voice so well. I say I never heard your voice so well, I never heard your voice, not half as well as I heard it tonight...

a man says: you're so far away, you're so far away, you're on one side of the world and I'm on the other. I send a message to you:

1. NOT FOUND.
2. A country that moves in and out of existence according to a dream.
3. AND DO NOT NAME THE THING YOU LOVE.
4. AND DO NOT NAME THE THING YOU LOVE.
5. AND NEVER NAME THE THING YOU LOVE.
6. fifteen miles of primetime terror.
7. I am here to tell you I was happy.
8. A THING NOT KNOWN OR SPOKEN.
9. ENTER 'Y' TO TERMINATE THE FILE.
10. And this, this is how the nights are, when it rains.

Club of No Regrets

Forced Entertainment
Text by Tim Etchells

'On the edge of a dark woods the scenes of strange play are enacted at gunpoint...'

Club of No Regrets was Forced Entertainment's 10th project for theatre spaces. In it a central figure, Helen X, who claims to be lost in the woods, orders the enactment of a series of fragmentary scenes by a pair of performers inside a tiny box-set, centre-stage. The box-set is a crude plywood room with sawn-out windows, the walls of it painted black and scrawled with writing and drawings in chalk. Behind this crude house is a large plywood wall also painted black and covered in chalk drawings which depict an overgrown cityscape, the whole picture blurred and distorted with smudged chalk.

To facilitate or perhaps hinder the enactments ordered by Helen, a second pair of performers function as stagehands or captors who, having tied the other two to chairs and threatened them with guns, proceed to bring them the texts and props they might need for the performance. The enacted scenes are replayed many times as though Helen is unsure as to their true order or correct arrangement. The scenes themselves, reproduced below, are fragmentary and to some extent incomplete, unconnected sections of made-for-TV dialogue, thriller nonsense, love story, psychic detection. Each scene is titled, the titles drawing attention to their found, cliched and more or less iconic status. The scenes are framed by a further text from Helen, a confused narration of her fairy story/history which she calls *Club of No Regrets*.

Collected together here are the key texts spoken during the performance; those from the central figure Helen X and those enacted repeatedly as 'scenes' by the performers inside the tiny box-set. The texts are presented in order as they appear in the performance, excluding the considerable repetitions and without annotation. Immediately following the text is a short section which maps the structure of the performance and makes some account of the action-track surrounding the text.

Like *Emanuelle* before it, *Club of No Regrets* creates a fiction in which theatrical material is being ordered, enacted and explored by the protagonists. Its movement is from a chaotic enactment of its scenes to a transformation of the same material via repetition, interruption and gradual mutation.

Club of No Regrets lasted one hour and 25 minutes. It was conceived and devised by Forced Entertainment under the direction of Tim Etchells. It was performed by Robin Arthur, Richard Lowdon, Claire Marshall, Cathy Naden and Terry O'Connor. The assistant director was Ju Row Farr, design was by Richard Lowdon, lighting by Nigel Edwards and soundtrack by John Avery.

Helen Text One

Helen (Terry) alone on the stage, wandering, consulting her notes.

Helen: [*Reading*] 'Piecing Together Torn Paper. Simple as this work may appear yet it none-the-less presents numerous difficulties, and is often very awkwardly carried out. An investigator often receives numerous torn pieces of paper of small size, the content of which, once pieced together, is of the utmost importance ... '

I'm lost. It's no bloody good. Can't see anything.

I'm lost in an overgrown city and with each passing second I'm growing more tired. I try to keep track of where I'm going but all these trees and buildings just look the same and the bread I drop gets eaten by wild dogs and the string I trail behind me is all tangled up in the gutters. Can you hear those wild dogs barking? Yes.

I'm scared. Can't see anything.

Some parts of this history have been censored and other parts of it have been, um, forgotten.

'Hello, hello, hello everybody ...'

What's that got to do with me? Nothing. Shit.

I'm racing. I'm going too fast. I'm going ... My heart's racing. Look at these dirty mouldy leaves on the floor. I've shot up this stuff that makes time run fast forwards and now it's starting to take effect. The cops are after me and they've shot up the same stuff, only the stuff they've shot up is stronger than the stuff I shot up so they'll end up further into the future, waiting to catch me ... Good.

Some parts of this history are lost, other parts of it are all broken. All the persons herein depicted are fictitious and any resemblance to persons living ... or dead ... is purely coincidental ... Shit.

I'll try something else.

I'm in trapped in a falling building. There's a power cut. Can you find the light switch? No. OK. Night's falling fast. Now I'm trapped in a different building: Help! Help! Now I'm trapped in a worse building. Can you reach the door from there? No, I don't believe I can. Shit.

I'm running away. I'm lost and ... I'm running down these tangled streets ...

I'm running ... Hang on.

[*Reading*] 'It is possible to imagine that in the remotest quarters of the Universe there exist entire galaxies of anti-substance. There atoms and molecules are formed entirely of anti-particles ...'

Right.

[*Reading*] 'Now, let us take an extravagant case. A being from this anti-world reaches earth. He could only survive in a "power dome", a sphere which separated him from our substance. And now he falls in love with someone from our world. This could bring about a cosmic tragedy because their first kiss would produce a colossal explosion due to the contact of substance with anti-substance ...'

OK.

Some bits of this history have been censored and other parts of it have been, um, stolen.

I think I have a bad luck name since in all history I share it only with a small-town plumber and two useless embezzlers who worked at the post office. My name: Helen X. I'll write it down so I don't forget it. I was born in a bad luck time, in a bad luck place just like this one, on the same day as a solar eclipse on TV, the most beautiful but very very bad luck thing.

I'm lost and I'm lonely. I'm losing things fast. I dropped some money back there somewhere. Two, no, change it, three pints of blood went right down the drain after a pub fight! I already lost my fingerprints in a game of cards. My name is Helen X. Soon I won't be a person at all, just a sad collection of bits all lost in the woods.

Good.

I have to think positive. I'm getting somewhere. I am getting somewhere. Perhaps I'll lie down and cry. No, bad idea—I'll sing to keep my spirits up. [*She sings, tunlessly ...*] Frank Sinatra never wrote a song about this place—he wasn't fucking good enough.

Some parts of this history have been censored and other parts of it have been, um, forgotten.

This history ...

ALMOST PREGNANT, a true life story by HELEN X. No.

The SHELL GARAGE's History of Mud. Part one in a series of eight.

No. No. No. No. No.

MY OFFICIAL LIFE ON THE RUN. By Helen X in conjunction with Jackie Onassis, no Jackie Collins ... Shit.

CLUB OF NO REGRETS.

Yeah. CLUB OF NO REGRETS. Being an extraordinary story told to keep the dark at bay, one night when lost in a strange town. CLUB OF NO REGRETS.

A spell might help me. What about a spell: [*She reads the titles of spells from a book*] TO CALL UP SPIRITS—no. TO PRESERVE YOURSELF FROM LOSING BLOOD—no. TO HEAL AN INJURED EYE—get someone to piss in it—no.

TO CALL UP DEATH, no I'm going to change it. TO CALL UP DEATH and TO GET OUT OF A TERRIBLE TERRIBLE PLACE. Yeah.

Tie a string on a branch, and to the string tie some paper, bearing thereupon these words: SUPER TRENDY DISCO, NO DENIMS / OF ALL AMERICA'S MYSTERIES NONE REMAIN.

CLUB OF NO REGRETS.

Scene 59: A Procedures Scene

A: Half of my officers were themselves arrested this morning due to some administrative blunder in the East side of the city. Can you imagine that?

B: It's terrible

A: I had some thoughts about procedure. I thought I'd run them past you. That OK?

B: Yes

A: We're agreed that during the search attention should be paid, not only to all details but also to all trivia. Those carrying out the search need to understand, instinctively, that everything in the area has its own intrinsic importance.

Scene 93: A Questions Scene

A: When did you first discover that the world was magic? When did you first discover that you caused magic in the world? When did you first discover that there was magic in the world?

Telegram One

DEAR NO-ONE I HAVE WALKED TO THAT BIT OF THE PARK WHERE THE TAPE SAYS POLICE LINE DO NOT CROSS AND I HAVE CROSSED IT . + . STOP . + . DO NOT TRY TO FIND ME . + . STOP . + . COS I'M A KIND OF HOMEMADE BOMB, DESTINED TO EXPLODE PRETTY SOON . + . STOP . + . BETTER FOR YOU IF YOU AREN'T NEAR ME THEN,

BETTER FOR EVERYONE . + . STOP . + . OH YEAH AND I SUPPOSE IT'S NO SURPRISE I'M PREGNANT . + . STOP . + . FOR THREE YEARS I HAD NO SEX WITH ANYONE, I TRIED TO FORGET I EVER HAD A THING CALLED SEXUALITY THEN ONE LITTLE FUCK AND I'M PREGNANT IT . + . STOP . + . IT'S GOING TO BE A GIRL I'M SURE AND SHE'S GOING TO BE PERFECT AND I'M GOING TO CALL HER GRIEF ...

Helen Text Two

Night is falling fast. I try to tell myself a story, call it CLUB OF NO REGRETS. Can you see those lights? Are there some lights left on in that building? No.

Telegram Two

DEAR NO ONE I'M SO UNHAPPY I'M GOING TO GET INVOLVED IN BAD PEOPLE TO TRY AND GET MYSELF MURDERED . + . STOP . + . YOU KNOW WHAT IT'S LIKE THESE DAYS — YOU WAKE UP EMBROILED IN A GREAT ADVENTURE AND THE NEXT THING YOU KNOW YOU'RE THROUGH THE FUCKING LOOKING GLASS INTO WEIRD WORLD . + . STOP . + . OH YEAH THINGS ROUND HERE HAVE CERTAINLY CHANGED STOP IN MY DREAM I'M NOT SURE WHO I'M SUPPOSED TO BE . + . STOP . + . YESTERDAY I FOUND A NOTE BY THE BEDSIDE TABLE BUT IT WASN'T IN MY HANDWRITING . + . STOP . + . THE NOTE SAID I'M OLD, OR GETTING OLD . + . STOP . + . THE NOTE SAID I'M HIDING BUT I'M NOT SURE WHO FROM ...

Scene 15: A Look How I'm Crying Scene

A: Look how I'm crying. Don't you care at all? Look how I'm crying
B: I don't want you to leave
A: Where am I going? What am I going to do?
B: I have pretended for so long that everything is fine.

Helen Text Three

I'm sweating. I stop at a call box, call all the people I know in this place, but get no answer. I call 0898 666 555 ELECTRIC LESSONS FOR GIRLS. I call 0898 777 888 ETERNITY NOW. I call 0898 444 333 GULF WAR DIARY. I call 0898 333 222 LOST IN THE WOODS. A leaf falls from a tree. Can you see that leaf falling? Yes.

Scene 6: A Troubled Scene

A: Queen of Nothing we call upon you to help us ...
B: Today I am troubled, I am troubled, cease to speak, cease to walk. I am troubled by voices. I call on Our Lady Of Car Parks to help me. I summon her, help me break loose from these bindings.

Prince of Lie-Detection and Broken Promises, I am coming dressed in rags to meet you. Queen of Nothing, mistress of the air and of satellites we have not seen you, it has been long since we've seen you. Oh can't you see I have no skin and no bones. I am coming dressed in rags just to meet you.

Helen Text Four

'Every person who comes under surveillance is given a special name. This name should be short (of one word that should charcterise the appearance of the observed or express the impression he creates; and it should enable one to judge wether it relates to male or female). One should not give simillar names to several persons under surveillance.'

OK. That's given me a clue ...

Telegram Three (Robin)

DEAR NO ONE . + . STOP . + . THE VOICES AND NOISES IN THE NIGHT ARE SCARING ME NOW . + . STOP . + . I'M INSIDE A CITY OF LIVING FAINTING BUILDINGS AND NOW IT'S GETTING DARK . + . STOP . + . DO YOU THINK THAT A ROOM CAN BE HAUNTED BY THE GHOST OF ITSELF? DO YOU THINK OUR BODIES KEEP THEIR GHOSTS STORED DEEP INSIDE THEM? IN MY DREAM I HAVE BEEN GIVEN A JOB AND I'M GOING TO DO IT: TEN THOUSAND IN CASH AND A CAR AND FRIDGE FREEZER TO KILL SOMEONE WHO NO ONE WILL EVEN MISS SURELY THAT ISN'T SO MUCH A CRIME AS A MINOR BENDING OF THE RULES HA HA . + . STOP . + . OH YEAH AND BY THE WAY DON'T CALL HERE AGAIN IT'S DANGEROUS ...

Scene 35: A Shoot-Out Scene

A: Ahhh.
B: What is it?
A: I think I'm hit. I'm seeing colours. I'm thinking in shapes. Hold me. Talk to me.
B: Oh god.
A: Talk to me, speak to me.
B: What do you want to hear?
A: Anything, I'm dying aren't I. I'm going down, just tell me something.
B: It's ... It's OK. You're not dying. Just ... listen ...

Helen Text Five

To get released from prison. No that's no good, I'm going to change it. To be released from prison or some terrible place. Promise to break a street lamp at near midnight. When you get to the prison gates and still find them locked say magical words. Say: 'What's shaking, what's shaking, the earth, the house and me, maybe...'

Right, we'll try it again.

Telegram Four (Robin)

DEAR NO ONE . + . STOP . + . I HAVE RENTED A ROOM IN A GOOD PART OF TOWN . + . STOP . + . IT'S BIG AND CLEAN BUT THERE IS SOME NOISE FROM THE ROOMS ABOVE AND BELOW . + . STOP . + . OH YEAH I FOUND A KNIFE BENEATH MY PILLOW . + . STOP . + . AND I THINK I MIGHT HAVE USED IT . + . STOP . + . WHEN I LOOK INTO THE MIRROR I CAN SEE MY LIPS ARE MOVING BUT I'M NOT SURE THE WORDS ARE MINE OH AND BY THE WAY I MISS YOU, THE WALKS WE'D TAKE IN THE WINTER GARDENS, THE PEACE WE HAD WHEN WE SLEPT EASY IN BED ...

Telegram Five (Claire)

DEAR NO-ONE . + . STOP . + . I AM CERTAIN OF ONE THING ONLY . + . STOP . + . AND THAT'S MY LOVE FOR THIS WORLD STOP IN MY DREAM I'M A PRIVATE DETECTIVE RIPPED OUT OF A NOVEL AND DROPPED IN THIS PLACE . + . STOP . + . I HAVE BEEN THINKING ABOUT STUFF . + . STOP . + . YOU KNOW THE KIND OF STUFF IT'S HARD TO TALK ABOUT . + . STOP . + . HAVE YOU NOTICED THE STRANGE CHANGES OF ONE'S BODY WITH AGE? HAVE YOU NOTICED THAT? HAVE YOU NOTICED THE POWER CUTS GETTING MORE FREQUENT? HAVE YOU EVER BEEN SCARED?

Helen's Questions

[*To Robin*]

Do you believe in extra-terrestrial beings?	Yes.
Do you believe that culture is politics?	I don't know.
Have you betrayed anyone?	No.

[*To Claire*]

Have you betrayed a country?	No.
Are you afraid of the dark?	Yes.
Have you killed anyone?	I don't know.

[*To Robin*]

Why is it against the law to change your name?	I don't know.
Do you believe in ghosts?	Yes.
Where are we now?	I don't know.
Is it true that you think you've fallen in love?	Yes.

[*To Claire*]

Do you like rain?	No.
Do you know spells?	Yes.
Tell me one.	No.
Have you ever been to Persia?	Yes.
What's it like?	I don't remember.
What colour are your eyes?	Blue.

[*To Robin*]

How many scars do you have?	Three.
Do you think suicide is an acceptable moral option?	No.
Do you have any illnesses?	No.
Do you know spells?	Yes.
Tell me one.	No.

[*To Claire*]

Do you sing in the bath?	No.
Do you swim in the ocean?	Yes.
Where are we now?	I don't know.
Do you believe that you are about to die, as a result of the injuries you have received?	No.

Helen Text Six

I've come to a clearing in the woods but the trees are made of ice, the branches hard as iron. I tell myself a story to keep warm. Ghosts are coming out of the buildings. I've come to a clearing in the woods.

'What are the prospects of a journey to the furthest star? Today we can only say that a return journey to stars nine or ten light years away would take not less than 25 years. It would not be rational to embark passengers who would never return to earth but have to spend all their life on the journey. Nevertheless.'

I'm in a frozen building. What's that? I can hear voices. Where? From far away. They yell: COME OUT COME OUT AND GIVE YOURSELVES UP! COME OUT COME OUT ALL FUGITIVES WHEREVER YOU ARE...

I've come to a clearing in the woods but the trees are made of ice, the branches harder than iron.

'Readers are warned that the sketch maps and boundaries here are provisional, approximate, unreliable and wrong. Nonetheless I have furnished them, for as my text is no more than a pack of lies they can do no harm…' Right.

This history, being an account of lostness, trees, woods and told with complete accounts, no, complete depictions of various treacheries, epic gun battles and escapes.

Telegram Six (Claire)

DEAR NO-ONE . + . STOP . + . WHEN I LOOK OUT THE WINDOW I CAN SEE THE WHOLE CITY IN ALL ITS SPLENDOUR . + . STOP . + . WHAT A VIEW . + . STOP . + . WHAT A VIEW . + . STOP . + . BUT WHERE ARE THE PEOPLE? IN MY DREAM I'M FALLING DEEPER AND DEEPER INTO A BLACK HOLE CALLED THE NIGHT . + . STOP . + . I'M FALLING AND I'M FALLING AND I'M FALLING AND YOU'RE FALLING WITH ME . + . STOP . + . WE'RE FALLING AND FALLING AND THERE'S NO END TO IT . + . STOP . + . DON'T KNOW IF I'LL WRITE AGAIN I'M RUNNING OUT OF LUCK…

Helen Text Seven

I've come to an invisible wall. I've come to an invisible wall that stretches high into the heavens and down into the ground. I write on the wall. HELEN X. HELEN X. HELEN X. Then I write magical words. SORROWS OF PART-ING/JOYS OF MEETING. OCTOBER LANGUAGE. NEW LOVE. I've come to an invisible wall..

Helen Text Eight

This terrible woods.
When did you first discover that the world was magic?
When did you first discover that there was magic in the world?
When did you first discover that you caused magic in the world?
Dear No One I've come to a clearing. I'm lost. I've reached a clearing in the woods. Night's falling fast. I tell myself a story, call it CLUB OF NO REGRETS.

Can you see those lights? Can you see? Are there some lights left on inside that building? Yes.

What ghosts are these? What strange signs? What things?

I have thrown myself out of the world and all the police on the whole earth are after me 'cos I have dared to be alive and I have no respect for the law. I've come to a clearing in the woods only the trees are made of ice and the branches are harder than iron. I tell myself a story to keep warm. Ghosts are coming out of the buildings. I'm lost.

What's that? I can hear voices. Where? from far away. I can hear voices all yelling in the night. What do they say?

They yell:

Look how I'm crying, don't you care at all? Look how I'm crying.
I don't want you to leave.
Where am I going? What am I going to do.
I have pretended for so long that everything is fine.
When did you first discover that the world was magic?
When did you first discover that there was magic in the world?
Ahhh. I think I'm dying. Tell me anything. I'm hit aren't I? I'm dying.
It's OK. It's OK. You're not dying it's OK. You're not dying, just listen.

What ghosts are these? What strange signs? What things?
Night's falling fast. I tell myself a story, call it CLUB OF NO REGRETS.
I've come to the very heart of the woods and there's no going on. I write my name: Helen X. Helen X. Helen X. And then I write magical words. I write:

Queen of Nothing. Queen of satellites and fax machines. I am coming dressed in rags just to meet you.

I have thrown myself out of the whole world.
I have thrown myself out of the whole world.
I tell myself a story, call it CLUB OF NO REGRETS. Being an account of lost-ness, trees and woods. I've come to the very heart of the woods. The trees and the branches so thick I have to cut through them with a knife. Brambles tear at my legs. The city like a woods, like a terrible woods.

I've come to the part of the woods that's the very heart of it. Some parts of this history are look how I'm crying, don't you care at all, look how I'm crying, what am I going to do? Queen of nothing, mistress of the air, we call upon you to help us. Oh can't you see I have no skin and no bones. I am coming dressed in rags just to meet you. Ohh ohh I think I'm hit. Ohhh.

What ghosts are these? What strange signs? What things? I can hear voices. Where from? From far away. They're yelling into the night. They yell: 'Tell me something, tell me anything, tell me, please.' I have come upon the thickest part of the woods. Brambles tear at my legs. Voices yell: 'The sketch maps in this history are wrong.' The city like a woods, like a terrible woods. We're agreed that those present at the search should take the utmost care not only over all details but also over all trivia. Look. A leaf falling. Can you see that leaf falling? Yes. I have thrown myself out of the world.

Are there lights left on in that building? Look. Look. There are lights left on in that building and there are people moving there. What ghosts are these? What strange things? What signs? Look. Look. There are lights left on in that building and there are people moving there.

What ghosts are these? What strange signs? What things? Nights falling fast. I tell myself a story call it CLUB OF NO REGRETS. Dear No One. I have come upon the very thickest part of this woods. Can you see those lights? Yes. Can you hear those birds sing? Yes. Do you like the moon over the city? Yes. I like the moon over the city. Some parts of this history are thoughts about procedure, I thought I'd run them past you, yes.

What ghosts are these? What strange signs? What things? Dear No one. I've come to the very heart of the woods and here the branches are as hard as ice. I've come to the very heart of the woods and I cannot escape. I've reached a point and there's no going on. There are branches behind me and thick branches blocking the way ahead. Dear No One. I'm trapped and there's no moving and there's no going on.

It's nearly (cough) midnight. I think it's time for the big escape routine. The one for getting out of the woods. Can we have the music please?

Helen Text Nine

I had feared the distant journey would weary our dreams, but I am on a knife-edge of happiness tonight. Time is late, and we shadows are fading. Forgive me: I am made to write as a witness, in difficult times.

Kings, thieves, usherettes, lords, liars, gunmen and prostitutes: all those who would know magic: take this book and have it read to you:

over the BRIDGE OF KISSES
left at MURDER STREET
to the BIG STATUE OF SOMETHING RARE
through the subway near DIFFICULT HOUSE
to the END OF THE WORLD
and then, for those that find it, on foot, to CLUB OF NO REGRETS

Thank you, goodnight.

Structure of the Performance

What follows is an attempt to map or diagram the structure of *Club of No Regrets*. The position of the various texts in the piece is indicated alongside notes and annotations concerning the action track and tone of the performance. Throughout the piece Helen calls for the scenes to be enacted again and again, repeating them, switching their order. Helen is erratic, jumpy and volatile, declaring that the scenes are 'completely wrong' or 'too sad' or simply 'too black and white'. Her struggle is to get them in the right order, or, more certainly, to forge some more poetic sense from their unpromising substance.

As Helen calls for the scenes to be enacted, Richard and Cathy function as brutal stage-hands who bring texts and props to enable the performance. Their action is often disruptive — drawing one's attention away from the scenes themselves, obliterating dialogue with noise and distraction. The annotations for the piece give only a crude and partial account of the action and of Helen's more-or-less impromptu responses to it.

Helen Text One
Helen wandering, reading and talking to herself in the darkness of the stage.

Robin and Claire enter as somewhat reluctant performers, with Richard and Cathy as stage-hands. Robin and Claire are gagged and bound to chairs using parcel-tape. Helen is above the set, looking down into the room, consulting her papers and drinking from various bottles throughout the piece.

Scene Order	Staging Notes/Terry's reactions
BLOCK ONE	Robin and Claire are bound and gagged throughout.
A Procedures Scene	Text largely inaudible, glasses brought for Robin and Claire.
A Questions Scene	Text obscured by Cathy banging behind set.
	Helen: Is that it?
A Questions Scene	
Telegram One (Claire)	Claire still gagged, text inaudible. Helen leaves her place overlooking the room to come down stage left.
Helen Text Two	Helen returns to her vantage point.
BLOCK TWO	Robin and Claire are bound and gagged throughout.
A Procedures Scene	Interrupted by constant changing of props in the room.
A Just As They're About To Kiss	Robin and Claire hop towards each other, bound to their chairs.
The Telephone Rings Scene*	The telephone arrives late, the scene an absurd failure.
Telegram One (Robin)	Helen: Completely fucking wrong. We'd better do another.
Telegram Two (Claire)	Claire is still gagged text inaudible. Helen has her head in her hands.
A Look How I'm Crying Scene	Helen: Too short we'll have to do it again.
A Look How I'm Crying Scene	Robin's mouth has finally been untaped.
A Troubled Scene	Robin cut out of chair by Cathy using knife, Richard pushes the standard lamp into the room through the window.
A Questions Scene	Claire's mouth untaped, a gun placed in Robin's hand. Helen leaves her place above the room to come down stage left.
Helen Text Three	Helen returns to her vantage point.
BLOCK THREE	
A Look How I'm Crying Scene	Water from bottles thrown onto Robin and Claire's faces as tears.
A Questions Scene	Text inaudible again due to Cathy banging behind the set.

A Look How I'm Crying Scene	Glasses doused with water for tears.
A Questions Scene	Helen reads aloud from a book as the scene proceeds.
Helen Text Four	As Helen reads Richard and Cathy bring a coloured shirt for Robin and a dressing gown for Claire, gesturing at gun-point that they should put them on.
Telegram Four (Robin)	
A Shoot Out Scene	A trickle of fake blood sprayed on Robin, a single squirt of talcum powder sprayed in the air as smoke. Richard with a gun through a window of the room.
A Troubled Scene	Richard and Cathy pelt the windows of the room with 'rain' from bottles.
	Helen: It needs more colour.
A Troubled Scene	Cathy puts a blue shirt on the table, more water thrown in the windows.
	Helen: Too black and white.
Helen Text Five	Helen pacing behind the set, then returning to her place.
A Troubled Scene	More water thrown in the windows, Helen ghosting Claire's words.
	Helen: I've completely lost the thread of it …
A Kiss/Telephone Scene	The phone arrives just in time to disrupt the kiss.
A Kiss/Telephone Scene	The phone arrives just in time to disrupt the kiss.
A Kiss/Telephone Scene	The phone arrives just in time to disrupt the kiss.
A Kiss/Telephone Scene	Helen given microphone.
A Kiss/Telephone Scene	The phone arrives just in time to disrupt the kiss.
A Drug Trip Scene	CHAOS: Richard flashing the practical lamp on and off, drawing circles of light in the air, Cathy throwing talcum powder into the room
	Helen: More cops! We need more cops, we'll have to do it again.
A Drug Trip Scene	Helen waving a tin-foil star, whoops and yells, circles of chalk, Claire crying into the telephone.
Telegram Four (Robin)	
Telegram Five (Claire)	
A Kiss/Telephone Scene	The phone arrives just in time to disrupt the kiss. Robin and Claire have been parcel-taped to the walls of the set by Richard and Cathy —since they cannot move the scene is a dismal failure.
	Helen: Shit.
Helen Questions	Helen enters the room and poses questions to Robin and Claire.
Helen Text Six	Helen returns to her place above the room
BLOCK FOUR	Richard and Cathy no longer pass text to Robin and Claire, except for telegrams.
A Procedures Scene	Robin and Claire still taped up.
A Questions Scene	
A Troubled Scene	Richard and Cathy deluge the room with water, talcum powder and leaves.
A Look How I'm Crying Scene	
A Kiss/Telephone Scene	
Telegram Six (Claire)	
A Drug Trip Scene	More manic than ever.
A Shoot Out Scene	Claire's face and neck sprayed with blood.
	Helen: Oh, she's dying, she's dying, oh God, she's dying …

A Questions Scene	Robin shouting against the music.
A Shoot Out Scene	Robin's face and neck sprayed with blood, leaves and talcum powder thrown into the room.
	Helen: Oh, he's dying, he's dying, oh God, he's going to die …
A Look How I'm Crying Scene	Helen: It's too sad, we'll have to do it again.
A Look How I'm Crying Scene	Helen leaves her place above the room.
Helen Text Seven	Helen returns to her place above the room.

BLOCK FIVE

Helen calls the scenes faster and faster. Richard and Cathy are running themselves into the ground. They pile on the leaves, talcum powder water and fake blood. Robin and Claire are soaked, their voices at their limits from shouting.

A Questions Scene
A Troubled Scene
A Just As They're About To Kiss The Telephone Rings Scene
A Just As They're About To Kiss The Telephone Rings Scene
A Just As They're About To Kiss The Telephone Rings Scene
A Look How I'm Crying Scene
A Drug Trip Scene
A Troubled Scene
A Questions Scene
A Look How I'm Crying Scene
A Procedures Scene
A Troubled Scene

Robin and Claire give up enacting the scenes. They stand in the centre of the room as Richard and Cathy deluge it with water, leaves, smoke and sprayed blood, the 'stage-hands' continuing to do the special effects and props-continuity long after the actors have stopped. Frenzy. Helen continues to call scenes in random order, doing the dialogue herself, mis-remembered, jumbled, confused. In the end the music lulls.

Helen Text Eight

Helen calms and continues to speak, leaving her position above the room and moving to the front of the stage. Richard and Cathy gently arrange objects in the room as she speaks: delicate arrangements of books, guns, leaves, bloodstains.

After a time they stop arranging objects in and around the room, and assume Helen's previous position looking down into it at Robin and Claire who are still embraced. When they've looked for a while they get down and start to clear the crude room set and all the things in it, leaving Robin and Claire embraced alone in the centre of the cleared space, visible against the backdrop wall of chalked buildings. Robin and Claire drop their embrace and join Richard and Cathy at the back.

Terry calls for the music for the 'big escape routine'.

CODA:
CHAIRS DANCE / ESCAPE ROUTINE

R&B music plays.

Richard and Cathy are bound to chairs with parcel tape and gagged. A frightening dance follows; somewhere between brutal ballet and the climax of some well-dodgy thriller. They struggle to escape, madly slipping and falling over as Robin and Claire dance. Often the chairs break.

Meanwhile Helen chalks a circle on the floor at the front on each side of the stage. Using the knife and a hammer, running from side to side of the stage she dances, a thrashing with the knife that suggests her cutting her way out of the woods. Richard and Cathy escape from the chairs and immediately tape-up Robin and Claire. The R&B music ends. Richard, Cathy and Helen/Terry are all breathing hard. Piano music comes on and the escape routine repeated in another key by Robin and Claire. Helen stays at the front, her 'getting out of the woods' dance going more and more slowly. Robin and Claire escape. The piano music ends. There is silence.

Terry pours water on the chalk circles on the floor at the front, erasing them with her foot. She walks to the right hand side of the stage, takes off her wig and picks up the microphone. The others watch as she speaks.

Helen Final Text

★ There are two scenes that Helen calls for which involve no written dialogue. The first is entitled *A Just As They're About To Kiss the Telephone Rings Scene* and in it Robin and Claire make their way toward each other in the tiny room, get closer and closer as if they are about to kiss and then break off at the last moment, usually prompted by the noisy arrival of the disconnected prop telephone. Richard and Cathy change the meaning of this scene (and others) by placing props into the hands of Robin and/or Claire as it is enacted. A Robin advancing on Claire to kiss her is transformed by Cathy arming him with a large rusty saw for example, or by the addition of an old bottle-thick pair of glasses.

The second scene which does not feature written text is entitled *A Drug Trip Scene*. The action for this develops and changes throughout its various repetitions but it basically consists of Robin and Claire feigning hysterical and/or manic hallucinations while Richard and Cathy draw circles on the walls of the room in chalk, make the hands of the prop clock go round and round very fast and use a practical lamp to crudely create the effect of shifting, swimming and flashing lights, and place objects and bursts of smoke (talcum powder) in the room to disorientate Robin and Claire.

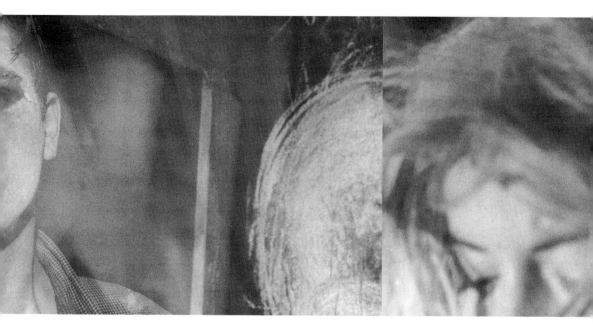

Speak Bitterness

Forced Entertainment
Text by Tim Etchells, with Robin Arthur, Richard Lowdon, Claire Marshall, Cathy Naden, Tim Hall, Sue Marshall and Terry O'Connor

Speak Bitterness was first presented in 1994 and has subsequently been shown in both theatre and durational versions, the latter lasting up to six hours. The essence of the piece is a line of people making confessions from behind a long table in a brightly lit space. The litany of confessions, read from the text which is strewn across the table in the performance area, ranges from big-time stuff like forgery, murder or genocide to nasty little details like reading each other's diaries or forgetting to take the dogs out for a walk. Dressed in suits the performers meet the gaze of the audience, speaking softly and drawing them in. The text draws on the diverse cultures of confession in, for example, contemporary chat shows, churches and show trials. *Speak Bitterness* was a break in style from Forced Entertainment's previous work, in that it was primarily text based and that it eschewed the fast-paced, physical and collage structures commonly used in our previous performances.

Speak Bitterness itself, in either durational or theatre version, uses the text as raw material through which relationships between the performers themselves and between performers and audience might be constructed. The confessions are read, whispered, shouted. They are erased with laughter or hesitation. Confessions come in single lines, in fast-paced exchanges between performers and in long monologues and lists. The performance may appear to be sincere, bitter, preposterous or even absurd by turns. The thing which holds it together is the sense that the performers are, through the medium of the confessions, measuring themselves against the possibilities of human misdemeanour and wayward behaviour — from the largest political crimes to the most banal of daily errors.

Project history

Speak Bitterness began as a durational performance for the National Review of Live Art in Glasgow (1994). In this frame the piece lasted five hours and the public could stay, leave or return according to their own wishes. There were never more than 20 people watching at one time and often as few as two or three: intimate witnesses in the small tarpaulin box which designer and performer Richard Lowdon created to house the piece. Fully lit, the public faced the performers directly over the long steel table which ran across the space.

The text drew on short passages of confessions material I had written for (*Let the Water Run its Course) to the Sea that Made the Promise* (1986) and for *Marina & Lee* (1991). A large additional amount of new material written by me was then augmented with writing from performers Robin Arthur, Cathy Naden, Tim Hall and Sue Marshall. This writing was edited by me and further augmented by improvisation from the whole company.

Like subsequent durational presentations of *Speak Bitterness*, the Glasgow version was not structured beyond an outline of simple performance rules and strategies. In this version, the piece unfolds in real time: an encounter between the public, the performers and their decisions on the day. Subject to the influence of desire, tiredness, accident, whim and impulse, this version of *Speak Bitterness* remains, like its theatre counterpart, at all times framed by the simple device of the confessions — everything spoken will be confession, using the pronoun 'we', and either drawn from the text on the table or made up on the spot.

The theatre version of *Speak Bitterness* was developed during summer 1995. We took the same blue tarpaulin box and adapted it as a stage space — losing one wall to create an open rectangle that the audience looked into. Strings of bare bulbs hung over the performance area and were extended over the auditoria of venues we toured — lighting the audience slightly and sustaining a sense of being in the same room as the performance.

In dramatic terms we tried to preserve the feeling of the Glasgow durational (spatial and performance intimacy, a sense of real-time process, etc.) whilst adding enough in the way of structural architecture (narrative or musical development) to keep a theatre audience engaged for an hour and a half. Rehearsals involved the usual glut of improvisation based, in this occasion, on the reams of confessional texts. We used video a lot — playing back rehearsals and analysing them. We set and scripted sections out of successful improvisations and then combined these sections into various different orders. We also left whole sections of the piece unscripted so that performers would be free to choose new lines in each performance, or to interrupt each other, speaking in a different order each night in various sections. Our aim was for an architecture/structure in the piece that did develop — leading you in and taking you places — but one that seemed live, accidental, spontaneous.

Speak Bitterness was conceived and devised by Forced Entertainment under the direction of Tim Etchells. It was performed by Robin Arthur, Richard Lowdon, Claire Marshall, Cathy Naden, Tim Hall, Sue Marshall, Terry O'Connor and Tim Etchells (in the durational version only). Design for the piece was by Richard Lowdon and lighting was by Nigel Edwards. The soundtrack was by John Avery.

The text as presented here is a wide range of the confessions material from the piece.

We're guilty of dice, of teletype and needles. We spread true rumours and wrote false receipts. On game-shows we cheated and on quiz shows we lied. We lay at home with the 'flu and a hangover. We made the heartbreak face and then we smiled. We stank of chlorine and fists fell on us like the rain. We made a mockery of justice and a mockery of the American/English language. We doctored photographs, carefully erasing figures and substituting stonework, pillars and curtains to make it look like George Michael had stood on the balcony all alone. We sacked the town, we painted it red. We slipped through customs at Nairobi International, without even being seen. We were exiled kings, useless princes. We revamped our image, we were really working class. We made the crowd blush, we were driven by demons whose names we couldn't even spell. We were white-collar criminals, haunted by our pasts. We told Mrs Gamble that Helen was with us when she wasn't. We were ex-cons trying to go straight. We thought that Freud was probably right about laughter. We had no moral compass, or if we did have one it had been badly damaged during the frequent electrical storms. We're guilty of heresy and hearsay, of turning our backs to the wall. We saw Arthur Scargill's blue movie cameo. We lied when it would've been easier to tell the truth. When we broke the law about satellites there was no one to stop us or care. We sent death threats by fax machine and kept a list on a computer of the people we were going to kill. We put the bop in the bop shee wop. We loved each other too much. We held each other's hands. We spat in the beer when no one was looking. We're guilty of murder, arson and theft. We crashed the spaceship on purpose. We got drunk too often, we nobbled horses, we made each other bleed. We knew that a professional foul inside the 30-yard box could lead to a penalty but in the 83rd minute we felt there was no choice—some of us went one way and I went the other, sandwiching the bloke and bringing him down hard—the referee was a Hungarian and never saw a thing. We were cold callers, scared of kryptonite. We were class traitors, cry-for-help shoplifters, we were murderers of sleep. Everything was a movie to us. We hacked and hoodwinked, we wounded with intent. When the food-aid arrived in the lorries we started shoving and pushing. We had nose jobs, chin jobs, eye jobs, tummy tucks and bum sucks. We were bloody fools. We're guilty of that look people have sometimes when they daren't speak their minds. We confess to radium, railways and romanticism. We were jealous of Helen Sebley's personal transformation. We never made the rendezvous. We were deathless, never fading. We ate pet food straight from the can. We dipped our toes in the water and we got our fingers burned. We had a truce on Christmas day. In the last years of our rule we deteriorated both physically and mentally—we planned to eliminate even our most loyal supporters. We went to Blackpool and got caught in the act. We stuffed the ears of men with false reports. We confess to oil rigs and pylons. We're guilty of landslide victories and throwing in the towel. We looked at pictures of rare skin diseases. We got drunk and got tattoos. We cut to the quick and were frozen to the bone. We read books to avoid conversation. We confess to the dimming of streetlamps on long tropical nights. We thought thuggery was better than common sense. We didn't like modern Britain. We thought modern art was a load of shit. When we started to go bald we grew our hair long in one of those Bobby Charlton hair-cuts, with a very long very thin strand of side hair plastered all over the bald bit at the front. We were cowards, strictly black market. We became nocturnal, inward-looking, scared. We set men a new standard by which to measure infamy and shame. We lived on a diet of speed and chips. We fell off the earth. We cut off the hand of an evil-hearted pirate called Captain Hook in a fair fight; we threw his hand to a crocodile which had also eaten an alarm clock. The crocodile so enjoyed eating Hook's hand that he followed the pirate around all the time, hoping to get a second helping — but the tick tock tick from the alarm clock he'd swallowed always warned the pirate of the crocodile's approach. We made false economies. We were one of those double acts from way back — on-stage it was all love and laughter — offstage we never spoke. We pissed on the flag. We made a soap for black people. We told long boring anecdotes. We worked for £2.90 an hour. We gave Helen 15 minutes to pack her bags and get out of the house. We never thought; we never danced at weddings. They invented a new classification of lunatic just for us. We wrote biographies without bothering to research or ask permission. We lost the front door keys. We dressed Geisha and looked ridiculous. We did that Sharon Tate. We used laser treatment on hapless immigrants. We stood outside the prisoners' doors all night and whispered nonsense so they couldn't sleep. We sang the songs of streetlamps and paving slabs. We kept a boyfriend in waiting. We dug a few graves in the football pitch and buried the bodies at night. We were not quite at home in the world. We made a film called AMERICAN BONDING CRAP — it was mainly for boys but some girls liked it. We invented a TV channel called THE MONEY CHANNEL — 24 hours of nothing but long fingers handling money — it was a hit all over the world. We blazed the trail, set off rockets and yelled from rooftops. We were small-minded, rusty after too many years. We were wankers. We were loons. We staged long and titillating fights between Good Barbie and Bad Barbie. We held our savings in Deutschmarks, under a bed. We confess to autumn leaves, to fatherless children and shiftwork, we were regrouping fighters, looking for somewhere to sleep. We served up the beer in cups made from human skulls. Our trade was to traffic in human misery. We sold the records that we'd bought in our teens and which were no longer fashionable. We were bored of the poor. We killed the first daughter of all English greengrocers in an attempt to avoid any unfortunate recurrences of the last 10 years. We confess to intercoms, faxes and prohibited places. We are guilty of arsenic, poor-laws, pass-laws and slightness in the face of adversity. We said we were the best there's ever been. We fucked around. We sniggered at a Scotsman's account of an alien attack—they ripped his trousers and left him in the pub. We invented rain-glare on tarmac and UHT cream that you could squirt from a tin. We were sceptics who didn't believe in anything. We drew our own blood with a syringe to make ourselves anorexic, we injected ourselves with yeast to make the blood clot, we injected red dye to make the blood more red, more red when we were bleeding. We crept out when everyone else was fast asleep. We had eyes like the stars, we talked to the trees. We named our sons THIRSTY, LUCKY and MEMORY. We sat up some nights and talked about the future of history. We talked about doing time. Our lives were like a soap made in heaven. We cut open our own bodies to try and find the evil in them, we found nothing, lost a bit of blood, needed stitches. We confess to wasting promises. We wrongly prescribed medicines. We turned down the title Miss Scunthorpe Evening Telegraph. When morning came we changed our stories. We confess to fraud and to forgery, we're guilty of coldness and spite. We gave up too easy, hit our children too hard. We dropped atom bombs on Nagasaki, Coventry, Seattle, Belize, Belsize Park and Hiroshima. We were rightly arrested under Sections 7 and 23 and rightly charged under Section 45. We planned the overthrow of governments and holidays in the summer. We put love first, broke our legs playing rounders. We filmed events in which we could not intervene, events that spilled out of control, events that didn't even exist. We altered documents and photographs to disguise the location of people and places that were dear to us. We confess to trade routes, comedy scenes, kitchen knives and libel. We confess to microphones, water and polygraphs. We needed help but we wouldn't take it; we wanted spiritualist ends through materialist means; we lacked faith and therefore patience; we spat on soldiers in the street. In a parody we published high state officials were portrayed in an insulting manner—the public and premeditated humiliation of their honour and worth was reproduced widely in the mass media in an unseemly and counterproductive fashion adding greater insult to our already reprehensible words. We wanked off for money. We were at Tet and May Lai. We kissed Paul on the mouth before we killed him. We had butterflies. We wanted to write love songs, really good love songs that would really last but we didn't know music and we couldn't write. We had unorthodox thoughts about the economy, we burned people's faces off with a blow-torch. We were inadequate, indifferent and afraid. We launched the death-ray. We passed off crap as good stuff. It was our job to insinuate strange objects into the crowd scenes of cinema—the man carrying a surfboard in *Anna Karenina* at the station, the child in Bertolucci's *1900* who's wearing a bum-bag and the woman in *Basic Instinct* who's leading oxen to the slaughter—all these were our work. We confess to lip-synching, eye winking and overturned lorries. Our good deeds would not take much recounting. We found each other lost and wanting. We waited till Paul was drunk and then we beat the fuck out of him. We went to the dogs, we drank our own tears, we farted on the first date. We said the Lord's Prayer backwards. We fell asleep in the middle and so didn't understand. We killed children. We practised false chemistry and worshipped graven images. The company we set up was fictitious — just a trading screen for another company which in turn was just a trading screen for a third company and so on — you could chase the money halfway round the world if you wanted and still never find the place that it ended up. We drank our own tears, we bathed in Diet Lilt, we had to get up in the night with a stomach ache. We had the doubts of daytime and the doubts of night-time. We perpetrated a hoax. We shot people in the head. We thought in shapes rather than words. We wouldn't talk about things, we just bottled them up. We photocopied our own semen and excrement. We bargained for immunity. We watched the light changing; we loved the sky; we dreamed in black and white. We rumbled with other gangs; we dreamed of drained swimming pools; we went into shock for a year. We didn't give anything, we were just there. We shouted for so long and we kept shouting until it didn't even sound like our voices any more. We told simple stories to children. We put family first. We were opinionated and sloppily dressed; we burst into tears. We confess to driftwood, safe-breaking and teletype; we said 'Come on, come on, let's drink and make up …'. We were stowaways. We left tapes with bad instructions. We wouldn't read novels at all because we found ourselves so taken over by the characters. We dreamt of hammer blows. When we looked back at the Super 8 and video of ourselves we could not recognise anything. We were cop-killers; we were comedy sub-plots; we got jobs teaching sarcasm to censors. We're guilty of astrophysics and heavy gases; we confess to truth serum, old tricks and stratagems. In the ID line we smiled; in Tesco's when we saw each other again we just pretended that nothing had happened. We found a way of digitising death. We confess to canned laughter and circular saws. We were cheeky little monkeys that need teaching a lesson. We dreamed of Tokyo, snow monsters and John Ford on his deathbed. We stood at the altar but couldn't say the words. We gave Cabinet posts to all of our mates. We tied cans to the back of Marvin Gordanna's hearse — it's what he would've wanted. Each morning when we put the kids on the bus to school we took their photographs — it was less a piece of photography and more an act of magic — making talismans to try and ensure that they'd come back OK. We confess to never having an original idea; we feigned disapproval of things we'd done ourselves; we loved the rush of wind and ran when the lorries thundered by; we said 'Hold on, hold on it won't be long now …'; we sat back in a pose of indifference; we stank of sweat and the Yankee hash. When a few housing benefit cheques arrived made out to Greg Samson we used them to open a building society account in that name and then cashed the cheques. We were antheads, chickenheads and snaggle-toothed deviants. We were just a bunch of fucking arseholes. We had unnatural talents; we used supernatural means. We confess to night vigils that left us tired and lonely; we wept with the aid of glycerine and caught the red-eye home; we struck it lucky on the hit parade; we knew god-damned all there was to know about the rumba; we didn't want to blow our own trumpet but it blasted anyway; we said 'Oh, any old how darling, any old time...'. We held a shredding party in the basement at midnight. We sat with our backs to the wall and posed full-frontal. We lived in a city of fainting buildings; we lived in difficult times. Our smiles suggested something more of surgery than of pleasure. We sat by Rachel's bedside and read stuff to her, hoping to wake her from the coma —we read her Tolstoy and *Peter Pan;*, we told her stories; we told her all the wrongs we'd ever done. We thought cheap thoughts in risky places. We called our children Dawn, Leslie and Lisa-Marie, Chantale Duran and Young Whipper Snapper. We went on 'Swap Shop' the same day that Edward died. We were often seen in the background of other people's holiday snaps, blurred, out of focus, staring downstream. We had identical operation scars, it was too uncanny, just something meant to be. We designed the Bull Ring Centre. We had enigmatic smiles. We wanted to be Michael's love child because he had such deep-set eyes. We were dizzy with happiness. We saw ourselves as commodities. When we got to the island the natives told us they looked after a huge monkey god called King Kong—we thought it would be a good idea to capture it and take it back to New York to exhibit—the rest is history. We took what we could get, we took the fifth. We did long slow kisses that lasted three days. We confess to tidal waves, hurricanes and magnetic storms. We're guilty of everything. We were clumsy—we got lipstick on our boyfriends trousers. We loved language. We hated Jews. We dated Asians out of curiosity. We knew the place but we didn't know the time. We sent dirty faxes. We signed our names. We christened our children DEATH, SOLITUDE and FORGETTING. We ate like pigs and never left home. We confess to mud and bleach. We perpetrated a fraud. We ordered the prisoners to take a walk for a while and stretch their legs. We held a wet T-shirt competition for the women and a wet trousers competition for the men. We were scum. We passed out drunk on the floor of a garage. We watched a film with bad language, it got four stars. We wrote death threats to ourselves. We made a film called OUT OF SOUTH AFRICA. We made false promises. We never sat down. We tried to bring about the false death of President Kennedy—false in the sense of coexistent or alternate. We left the best bits on the cutting-room floor. We sulked and skulked and stamped. We confess to breaking three ribs in our sleep. We said we'd speak again soon and then never called back; we were accessories; we gave names, names and more names. We mistranslated; we drove too fast. We admit to announcing personal problems instead of the next train approaching platform four; we asked awkward questions on the Granada studios' tour. We never had our fill of bombing and shooting; we were cry-for-help shoplifters, bingo callers with cancer of the throat. Long after Stalin died we pretended he was alive — wheeling him out for public appearances, waving his hand from the balcony. We never wore seat belts. We got rumbled and frisked. We found panoramic views. We transmitted deadly advice. We switched labels just before the checkout but didn't realise that the barcode would betray us. We never spoke another language. We flipped channels quickly when the film got embarrassing. We wrote in to the magazine WIFE BEATER MONTHLY. We peeled the skin back and looked. We made no difference, we made no sense, we were the worst kind of people in the world. We're guilty of bright light and rum. We altered flight paths and planned alternative routes; we confess to static, break up and climactic change. We broke into phone boxes. We weren't comfortable in our skins. We were witches. We stole hotel soap. In the scene of community singing filmed in an air-raid shelter and designed to show the good-will and high spirits of Londoners during the Blitz, we were the ones in the background whose lips were hardly moving. We were bloody fools. We were sick as a parrot. We ran a numbers racket and we dug our own graves. We were loons that danced naked at harvest time. We never wanted children anyway. We confess to zinc and shopping malls, to bad dreams and collectivisation. We fucked the economy. We talked about democracy. we stole some electrical equipment which looked expensive and complicated but which we couldn't understand; we plugged it in at home and got some nasty burns — objects began to arrive from the future, we were puzzled and then later imprisoned. We made small talk. Some of the paperwork we submitted was a little bit irregular. We asked the hairdresser about his recently dead father. We stole fish. We worshipped cruel Aztec Gods. We were careless with the truth. We patented an obviously crackpot device for listening to the songs of angels. We built extensions on our houses without the necessary planning permission. We treated people like scenery, we treated the whole place like a hotel. World War 3 was just a thinly painted backdrop for our love. We kept lifting up the curtain and peeking behind. We hit rock bottom, we found our own level; we tried to guess the presents by feeling through the wrapping paper. We filmed events in which we could not intervene, events that spilled out of control, events that didn't even exist. We hated robbing banks — it got boring after a while. We handcuffed Lee Morris to the railings in the playground and pulled his trousers down. We lived a harsh fast life; we were glad to be alive; we didn't have an opinion on anything except how crazy the world was. We're guilty of attic rooms, power cuts and bombs; we confess to statues, ruins and gameboys. All we wanted to do was to tempt into life things that were hidden and strange. We went into town and stopped dead in our tracks. We had a bag full of controlled substances hidden in the toilets. Our hobbies were card-playing and time-wasting. We drank too much champagne. We were a slick act; we were stadium rockers — every mumble, every gesture every bit of impromptu patter was the same at every gig — all over the world. We had HUNGER for breakfast and STARVATION for lunch.

We were suicide bombers. We made a film called STREETS OF YESTERDAY. We're guilty of heart attacks, car crashes and falling off bridges. We agreed with Albert Einstein the scientific genius. We were sheep, eye-witnesses, minor clerics, prostitutes and baseball fans. We dreamed of heat and of solitude. We wished for peace, or a cease-fire at least. We cut the head off a live rooster and drank the blood—we thought it would help. We fucked our brother. We were smugglers, heathens or pirates. We lied about our age and then hoped for better things. We showed a gun in the first act, in a draw, hidden under some papers; the central character kept staring at it and mumbling, crying almost, but we weren't prepared to let her use it; the dramatic tension was all wrong and so by act four the audience were still wondering what the gun thing was all about. We burned effigies of trade negotiators. We were fraudulent mediums, working the crowd. We were not beautiful or especially bright but we had the strange gift of being remembered. We were hate-filled children with ice in our veins. In interrogation our voices got quieter and quieter, and the detectives, not wishing to break the mood, got quieter and quieter too, until, by the end of it, stage by stage, we each were only moving our lips and no sound came out, the tape-recorder running for posterity. We altered the limits of human action; we loved a piece of time too small to give a name. We came to the place where the tape says POLICE LINE DO NOT CROSS and then we crossed it. We were funny without meaning to be. We listened to 'Stairway to Heaven' 13 times in row. We played in the show houses on the edge of the estate. Long periods of boredom were our fault. We spent long hours at the bus stop; we were long-lost cousins in love. We liked the way Sarah smiled; we liked the smell of napalm in the morning. We missed episode two; we lied through false teeth; we watched repeats of everything; we did thankless tasks. We were continuity flaws. We jumped ship before the world had taken one full turn. We took three sugars in our coffee. We confess to parricide, conspiracy and Pearl Harbor; we all wore clothes our mothers made. We were blacklisted in car manuals. We evacuated whole communities over-night; we buried our pasts in shallow graves. In the baths we spontaneously combusted and in the park we talked while the kids played on the climbing frame. After a long time of fake deliberation over the menu at the motorway services we went for the special offer RECESSION-BUSTER BREAKFAST (two kids eat free with two adults). We confess to personal interest, hobbies and irrelevant experience; we are guilty of landing awkwardly. We are responsible for the coasts and the moors and cumulus clouds and great vistas and vast landscapes and poignant winters. We read the map the wrong way up. We confess to sarcastic suicide notes, to Aeroflot and diagrams; we sniffed lighter fluid and spat through our teeth. We took the gunshot; we took the ricochet, that's all there is to say. We were extras, walk-ons, stand-ins and losers. We were just there to make up the numbers in some of the crowds scenes. We knew we were gay from the age of 5. We had 'plastic surgery' to look oriental or black so we could supposedly report on what it was like to be different—we reported our findings on Good Morning Television to the pleasure and interest of Richard and Judy. We confess to knowing Sam and refusing to wave to him. We bled in open spaces; we climbed without a rope; we revealed secrets to the Russians and cheated for small change; we were cautioned for loitering under Section 35. We were test patients, sat in a hospital room and waiting for the side-effects. We got mixed up, we got into the occult. We dreamed the whole of the Second World War before it happened. We had the faith of no faith. We thought that less was less. We failed the breath test. We gambled everything on the chance to win diamonds, camcorders and holidays. We were bogus asylum seekers, bogus refugees; we travelled through the German night; we met the German girl. Our marriage was just part of a plan to blow up the train. We had sex in the visionary position—he sat on one side of the room and I sat on the other, masturbating and staring at each other in a mixture of fear, desire and disbelief, certain in the knowledge that even if we came together we would not come together at all. We stayed up after midnight. We were described by photofits. We sighed when the evening had to end. We were invisible. We sadly lacked in the subject of botany; we switched the bags while no one was looking. We noticed, not for the first time, the look between Carol and Jessica's boyfriend Martin Gardener. We christened diseases with beautiful names; we cut off the villages and sealed off the streets. We drew the curtains when the window cleaners came. We mispronounced URANUS and SCHEAT. We thought we were funny, funnier than anyone had ever been. We took afternoon naps when we should have been working. We fell in love with every co-star. We cheated at cards. It took us three hours to cut off the head with a open knife. We dreamed about dinosaurs and planes crash landing in back gardens. We never said how much we needed each other. We washed up badly. We never thought. We never danced at weddings. We got tattoos done on our foreheads saying PAX AMERICANA. We confess to aborting our children for research, killing our parents for the house and putting granddad in a home. We were not at our best in the mornings. We did not feed the neighbour's cat. We lost the thread. We laid down our lives for someone else's country. We smiled invitingly at Antoine, thereby raising expectations that we had no intention of fulfilling. We frequented gaming hells, low hostelries and the late-night supermarket on Jasmine Street. We passed folded notes and whispered at the back; we sang off key and stared at the person to our right. We weren't ready for our opening night. We were sex tourists; we liked Steven but he smelt funny; we told stolen jokes on *Pebble Mill*. We sold defective oven gloves door to door. We lived in clutter. We were top of the pops. We stayed out past bedtime, past curfew, past caring. We knew what we were doing. We looked on at the ecstatic twilight of technological society. We saw nine great motorway pile-ups. We were always interested in missing things — time, people and history. Our lounge was like Bosnia — divided into two — the two of us looking shell shocked across space. We cut the crime rate by introducing a new system of counting. We said 'Don't call here again it's dangerous'. We spoke OCTOBER LANGUAGE. We dreamt of hammer blows; we trained as cosmonauts in Star City. We were spastic bashers. We were captives of our metaphors. We wanked off for money. We tried to export things without all the proper documents; it wasn't deliberate fraud but you could see why the customs men at Ramsgate were suspicious — they kept looking over the paperwork and tutting and then making phone calls to man in one of the other portacabins. It was 3am when they let us go, and only then because it was the end of their shift. We told mortician jokes at weddings. We betrayed our friends through silence. We were lonely for 12 years. We loved the way the rain ran off the windscreen. We fenced stolen farming equipment. When the mermaids tried to warn us we threw stones at them. We snored loudly while other people were trying to eat. We read novels with unhappy endings and then later wouldn't read novels at all because we found ourselves so taken over by the characters. We wept for slimmers. We learnt how to fly. We were intellectual pygmies. We flung mud, we dug up mass graves. We played truant. We taught Russian roulette at A level. We dubbed silent movies, we coughed in dramatic pauses. We chanted meaningless or silly slogans to put the other marchers off and when the stewards tried to stop us we ducked under the crash barriers and ran off into the park. We played musical chairs. We believed in the spirits of dead astronauts. We were scared of volcanoes. We sent each other used underwear through the post. We countenanced forever as an expression of mortality. We honoured without exception all church architecture. We said 'Love is like floating in duckweed'. We were dead meat. We stand accused of Saturday nights and early Monday mornings. We were jealous in a sensational manner. We used supermodels in war documentaries — they were excellent. We were poisoners. We put the last buffalo to sleep. We went to Stonehenge and didn't like it. We ate Kimberly Saunders' arm. We watched a man die in 6 inches of water. We're guilty of making weak tea; we drove madness into the hearts of good folks; we broke all the rules of ice hockey in one day; we forged doctors notes; we could never return. We broke down doors, smashed windows and blamed Philip Lawson. We took a lot of liberties. We took advice from demons. We pretended to know people. We took too long getting ready. We inflicted vicious attacks and horrible injuries; we stole from a warehouse on Last Minute Street; we practised bizarre interview techniques; we idolised Raymond and Lesley. We liked uniforms and signs of obedience. We held him down — it was fascinating. We had piss stains on our trousers. We had no hope. We linked our arms and skipped in a desperate imitation of *The Wizard of Oz*. Our philosophy was do them before they do you. We fingered our arses. We thought we were relatives of Robert Duvall — but we weren't.

We confess to rubbing up against tables. We redrew maps to slowly excise certain areas — this was a slow technical distortion (nothing as crude as omission) by which unwanted areas were minutely compressed over long periods of time. When the government changed, and with it our political fortunes, we had to slowly distort it all back. We sniffed lighter fluid and spat through our teeth. We took the gunshot, we took the ricochet. We came from a country where smiling was considered dangerous. We were tricksters, pranksters, practical jokers — we put meat in someone's tea; we left the bedroom looking like a raid; we wore funny noses, bow ties that went round and round — for the grandchildren we pretended to be powered by electricity — drawing energy from the light bulb in the centre of the ceiling and moving in a strange jerky way. We blocked the fucking fast lane. We rang the wrong number twice, no, three times. We brought the same magazine for years. We had tattoos done one our arses saying LONG LIVE THE HEROISM OF SENSELESS PURSUITS. We had tattoos done on our heads saying LET NO MAN ENTER HERE. We had tattoos done on our stomachs saying WHY EMPTY? We ran out on Vic — it was a gamble. We missed a train. We were death mechanics. We were sleep throwers — when we woke up in the mornings there was nothing near us. We were loud drunks and fornicators. After dark was a time of hate and burning for us. We fell asleep at the wheel and woke up some miles down the road. We were pirates. We were lawless. We sailed beneath the black flag. We had our hands in the till. Stumbling lost and disorientated, we realised the world was full of dames. We confess to bellowing sweet nothings. We believed in UFOs. We believed that Jung was probably right about women. We believed that truth was always the best policy. We dealt in imaginary videos. We got drunk on half a pint. We entered the wrong room and backed out hastily. We had sexual intercourse that night, not once, but 17 times. We sent our daughters off into prostitution and one of them came back dying of AIDS; we could not understand why she was dying, or even that she was dying at all — with her sweats, her blisters and her strange agonised deliriums we thought she was becoming a shaman, a magic priestess, but it didn't work out that way. When the lights went out we swapped places. We were YTS vandals on job creation schemes. We pretended to fall over outside a hospital. We lied about our age. We looked promising in mirrors. We lied twice, denied three times. We killed 10 men, burned 16 houses. We wrote two love songs twice on the trot, we made six threatening phone calls and six gentle apologies. We saw six crows sat on a fence; we wept 16 gallons of tears; we drank 14 vodkas, we issued several writs. We saw each other 57 times; we threw nine coins in the fountain; we threw 17 coins at the goalkeeper; we made three wishes; we had seven dreams; we had 10 seconds of silence, 10 years of peace, 10 scars on our arms where the rotor blades had hit. We tore five pages from the back of the book, we crashed 200 cars, fathered 39 children, walked backwards for nine days. We wrote six novels.

Section III

Journalism and Programme Notes

Journalism

What follows here is a mini-anthologies — one selected from various journalism, reviews and short pieces on other people's work that I've done in the last 13 years or so. The pieces I've chosen are responses both to high-profile international work, to touring and meetings with artists and to small-scale events I've seen in Sheffield, in Manchester and elsewhere. The through-line is challenge and inspiration — I've chosen pieces which I hope will link back to debates elsewhere in this book and raise bigger concerns than those local to the pieces I'm discussing.

I Wanna be Adored —
ICA Live Arts on Tour in the USA

I Wanna be Adored was written for the *Guardian* newspaper following a three-week tour of America undertaken by a whole crew of performance artists, dancers and theatre-makers, organised by Lois Keidan and Katherine Ugwu, then the directors of Live Arts programme in the ICA. The tour took in PS122 (New York), The Walker Arts Center (Minneapolis) and Highways Performance Space (Los Angeles) — all of them more or less legendary venues in the development of contemporary performance in the USA. The piece is a fragmented document in text form, bearing witness to some of the people we met, the places we saw and the artists on the tour. Most centrally it describes an outsider's reaction to the American political and cultural situation in the wake of the Culture Wars.

Over three weeks in February and March 1996 the ICA's *I Wanna be Adored* tour took 12 British performers on a three-city, 2,500-mile tour of the USA, from permafrost to desert, via gun-shops, Hollywood and the biggest mall in the world to the best-known of America's alternative venues — Highways in Los Angeles, PS122 in New York and Walker Art Center in Minneapolis. This tour — a kind of best of British new performance work — whisked US audiences far from the easy exports of heritage, glamour and Shakespearean West End. From the crowd-baiting stand-up of Ronald Fraser-Munro, through the intimate exploration of identity in Susan Lewis's choreography and the wild Asian-camp lip-synch of Sarbjit Samra to the speculation on contemporary England produced by my own company Forced Entertainment, the package showed a Britain in contradictory fragments — a Britain (like America) in which ethnicity, sexuality, national identity, social and artistic agency are all very much at stake.

4 March. In New York I wake early each morning, surveying from the bed the cramped territory of my phone-less, sink-less, TV-less box room, reassured somehow by the sounds of the city outside and watching the curtain shift in the breeze. At 6am the city is already a chaos of dogs barking at aeroplanes, stray footsteps, cop sirens and arc welding on rooftops, but I only wake properly for a loud persistent banging in the cast iron pipes besides my pillow.

Clunk, the banging says, *clunk-clunk*, *clunk*, and I move quick though clumsy, knowing that this could be some vital moment in our rolling dialogue with America. *Clunk* the banging continues, appearing to come from a distant quarter in the labyrinthine Hotel 17, *clunk-clunk* — but before I can search bleary-eyed for a spoon with which to strike the pipes and reply, the strange communiqué has ended, replaced by a symphony of car horns ascending from the streets.

Foiled again. I'm left stood drowsy beside the bed, reflecting on what I've seen in America, reflecting on what I've heard.

26 February. A guy on a New York street corner, drinking booze from a brown-bagged bottle and making fervoured orations to the passers-by.

Ladies and Gentleman who would like to see me eliminate my lower intestine? Ladies and Gentleman who would like to see me eliminate my higher intestine? Ladies and gentlemen I will now eliminate the spleen...

Bawling on the sidewalk, intent on self-destruction, a large swig from the bottle after every sentence.

17 February. I sit in an office at Highways in Santa Monica, LA, with Jordan Peimer, outgoing programmer at the venue — a cluster of buildings off Olympic Boulevard sharing the homely feel of under-funded arts spaces across the Western world. I'm talking, asking questions and trying to get clear in my mind the complex genealogy of what American commentators call the Culture Wars — the combined skirmishes and flare-ups that make up six years of strife between American artists and the organised Right. Names float by me — performance artists like Karen Finley, Tim Miller, Ron Athey and Holly Hughes — many of them intimately connected with this venue — fine artists and photographers like Mapplethorpe and Serrano — all of whom have broken taboos, asking questions about art, audience and community. Jordan's soft speaking is a flood of Congressional denouncements, direct mail campaigns by the religious Right, venues and artists getting cut, defunded, castigated, and all of it in a country where even a Mighty Mouse cartoon can spark a Christian backlash and boycott campaign. I close my eyes and concentrate...

24 February. A 6-foot black man dressed in cardinal gear and carrying a whip is offering to 'thrash some religion' into the crowd. This is Minneapolis, and there aren't any takers. Cardinal Caesurae Cappuccino (one of three alter-egos for Ronald Fraser-Munro) raises his arms to declare his commitment to Saint Reebok, railing against Satan, born again on earth in the form of Pat Buccanni. It's the day before Dakota's primaries: 'Do not trust or believe in this man, my children...', he warns, 'no matter what tax cuts or incentives he may offer...' Who knows if America is listening.

15 February. If Sheffield or even London are cities, then from what we've seen LA belongs clearly to some separate species of human settlement — a sci-fi metropolis based on car parks and poodle manicure. Indeed, at times the odds against anyone from this strange place understanding any of the British work seem immeasurably bad. At the first performance as Michael Atavar talks about gay men loitering in cottages the crowd gives way to sparse uncertain laughter, seeing thatched rooves not toilet cubicles. When we speak about cites, or when Susan dances mixed-race identity, or when Sarbjit skits sentimental Country, we soon know or guess that these things mean differently here.

But, despite all this, the work really does succeed in contacting audiences; it's not the details of landscape that people yearn for after all, but a sense of the struggle and the people in it, and there's plenty of that to go round. If all else fails, we joke in the dressing room at interval time, there's always the international language of audience humiliation, for which Ronnie has a cruel and proven appetite.

17 February. Jordan Peimer is still talking: 'I'm deeply fearful about how venues like Highways can survive...', he says:

there really is a war getting waged here by a very conservative and intolerant group of people undermining the founding principles of the country — religious tolerance and freedom of expression. The thing that shocks me time and again is that these are the things I was brought up to believe as a child in American history classes and they're not true and they're becoming less true day by day. What we are seeing is this debate about who gets the right to speak, to exhibit and even to be seen.

3 March. The stage is a secular shrine bedecked with almost exhausted symbols of Irishness. Statues of the Virgin, bottles of Guinness, potatoes and recordings of Eamonn De Valera. In her sequinned dancing costume Christine Molloy of Desperate Optimists crosses the stage at speed, careful not to step on the square of 'genuine Irish turf' which she carried with love as illegal hand luggage in a plastic bag from LA. Behind her Jo Lawlor pulls down his black IRA balaclava and swigs a Guinness genially, emitting the occasional 'Whoop!' in support of the dancing. Talking about living in England, in exile, they ask the question repeatedly, 'What is the difference, for us, between staying and going?'

Days later they journey to Ellis Island where Jo and Christine pose for photographer Hugo Glendinning in the Immigration Hall. Jo's mother was born to Irish émigrés in New York and then shipped back home alone at age 11 months to be brought up by relatives. I imagine Jo's mother and her sea voyage home. The kind of journey you would never remember but also never forget. The kind of movement that might live inside you.

Holding her genuine 'Irish'/LA turf in her hands Christine explains to the New York crowd: 'I am trying to decide if the land is heavy, or if it is light...'

18 February. Performance Artist Ron Athey is laughing and laughing, his tattooed arms and pierced face looking slightly incongruous in the Hollywood Athletic Club where we're eating. When he speaks his humour always cuts against the content of his words, words that describe his own early brutal 'SM exhibitions' in gay nightclubs and his current status as an artist whose appearance in a venue (piercing, penetrating, scarring — pushing at the limits of the body) is more than likely to cause funding cuts and crises. In Los Angeles Athey's problems also extend to other sections of the gay and lesbian community:

> There's a kind of gay fascism around the look here — I remember we made a float for Gay Pride — this whole tattooed crowd of us and all these muscle queens were booing us. They're wearing these electric green polyester g-strings and they have these huge fake-tan bodies ... and they thought *we* were vulgar!

13 February. Walking on Santa Monica beach I am remembering a performance we made in 1986 called *Nighthawks* — a Sheffield company's re-version of an America it had never seen anywhere outside of books, paintings, movies and music. In this Chinese-whisper portrait we mixed up Edward Hopper with William Burroughs, Marshall McLuhan with Tom Waits, Elvis with Badlands. Even so the piece we made was never as strangely at odds with itself as the America we see 10 years later, in real life, in 1996.

18 February again. Seen as a potential weapon for the Right and speaking to the harsher side of contemporary gay sexuality Athey is unrepentant about his work:

> It's hard for gay performers who work in darker images or who take unapologetic views on AIDS. I mean work that isn't fighting for gay rights but acknowledging uglier things like being HIV positive and practising unsafe sex, or about the self-destructive

aspects of S&M ... things you're made to shut up about. It seems that if you go into your mind and pull out dream images it's easy to step on toes because you're not carrying an agenda for anyone ...

1 March. I am listing the bizarre phone numbers advertised everywhere—for information lines, sex lines, chat lines, businesses. There is 1-800-555-EASY, 1-800-666-WILD, 1-800-MATTRESS, 1-800-44-GIRLS. Best of all perhaps, in New York's Union Square subway station I catch a brief glimpse of an advert for something, although I never find out what, the number, in large red letters reading: 1-800-3-END PAIN. At a phone on the street I try calling it, but the line is busy for hours.

22 February. Minneapolis. Michael Atavar asks the gay men in the audience to jangle their key chains so he'll feel at home. There is laughter and a ripple of sound through the large auditorium. Of all the spaces we play this is the most established, the best funded, the most secure. Leading the venue in its reputation for radical performance and stalwarts of many Culture Wars run-ins, John Killacky and Bobby Tsumagari are quietly confident of their position and optimistic about the future.

> We've lost many thousands of dollars around these censorship controversies but we are a strong institution with a long history of supporting work that is at first bewildering or provocative ... from anti-fascist ballet in 1938 through Cunningham, Cage and Rauschenburg in 1963 to Karen Finley or Ron Vawter in 1993 ... this institution has that tradition of bringing in the people who pull the rugs out from underneath the community and the community supporting it and celebrating it.

A large block booking of gay men have come to see Michael Atavar and he is thriving on it, ad-libbing, playing gestures to the back. His golden Elvis suit, complete with bondage straps, is shimmering madly in the light ...

> It's only the blood that bind us together you know, it's only the blood, the piss and the come that binds us together, taking us together somewhere on a journey. I wouldn't lie to you. Believe me. How could I lie to you about something like that?

2 March. It's our last performance in New York and images of Sheffield cross-fade on screens behind us—tower blocks, churches, petrol stations. Richard is quizzing Terry about whether the work is optimistic or not, and she is trying to answer and each time she does Richard pauses and asks once again: 'Is the work optimistic? Is it getting more optimistic? Why do you think it has changed?' There is a kind of silence in the venue at this point in the show here as at previous performances, where you can feel people locking on to what's happening—to the heart of the work itself—to this question of whether art (or indeed anything) can change lives or change perceptions.

4 March. Back in the hotel. Outside my room there's a minor fracas over use of the shower. Perhaps the bloke in anorak and Red Indian head-dress is fighting with the old guy who breathes only from an oxygen cylinder, but from the voices it is impossible to tell.

Anyway I'm thinking back to my chat with John Killacky at the Walker when I asked about the question of optimism and art. And this is what he said:

> I grew up in the '60s and I continue to believe that art is essential and that it absolutely can change the world and as bleak as anything gets I want to be there to support artists—it's the

only light I can see in the world. Any cycle that's gonna go on—funding or not—you're not going to stop making your work, and to be moved like I was tonight, seeing your work here in Minneapolis, that was thrilling...I want to be part of that, no matter what...

Footsteps in the corridor, doors closing, silence.

Stella: Anne Teresa De Keersmaeker
Music by György Ligeti; deSingel, Antwerp, 12 April 1990

Stella, the seventh full-length piece choreographed by Anne Teresa De Keersmaeker, is both dazzling and self-confident. Earlier pieces, like *Rosas Danst Rosas* (1983), had a sharp uniformity and minimalism in which costume, setting, dance language and overall architecture were tightly pared down and controlled. Set against this came small details; tiny idiosyncrasies in the dancers' steps, brief individual moments of resting, of tying shoes, of smiling or of watching. No matter how much one admired these details and their provocative place within the work, the weight always lay, in the end, with the universality of the group.

Stella takes hold of this earlier work and, with a passing nod to contemporary theatricals The Wooster Group and Need Company, calmly breaks it all apart. Somewhere at its centre perhaps is the same chorus of women from *Rosas* or *Mikrokosmos*; women in temporary freedom from direct male power, women in simple black dresses, women who run together, tumble and fall. But there are big changes too. For a start there are few sections where the five women are pulled together in dance. Mostly they don't dance at all. Instead, they have verbal texts with accompanying movements, drawn from

theatrical or literary sources and which they continually attempt to perform. There are shared elements of content or theme in these texts, but there's no attempt to homogenise purpose or style; they are from different eras, in different languages, performed in different ways. The women rarely collaborate and, although they sometimes watch each other with interest, most of the interaction comes through their attempts to interrupt or upstage.

In this chaotic context the dancing serves as a binding agent, but it too has changed. The structures used are looser and cooler, and the drop-outs more frequent. The composure and speed we've seen before are challenged by humour and ungainliness, as though the women enjoy themselves, wryly refusing to conform. At other times the old composure is challenged by desperation, and the women roll and thrash as though scared that this dancing itself might not work anymore.

Like much of the best in new performance, *Stella* foregrounds the process of theatrical presentation. The space is a clutter of props and chairs, the hanging back and side walls only the backs of cheap theatre flats. In this space the women exist on two levels; as the black-dressed performers who dance, watch, change costumes and wait and also as the products of the found texts they're trying to perform.

These texts are drawn from Williams's *A Streetcar Named Desire*, Goethe's *Stella* and Kurosawa's *Rashomon*. The women are all defined by their uneasy relationships—with men and with themselves. One's an alcoholic; two are victims of rape; one's an innocent on her way to being hurt. The male world is present only in its looming absence; as they run, yell and laugh their way through the piece the women constantly undercut all their roles, gaining and shedding costumes to underline the change, dropping from high drama to a smile at the audience, replaying moments as though rehearsing, or looking away in discomfort when someone else goes too far.

The purer choreography and the self-generated content of the earlier pieces hasn't been replaced with theatre, found material and wholesale undercutting as part of some apologetic failure of nerve but because of a very clear contemporary understanding of the way we manage our identities In problematising performance, and in challenging the purity of her work De Keersmaeker asks questions about our abilities to construct ourselves for the world.

Such questions, dramatised or handed to us on a plate, would be pointless. Instead we are thrown into the thick of things; the demands and responsibilities of the audience are repeatedly challenged and brought to the fore. On the simplest level it is the women watching each other, with concern or with complete indifference that is very often represented on the stage, De Keersmaeker asks: 'What is it to watch?' 'What is it to witness?' 'What do we want?'

Later, in a section that uses Ligeti's *Music for 100 Metronomes*, the debate about our role takes on a mounting confrontational aspect. Here the metronomes are set moving in a delicate cacophony across the front of the stage and its soon clear that the performers will simply wait for them to run down. How long this section lasts in measured time I couldn't say, but by turns it's boring, tetchy, comic and sublime

We're present at an event which although public, often makes demands by being reserved, by taking it's time, by keeping its distance. At first we're bombarded with texts that we're unlikely to understand, or that remain cryptically incomplete. The text drawn from Blanche Dubois works especially well in this respect because what started life as dialogue is here only monologue, a series of nervous rhetoricals, rushed out to the audience with no real hope of reply.

Blanche's text becomes the nexus of a thousand aspirations and doubts: the private, the public and the artistic all bound together on the stage.

I don't know if I can turn the trick anymore

Is it dangerous to be tender?

Are you listening to me?

I don't know if I can turn the trick anymore

In their fluorescent-lit arena the dancers struggle with the fragments of their texts, their precedents and myths, just as we in the audience must struggle with ours.

In *Stella*, De Keersmaeker uses a form that perfectly suits the complexities of our contemporary situation. There are some structural weaknesses, especially the relative ill-definition of two of the dancers, but it does remain a considerable achievement. It may be bleaker and less transcendent than previous pieces, and it may also be a harder piece for traditional dance audiences, but in moving away from a collective optimism it has found a voice that is vital, effective and honest.

Three Works: Steven Taylor Woodrow

In his three separate works Steven Taylor Woodrow brings paintings to life (*The Living Paintings*), creates a hospital ward where the patients have sunk forever into their beds (*Going Bye Byes*), and finally animates a listless man and woman inside a building, classical temple from the outside and monochrome supermarket within (*Good Buy Cruel World*).

This latest work is something of a departure for Woodrow since in it the two performers are not fixed into walls or furniture but have free rein within an enclosed space. Although the shuffling, shelf-stacking man and the disdainful till-girl share the levelling monochromatic colouring and clothes of the earlier works, these two are perhaps closer to being full-blown characters through their situation and the dynamics of their unequal relationship.

It's powerful, resonant stuff, but these days at least our immersion in magic can never be total or unproblematic—key to understanding Woodrow's work is that the strong fictional invocation of place and character coexists with a clear sense of our presence in real time. Thus, the illusionist mechanics of the work, the durational discomfort of the performers, the sense of humans operating within simple rule systems, and so on, are all acknowledged (not disguised) aspects of our experience.

Woodrow's humanoids operate within clear constraints (spatial limitation, no speech, etc.) but their objectives are often fascinatingly fluid, allowing us room to project concerns and reasons onto them. More concretely, through physical or textual interventions, we can influence his figures; changing their lives, entering their spaces, double-guessing their games. At worst (say swamped by nearly 100 French school children all prodding, running and shrieking at the tops of their voices ...) this work can appear like a stall at some hideous avant-garde Euro-Disneyland of the future. But a look beyond the sound-bite boldness and the ad-man's titles reveals a vision and a set of concerns both distressing and important.

To speak with the paintings, to sit silently at the bedside in *Going Bye Byes* or to make purchases in the dead green light of *Good Buy Cruel World* is to try to engage with another world, to cross a line, to reach out and behave in what Richard Schechner might call a non-work, non-useful context. Each move anyone makes in respect of Woodrow's figures is a testing of the magical waters, observed closely by all present. Many people begin with a joke: offering a sweet, performing a shrug or a smile. Typically, interactions develop until the figures reject an advance, or subvert the interaction in some blocking, cryptic way. A woman offers her shoe to one of the paintings and then, after much business, the painting puts it calmly in its pocket, looking away. The woman stands, shoeless, perplexed, washed up on the shores of real time. In *Going Bye Byes* it's often simply the closing of the eyes by the bedridden ghosts that dismisses a person or a crowd—a closing of the eyes that speaks both of the performer's tiredness with this particular game and of the patients' terrible, inexpressible private pain.

These collapsing interactions stress an almost existential insularity in our relationships with the other (people, enchantment, art) but at the same time they do give us a brief taste of life in another country, a chance to step away from earth and look back.

They also give us a series of insights into power and how it operates in a spatial dimension. Paradoxically, the fixed, constrained beings of *The Living Paintings* and *Going Bye Byes* are more intimidating than the free agents of *Good Buy Cruel World*. There's something about the paintings' strong position high on the wall, combined with a culturally engrained mistrust of anything inanimate that's acquired life (usually by dubious means) that leaves us suspicious and (rightly) unsure of their intentions.

The beds, on the other hand, are people on the way to objecthood, receding like the TV dot at closedown, unable to enter any tactile or active relationship with anything. They are utterly powerless, of course, and the brutality of some spectators defies expectation. Perhaps that's why the beds are frightening too — because they force us to confront our own power, our own health and mobility, because the sight of another human as a passive object awakes a part of us we'd rather not address.

By freeing up the performers spatially in *Good Buy Cruel World* and making them individuals rather than part of a more or less identical set, Woodrow is taking us into new and not wholly successful territory. New, essentially theatrical issues arise out of the mobility and the more complex fiction that he hasn't quite worked through to conclusion. It's still very challenging work.

He's also keen here to use a new medium for interaction with the public. Bored perhaps with the array of polos, teaspoons and shoes foisted on the paintings and beds over the years, we are now invited to hand over something much more important: money. Prices for the slightly tatty monochrome merchandise (all stamped and dated by Woodrow) were both viciously arbitrary and unexplained, raising confusion (and occasional outrage) at an almost biological level. One might pay 100 francs for a sprayed green tin of food only to see another pay six centimes for an identical item. Any attempt at haggling was greeted with disdain and the confiscation of goods one intended to buy. On some occasions it appeared impossible to buy anything at all, since on producing money one was dismissed out of hand with a roll of the eyes.

Stepping into the magical world is always a charged, uncertain moment — it's good to know at least that money can't ensure safe passage.

My Body Did Everything I Asked It: Tony Mustoe and Alan Maclean
Sheffield, 1990

My Body Did Everything I Asked It is a performance by Alan Maclean and Tony Mustoe. Maclean is a Sheffield-based artist who, in works like *The Ratman* and *Ratman in the Rain*, has created a form and a persona in which to explore the interplay between individual masculine identity and language, mixing down-market stand-up rhetoric, stream of consciousness ravings, TV fragments and hook lines from once-popular songs.

These elements are all present in his latest piece, which employs a form that's part chaotic wrestling match and part chucking-out time sing-along. Set in a wrestling ring almost alive with coloured balloons, it takes on not the solitary, idiosyncratic interiors of *The Ratman* but the clumsy and prescribed attempts at social interaction by two men, isolated from each other, and themselves, by virtue of class, biology and culture.

In its reference to trash or popular performance forms (slapstick, sentimental songs, snapshots and wrestling) *My Body* is constantly opening the divide between a cultural slickness (or ease) and the needs and unkempt passions of its heart. In appearance *My Body* is a big mess, its technology temperamental or inefficient, its structure in danger of collapse. In contrast to Maclean's previous work, its control of our attention and of its own performance elements is slack and sporadic. What we see is not the careful, sculpted appearance of chaos but something approaching chaos itself.

Maclean and Mustoe switch from

brash yells to each other and to the audience, then converse in a series of desperate asides, break off their conversation to remedy some fault in the microphone or to stop the record player from running out of control. In this vibrant shambles images only half-appear, visible through a thick soup of deliberate deconstruction, accident and confusions. It's a significant contemporary paradox though, that here, as in many other performances, our pleasure is very much bound up with the failure of the piece, with its struggle to achieve.

The fascination with failure bespeaks a healthy distrust of glib or over-confident effect. Performance language has become self-conscious, self-doubting, hesitant. Nothing can be effortless now, and even if one does see something simple or perfect or whole (the hyper-real sets for Steve Shill's solo theatre pieces), or a moment that attempts a perfect narrative closure (I'm thinking of a tiny image towards the end of The Wooster Group's *St. Anthony*) then these things automatically, and quite deliberately, problematise themselves. Put perfection in a performance arena in our current climate and it hangs there, suspended in quote marks, an impossible thing.

In *My Body* no moment is whole, every second must be worked for and fought with, and in recognition of this it insists that if we are to have the pleasure of those moments we must also have the heartache, and the boredom, of the work. It's both impossible and charming to watch, a piece that judders and jolts along, allowing infinite space for us to renew and revise our readings of its world. The essential dynamic in this process is a twist: the twist that takes place as indifference or irritation in the audience suddenly gives way to emotion or laughter. As often as not, the triggers for these twists appear uncontrolled, flowing from the rhythm of the work; unrepeatable, unformed, half-conscious, comic, pathetic and entropic. Perhaps something will come of nothing.

The politics of all this struggle find echoes both in and all around the piece. Mustoe, Maclean's collaborator has slight cerebral palsy and often it's his inherently ambivalent relationship to the icons and structures of terrace culture that are brought to the fore. At its most compelling the fight here is with language, with a system of languages that lies always outside the two men, forever just out of reach. Mustoe's speech is often slurred and inaudible, just beyond hearing and it's set off well by Maclean's scrambled, rhetorical yells:

> Yer think you've got me do yer? Yer think yer've got me for half an hour. My it's hot in here. My bedroom's like a bonfire…

Time and again a moment shoots from the chaos, a moment where them words that can't ever be our own are made to speak clearly of our lives and our loves.

Of course there are some fine contradictions in the piece: a collaboration between a working-class man with cerebral palsy and a liberal middle-class artist automatically engenders a discussion about exploitation and about voyeurism. It doesn't take a Foucault to realise that by listing Mustoe's disability in the programme/invitation and at the same time omitting to mention Maclean's own dyslexia which has continually informed and enriched his work, a hierarchy of naming and consequently of power has been set up.

At times in *My Body* the power relationship between the two men seems fraught, uneven, patronising. The use of slides of Mustoe's family and a rambling autobiographical text by him, without a balancing or counterpointing personal narrative or images from Maclean allows an unevenness of emotional investment from the two to creep in. It's a minefield of a piece, but what carries one through, I think, is the fact that the two are willing here to struggle in public with the issues, to work through the power games and the boundaries of class and languages, often in a knowing and mock-antagonistic way, if not in a belief that there's a resolution (*My Body* won't offer us that...) then at least in a determination to get on with the job. Here are two men, *joined together in a fight*.

The Hour in which We Knew Nothing of Each Other: Peter Handke

Peter Handke's *Die Stunde Da Wir Nichts Voneinander Wussten (The Hour in which We Knew Nothing of Each Other)* is an ambitious 35-performer work which mobilises the massed ranks of the urban everyday in pursuit of a large-scale theatrical poetic. In a design of hallucinatory clarity (Gilles Aillaud) the stage indicates an outdoor space somewhere between a street and a public square. Low white-walled buildings on the left give way to roadworks, a statue and a car, the latter casually draped with tarpaulin. A string of telegraph poles in false perspective run a huge diagonal through the space and against the clear blue sky that marks the back wall of one of Berlin's largest stages.

In the two hours of Handke's work this space is crossed and recrossed by some 300 characters, none of whom speak, from power-dressed yuppies to lone joggers, from down and outs to cops with guns, from Moses to John Wayne with Charlie Chaplin in between. Divided into movements by the billowing of a translucent curtain, the piece shifts between a kind of quotational naturalism of walks, gestures and tics towards a proto-dance that's made from gestures repeated and magnified. Each time the dance arrives, or a movement completes itself the curtain cuts through, blown by an unseen wind as it falls across the stage, wiping the picture clear and empty, scattering the characters into the wings like so many leaves.

In pursuing and remounting the everyday theatrical in a framed theatrical setting Handke and director Luc Bondy have hit difficult terrain. The choreography we may spectate from a café table or a bus window, after all, knows no single author, and is the product only of hundreds of individual and unknowable negotiations about pace, territory and presence. The work of this choreography (written about in Michel de Certeau's *The Practice Of Everyday Life* [1]) is practical, rooted in real time and permanently in flux. The choreography of the street is both individual and social, hidden and performed. It is before us but not for us, written through the space of the street itself, and by the contingencies of necessarily individual practice and spectatorhood.

The Hour in which We Knew Nothing of Each Other (in this production at least) has none of these qualities. The performances shun privacy and simplicity in favour of high-panto at every available opportunity, homogenising both characters and audience in the process. Meanwhile the local structures of the work; visual puns and stereotypes, mini-narratives, and so on, also mitigate against any integrity for the individual fragments, fictions or images presented. This is a real problem that threatens to undermine the whole workings of this piece. Where The Wooster Group or even Robert Wilson, whose performances are often staged at Schaubuune, use collage they do so with a keen sense of the haunted autonomy of the fragment — of the links *and* separations between discrete objects in a spatio-temporal frame. Not so this production.

Bresson, who is invoked by Handke in the programme, once said that 'the flatter an image is, the less it expresses, the more easily it is transformed in contact with other images...', [2] but there's little flatness, little blankness here. At worst the images are over-expressed, like a join-the-dots puzzle that's already been done, leaving no space between lives, fragments or fictions for a watcher to explore.

Throughout the piece, to be fair, there are glimpses of what this work this might have been—gorgeously blank non-meetings in the space, images as crisp, clear and resonant as they are undecidable. The latter sections especially, in which snow falls on a diagonal, covering a carpet that's been rolled across the stage and around which the entire cast are positioned; sunbathers next to wounded soldiers, next to Bavarian tourists, are precisely more private and thus engaging—before us, but not for us. Such moments are too few and too far between and still they present problems. Handke and Bondy's magical-naturalism invites tendentious and recursive comparisons between the world of *its* street unconscious and the streets the world outside. Is this substantially young, substantially white crowd meant to be universal? What's that supposed to mean? Finally it's perplexing to find that a writer like Handke whose text-work has so questioned and *staged* the construction and the work of writing, of language and its reception here has a production which so erases process in any visible form. Neither the work of the theatre (bodies producing fictions) nor the work of the street (bodies in the live negotiation of space) finds any real expression here. It is rather, unwittingly one suspects, a piece of almost pure spectacle.

Notes
1 *Arts de faire* (Union Generale d'Editions, Paris 1980), translated as *The Practice of Everyday Life* (University of California Press, London, 1984)
2 Quoted in *Schrader on Schrader*, Faber & Faber, 1990

New American Performance: Woosters, Wellman and Vawter

Terminal Hip (performed by Stephen Mellor) is a slippery tangle of free-market voices all seeking air-time in the same white male brain—a blurted channel hop through the lingua franca of TV-America. For writer/director Mac Wellman, language is a good stick to beat itself with and in *Terminal Hip* he takes the rhetorical strategies of the success seminar, TV evangelism and bar room philosophy, chops them, swirls them and leaves us nodding to the rhythm. For 50 minutes the piece jumps, melts and cuts between voices, seeming to make power visible and sparks of momentary knowing and pleasure fly.

The drama we're watching here, as in much contemporary work, is that of meaning's endless constellation and evaporation. The pivot of the drama is precisely our own watching and listening, our own agency in making sense of what there is. It's engaging and lovingly carried through. However, Wellman's desire to smash language runs side by side with a need to restore order, albeit a poetic one. This is a hard, if fairly inescapable path but it leaves this piece and Wellman's other LIFT presentation, the outdoor work *Bad Penny*, as somewhat safe, even civilised occasions, in which the bandwith of expression is distinctly, well, theatrical. Language, delivery and gesture all hint at mayhem, but it's never quite delivered, the danger somehow ducked.

Brace Up! too is a fairly safe piece, compared to *L.S.D* or *St. Anthony*, in which the layering of many found texts has been replaced by the doubling of a single one—Chekhov's *Three Sisters*. The performers are endlessly here in the flesh *and* on video, here on video *and* in the flesh, except hidden by screens, here, not here and then doubly here. The play too is doubled up, by translator Paul Schmidt and narrator Kate Valk, framing and demanding the events. When Valk asks: 'Isn't this the moment when a clock's supposed to ring?' a tape of a clock ringing conveniently plays. Valk is very audience-friendly but soon has the air of an over-enthusiastic tour-guide who won't let anyone out of sight lest they chance to discover something for themselves.

The video and audio tracks have got to be the most sophisticated and precise produced by anyone working in performance. The skill of the group is such that they can give each live moment its individual counterpoint in the mediated tracks, and they seem mesmerised by this ability, piling on detail after detail. The relationship between the parts of *Brace Up!* is often strangely *readable* though — when Vershinin says something boring we get a close-up of someone asleep, when the fire in Act Three is being discussed we get snatches of film showing, wait for it, a fire. At worst, through all this reiteration (via narration, soundtrack, video) one longs for something with, well, depth or even mystery. At best, though the piece pushes on through into a sort of hyper-normality, where the more straightforwardly things happen and are described the more problematic they actually appear.

The real high points are those when the narration drops out altogether — the 'Japanese' dances and the sections of speeded up movement, especially in Part Two. At this point it's clear that those championing this piece as a great contemporary Chekhov are seriously missing the point. In truth, when it goes for it, *Brace Up!* is an intricate meditative space, a surface whose beauty, speed and precision leave one in awe and in which the banal figurative elements (props, plots, characters) are remade in an almost abstract mandala — components in a strange transcendent dance of language, movement and video.

Ron Vawter's *Roy Cohn / Jack Smith* is for me the best of these four works. The unassuming structure (two monologues of white gay men) belies a passionate, complex theatrical experience. Negotiating the shift between the homophobic Cohn and the camp, rambling Smith I'm reminded of Bresson's remark that 'the flatter an image is, the less it expresses, the more easily it is transformed in contact with other images'. Indeed, The Wooster Group's aesthetic is rooted in a blank, pulled-back playing style in which the temptation to fill spaces with needless attitude is resisted, precisely as a mechanism to invite us in emotionally. In expert hands, like those of Vawter or *Brace Up!*'s Anna Kohler, blankness is not to be confused with coldness but becomes instead a hugely charged and almost polymorphously sexual state — the performer as a screen, empty, yet capable of anything.

The straightforward after-dinner-speech contract set up in *Roy Cohn* is soon upset by *Jack Smith*, and it's hard to keep track of the extraordinary, moving re-negotiations one has to make; negotiations around history and politics that are none the less intrinsically bound up with form, with one's ways of making sense. Again it's the drama of meaning's endless constellation and evaporation that we are watching. All through *Jack Smith* there are moments where I think back to Roy Cohn, or to Vawter playing Cohn, or both, measuring an incommensurable set of distances, slipping backwards and forwards, marking the space between three men. 'Emotion' as Paul Schrader wrote of Bresson 'is not denied, merely postponed'.

Recent Installation Works:
Index Theatre

Train up a Child In the Way He Should Go, Manchester Metropolitan University Gallery, April 1994. *The Alphabet of Dogs*, Oliver Machine Works, Manchester. Commissioned by the Boddington's Manchester Festival of Television and the Arts, 12–30 September 1994.

Based in Manchester Index Theatre make work haunted by the sweet and sour delicacies of a distinctly regional life and history. Such reflections on regionality have always been mapped over with a clear sense of the larger myths and forces currently at work in the UK landscape. In recent years the group have forsaken their intense and rather baffling deconstructions of theatre texts, shifting to a form that's brighter and looser. Since last year's *'66 to '99*, the company have also, like others working in new theatre, diversified their practice towards installation and gallery performance. The changes suit them.

In *Train up a Child in the Way He Should Go* and *The Alphabet of Dogs* ideas around voyeurism, anthropomorphism and childhood are very much in the air. The works are connected by a desire to deal with power and with its exercise in the everyday structures of cultural learning. Both pieces play on the idea of humans watching animals (bears in the zoo, dogs in the street) and on its ironic reversal—the notion of animals as uncomprehending spectators (or even inheritors) to human progress, culture, or lack of it. In each piece one's presence as a viewer is a significant part of the work, and becomes, by implication, performative.

In the past, Index seemed unwilling or unable to work with theatre's codes to satisfy that medium's problematicaly social audience. Narrative or rhythmical architecture—the creation of a 'satisfying shape'

to be experienced by a body of watchers over time—was always a site of difficulty and friction in Index's theatre. However, in the gallery context of single viewers, their work positively thrives—one's experience remains delicate and avowedly individual even as it edges towards imagining the social. Viewers of these installations then, experience narrative not as total (theatrical) architecture but as a series of personal eddies and ripples.

In *Alphabet of Dogs* meaning is repeatedly and enjoyably deferred by a shifting set of frames, both actual and intellectual. Moving from a white-walled room in which a monitor shows a pack of dogs chasing madly in a large dilapidated warehouse, one comes eventually to an internal window looking down on the site of the video itself—a warehouse that's now almost deserted. In fact, peering into the cavernous space below one sees only a kitsch plaster dog which sits staring at a huge screen, showing home-movie footage of the May Day parade in a Yorkshire town during the 1950s.

As a watcher one is very aware of the poised doubleness of this scene—humans watching a dog, the dog watching videotape of humans. The content of the tape adds a further irony, since the celebrations it shows consist mainly of badly costumed children enacting the great events of British History. So, a dog stares blankly at some nostalgic document, at history rendered as naive pageant, all in a now deserted industrial building that once housed useful work, and all in a country, which, according to *Alphabets* most obvious pun, has literally, gone to the dogs.

Train up a Child in the Way He Should Go also played games with the doubled positions of watcher and watched. In this more engaging piece, three performers dressed from head to foot in gaudy pantomime bear costumes lived out the long hours of gallery opening in a brutal steel cage. Spectators to this scene were effectively placed in fiction, as visitors to a perverse zoo—in much the same way as Stephen Taylor Woodrow's *Going Bye Byes* placed one at the hospital bedside. However, as soon as one found a role in *Train up a Child* the piece worked to destabilise it. In particular, the performers dressed as soppy-eyed bears hardly bothered to be bear-like at all; their boredom —sitting knees clasped, or hanging glumly from the bars of the ceiling, seemed more like that of a bunch of kids killing time at a bus stop than anything else.

Spiralling thus between human boredom and animal boredom, between the real and the fictional, *Train up a Child* also placed itself with skilful ambiguity at the meeting point between kitsch comedy and high melancholy. Reading from the biro scrawl which ran around the gallery walls —a stream of consciousness flit through Northern nostalgia, kids adventure and public toilet porn—I found this line: 'The sea is calm (rough); The ship is rolling; The wind is strong (light): are you a good (bad) sailor? ... Who could legislate these moments?'

Shirtologie!: Jerome Bell

Trained as a choreographer, Jerome Bell forgets the most of dance, as if, in the forgetting, something else might be possible. Working in a language of movement and image that could be described as a kind of delicate, humane minimalism, his interests are located just at the slippery, evocative meeting point between the physical and the philosophical—the body itself and the processes by which live presence is constructed, the processes of language and the relationship of language to objects (animate and inanimate), the process by which narrative (or meaning) is constructed, through the deployment of objects (animate and inanimate) in time and space.

Shirtologie! is 20 performers and a collection of T-shirts. An empty space, black dance floor, white light. The performers young—late teens to mid-twenties, a range of body types and human presences. The T-shirts second-hand—replete with the workaday slogans, logos, icons and pictures of international capitalist culture, much of it outdated; slogans for products or ideas you don't remember so well, numbers and dates (festivals, occasions), statistics, jokes, faces, admonishments, warnings, demands.

As playful as it is minimalist *Shirtologie!* is 'simply' a matter of deploying the people and the T-shirts in combination and arrangement—structures through time, pictures in space. The work of the piece is that of dressing and appearing— changing clothes, presenting oneself, in T-shirts—the body clothed, always in language, mainly in silence—the fragmented conversation of written slogans on neighbouring T-shirts—CHOOSE says one, VOTEZ says another, TAKE ME says a third and the eyes of the wearer flicker across those of the audience, looking for gazes to meet and looks to avoid.

Each of the sections builds slowly around a theme—the countdown, a count upwards from one to 20 and beyond, a set of linguistic puns, or even a kind of playing/punning with cultural iconography. After 50 minutes of silence there is music on the PA—Madonna then Nirvana. Combination games on the T-shirts—2 Madonnas, 4 Madonnas, a Marilyn, 2 James Deans to dance with, a Nike T-shirt and an Adidas T-shirt dancing together— the whole thing a sentence written in some second-hand pop-culture code. The last song: *Something in the Way*.

But whilst *Shirtologie!* explores the relationship between the various on-stage elements (performers, shirts, sounds, space), its primary concern is perhaps with the way these things are decoded, read and experienced by the audience, and with the ethical complexities of reading and being read. The relationship of performers to the public here is always under-articulated and through this remains fluid and complex — at once aggressive and inviting, curious and defensive. It shifts between these things constantly, managing to do so by staying blank and open to many projections. The paradigm moment in this comes quite early on, when the performers make a line in their T-shirts very close to the audience and simply stand still, to look back at us.

It is the kind of moment that happens a great deal in late-twentieth-century performance — a theatrical structure that privileges the chorus rather than the soloist or star — the blank and confrontational democracy of the 'line', the point at which the stage looks most like the auditorium. Deployed by Jan Fabre or by Pina Bausch, by Peter Handke or The Living Theatre, lines of this kind have been everything from revolutionary posturing to sculptural cigarette breaks — but in Jerome Bell's hands the line takes on a new fragility. There's a nakedness in the performers, clothed, a presence, a vulnerability and an unease. The public are uncomfortable too, not accused so much as worried, about the ethics of their gaze.

Only after what feels like five minutes does a performer remove a T-shirt, revealing one beneath: I THINK THEY'RE LOOKING AT US.

There is a silence again and more looking. And then a further T-shirt is revealed: RELAX.

Smiles. The performers shift posture, take their eyes off us, break the line. The deadlock is broken. There are audible sighs of relief in the audience, and a shifting of postures that parallels that taking place on the stage.

Descriptions of Bell's previous two works (one a 'choreography' of 10 objects/items from his own house and the other a presentation of four naked performers titled *Jerome Bell*) incite the idea that he is slowly and methodically building a more and more complex notion of stage presence. Indeed, in sequences like the one above Bell gambles everything in an attempt to change the way we are looking at the stage, an attempt which is linked to the construction of presences before us which are right at the very edges of what dance or theatre most often supply. Tuned in by the structure of the piece one can see the performers here — the rise and fall of breathing, the tics and gestures of faces and eyes — with an openness and in a spirit of 'nowness' that does not have a name. It makes *Shirtologie!* an inspiring piece.

Programme Notes

The programme notes for Forced Entertainment were written as introductions to the performance pieces we've made — quick, accessible ways of framing the concerns, style or ideas of particular works. Once again it's my hope that in this context they will chime with more general debates elsewhere in this book.

Some Confusions in the Law about Love (1990)

In New York this Christmas I saw a news item about Elvis Presley. I'd been there two days and my TV watching had been confined to end-of-year round-ups and a dull brush with *The New Adventures of Lassie*. In the round-ups I'd listed the most common words. Crack and AIDS were neck and neck, but, dead for 12 years and seven months, Presley really hadn't featured much at all.

The piece took a speculative line, asking just what songs would the King have gone on to sing if he'd continued to live? Would there have been an image change or a return to early styles? And what kind of promos would the King have used if he'd made it to the video age? In answer to these questions a version of Springsteen's *I'm on Fire* was set against a sepia toned promotional clip: an out-of-focus fat man in Presley glasses climbing endlessly out of a car and into the rain as he mumbled the words in a dubious way.

Back in England we talked about the glut of speculative Presleys, both living and dead. There are the ghost Presleys

contacted by mediums and psychics across the world; the fake-dead Presleys hiding out on islands in the sun; the spirit Presleys who call on lone housewives or ex-alcoholic truckers; the disguised Presleys sighted in supermarkets and mobile homes. Each has his own obsessions and messages for the world, his own reasons for dying or for living on.

The stories multiply, shatter, cross-refer, expand, and as they do so the real Presley fades. These mythical constructs are now almost independent of the person behind them. Slowly buried by his own ghosts and by his run away selves Presley is a blank sheet of paper upon which anyone's hopes, desires or wishes can be written. I know little and care less about the real Presley, but the network of fake ones draws me in.

This idea touches many nerves. We are all in a position where the first-hand experiences of our lives exist next to, and are combined with, images, myths and narratives drawn from TV, the print and electronic media, film and music. Most of our experience is second-, third- or fourth- hand. In this context the fake is more pertinent than the real. Cubic Zirconia better than diamonds, fool's gold more human than gold.

Theatre seems the ideal medium for these concerns because it's so inherently bound up in fakery. We flirt with our desires and we exorcise our fears by making these stories and lies,

In *Some Confusions in the Law about Love* the characters make fictions on a tacky nightclub stage; they act fragments from sex acts, love suicides and stories about Presley come back from the dead. It is beyond them to present these myths convincingly; the acting is awkward, the locations they speak of not convergent with their stage. It's a piece about people who want to go to Memphis, to Hawaii, to Japan. It's about wanting to escape from oneself, about wanting to fake one's own death, even about wanting to die.

Underlying the form of the show is a pathos, an anxiety about the way reality feels weakened, a fear that representation has failed us. The characters have a rag bag of media trash to support them, a language that's discredited, broken, inappropriate and a world that is shot full of holes. Just like the rest of us.

In the final sections of the show three of the characters are pretending to be naked and dead. They are covered in talc, like white ghosts, and have sad rubber sex organs held on with thick black elastic. They talk joylessly about how much they like drinking, drug-taking, and sex; the pleasures of the flesh.

On the second night someone, disgruntled, said to me, 'Well, if you're going to do that you should really take your clothes off…', and I knew that four years ago we did just that.

These days, in performance at least, fake sex organs are more interesting than real ones. They contain more about sadness and failure, more about faith and aspiration. In our work we've exchanged the shock of the real for a dialogue with the theatrical; its inherent codes of fakery and pretence. On-stage the characters are trying to build stable worlds and realities, an attempt we all share, an attempt that's both doomed and strangely charmed.

Club of No Regrets (1993)

> In my dream I'm a private detective, torn from the pages of a cheap novel and thrown into this world…
> (*Club of No Regrets*)

The quest for us, as usual, is to force the stories we do know to yield us the stories we don't.

Club Of No Regrets is a layering of diverse voices, actions and objects. Some way into the rehearsal process we saw a moment on TV. A man leading a woman with a gun, the woman's mouth sealed with parcel tape. Or maybe the woman had the gun and the man's mouth was sealed. It could have been abduction or rescue but since the TV volume was down and no one saw the start or the end of the film it wasn't easy to say. So this image drifts in from the edge of intention, from somewhere, its meaning already cancelled, or held hostage. We are catching things not from the point of focus but from the corner of the eye.

The fragments in *Club of No Regrets* (cop thriller, psychic chiller, fairy story and voodoo spells amongst others) we have found and vandalised or made up with familiar genres in mind. In the work these more or less recognisable shards are laid out in a pattern: the elements and their conjunction hint at narrative, but the pattern has more to do with music, with

meditative space. So the quest, in other terms, is to get the stories we do know to yield us the space beyond stories.

The strange dance between narrative and abstraction. Songs that cannot be sung. Impossible pictures.

We spend time to get things looking random, not produced by intention, making meaning that's born out of visible struggle. In *Club of No Regrets* a lost woman gives herself the name Helen X and attempts a story to keep the night away. Helen's intention is always thwarted by the inadequacy of her materials and by the unsuitability of her circumstances. Her intentions, like our own, are always scrambled by memory, written over and challenged by other intentions, other scrambled desires.

We don't seek a meaning that has been placed but seek rather the sense of meaning falling into place. A meaning that happens to happen, a feeling that tumbles, a feeling on the very edge of accident. A sense that comes because *that* happened and *that* happened and you were there to see it (but you always knew you could've seen something else, heard another line, caught another gesture). We're seeking a work that values the moment where you saw and connected. Where the job of piecing together torn paper is yours.

Club of No Regrets, then, is a performance about the work of seeing, about the quick joy of it and the slow joy of it and the hard work of it, too.

Red Room (1994)

Red Room was an installation performance made in collaboration between Forced Entertainment, photographer Hugo Glendinning and performer Will Waghorn. The work was presented as an ICA Live Art Commission in conjunction with The Showroom Gallery during the first two weeks of December 1993.

Using detective fiction and forensics as its central metaphors the work also drew on a range of everyday urban practices; the personal mythologisation of space, the chance observation of strangers, the finding of discarded letters or photographs. The work's concern was thus with the nature of evidence and with the piecing together of fragments and clues to create narratives.

Glendinning's photographs (raw material for the performance installation) recorded fragments of performance by Forced Entertainment in a range of urban sites, including tower-blocks, stairwells, phone booths, patches of wasteground, railway tunnels and the backs of cars. These photographs did not so much capture the staged actions or events as somehow appear to lose them. The performers are always falling out of frame, the event to be recorded slips away from us, the subject is blurred, out of focus or obscured. In place of a strong legible centre we only see details, absences, hints and the camera's struggle to contain the event.

For the installation a false wall was installed in the Showroom's front gallery, creating a complete blackout inside. Visitors to the gallery entered a darkened space which could thus only be navigated, and its contents observed, with the aid of a torch. This space served as a 'display space' in which Glendinning's photographs (heavily cropped) and fragments of text were

arranged on grids of string — the arrangement of these materials amassing and changing over the period of the installation.

In the rear of this front space a doorway led one to a very narrow corridor, 20 feet in length at the end of which a faint glow of red light spilled from the second gallery. Only by moving along the corridor and turning the corner into the second space could one discover the source of the light and the performer at work. The second space, revealed in this way, was also free of natural light, but lit the deep safe-red of a photographic darkroom. In this space Will Waghorn worked — printing and developing images, washing them and hanging them to dry, typing notes on a manual typewriter, recording others on a small Dictaphone. The benches in this room were strewn with cropped and discarded prints, with forensic dusting powder, with notebooks and texts about detection.

In its construction of space *Red Room* mobilises the viewer, turning the act of looking into its subject. The navigation of an environment (first blackened, then cramped and finally inhabited), the tracing of a trajectory with a torch, the choice of materials to illuminate for a second or ten-minute stare; all these acts seek to make our looking performative, aware of its construction. We're all first on the scene of the crime here, making stories, we're all scattered in the pieces, all joining up the dots.

Thinking about a space for performance, perhaps the first thing one wants to do is to get in there. To stand in it, to walk around, to sit or to run, to find through being what it feels like, to discover its comforts and discomforts, it opportunities and secrets. This doing is allied to watching — to observing other bodies and how they operate in a space — noting positions that dominate pictorially, positions that allow an overview, positions that are hidden, trajectories and resting points that seem written cunningly into the space itself.

This same process guides us whether we're making performance work for a theatre studio or for a site. In making studio work we always begin by building something, something between a set and a playground, however crude — building a space and then dreaming or finding what happens there. For our site-specific work the space is already built — all we have to do is explore. *Dreams' Winter*, created for Manchester Central Library, is the third project by Forced Entertainment for a non theatre space. Our first on-site research visit there saw us running round the edges of its circular, dome-ceilinged space, shouting, playing walkmans as we moved and dropping books from a great height onto its tables.

These attempts to test the space (its physical limits, its extraordinary acoustics, its ingrained still points and trajectories)

Dreams' Winter (1994)

Written for *Dreams' Winter* — a site-specific performance by Forced Entertainment involving 25 performers, commissioned for Manchester Central Library as part of its 60th birthday celebrations — this programme note takes a look at the way space in particular informs and influences performance.
A version of the text was also published in *Art Alive* magazine.

gave way, in time, to discussion and speculation. What kinds of actions does the space engender? What kinds of narratives get played out here? What movie scenes might one wish to film in this place?

The whole process for us is one of balancing things written into the library (actions, acoustic effects, fictions, texts) with a sense of things that work against the space—what would it mean to see a pantomime horse appearing round the corner of the bookshelves? or to see the aisles piled high with trees?

Since the company's formation in 1984 we've always felt the influence of a wide range of cultural practices. So it's been film-makers, musicians, photographers, fine artists and live artists with whom we've felt an affinity.

Working outside theatre space it seems that the dynamic confrontation between flimsy 'theatrical' elements (costume, fiction, props, wigs, placards) and the substantial material-real of a site is very much at the heart of our project. A series of photographs we created in 1991 with photographer Hugo Glendinning really bring this home—the pictures show 'characters' in costume whose names are declared on cardboard placards. The characters are stood in outdoor locations—in the middle of a river up to his knees stands a man with a sign saying A TERRORIST IN HIDING, beside an enormous factory wall, stretching to infinity stands a woman in a dress with a sign saying A TELEPATH (AGED TWELVE). One's eye goes instantly to the fissure between these theatrical gestures and the realness of the space that contains them—a fissure that changes everything, making the real doubt itself and the theatrical look strangely solid and true.

In *Dreams' Winter* we're working with texts and actions that belong in the library and others which (perhaps) do not. There are indexes, alphabets and phrases from a language lesson. There are voices which speak of being lost, of being at the edge of a car park, of being in the middle of a forest. There are sleepwalkers, wandering with their eyes closed; there are lost children trailing string behind them; there are men and women slumped over books as though dreaming the world. It's as though we want to invoke not just all the bodies that have moved through the gorgeous space of the library, but all the lives and stories contained in its books. After 15 July the Central Library in Manchester will be a changed, more crowded place.'

Hidden J (1994)

> Each of us has some ghosts he has to look after.

Maybe this piece started with a photograph we made with Hugo Glendinning in 1992. In it Richard sits slumped on the scrawny grass of a ridge that looks down onto Sheffield early evening, the lights of the city visible behind him, a suit jacket laid across his legs and a cardboard sign propped next to him saying simply FRANK (DRUNK).

That was the last port of call in that photo shoot but the wasteground where we shot FRANK was getting busier—lads hanging out, men walking dogs, kids running home, people headed off into town for Friday night. One bloke passed us, took in the whole scene—photographer, a

few people standing round with camera bags, sacks of clothes and Richard looking wasted on the grass acting FRANK (DRUNK). The bloke got right past us, headed for town and then turned, jerking his head towards Richard and spoke: 'That'll be me in four hours time', half smiling, half just stating a fact.

So this Summer we've been chasing FRANK.

In rehearsals Frank got drunk, then drunker, went to a wedding and a party. He met an angel and a devil. He railed at lampposts, trees and bushes; he cried. Rehearsals strayed in other directions too, hitting other worlds. Frank got confused with some stories that my brother sent me from Ghana, West Africa — about men who had curses put on them, about massacres in the border zone around the end of 1993. Frank got tangled with the jumbled stories of present-day Europe; with civil wars and refugees. Frank made a trip to the casualty department of a nearby hospital.

Some of these adventures, some of these confusions, some of these worlds have made it into the show. We hope you enjoy it.

Speak Bitterness (1995)

In a true story we read years ago two lovers were leaving Soviet Russia for America. On the day of their departure they set aside some time for saying a special and long-anticipated goodbye. Bags packed and plane tickets bought they took it in turns to stand on a chair in their kitchen and speak forthrightly to the small electrical device on the wall which they had always presumed was a bug — telling secrets to their suspected eavesdroppers, chancing wishes and confessions to the wall, to the city, to history and the night.

For us, performance and confession have always gone hand in hand. Seen in this way each show is a series of admissions or ownings up, not just to the things that one has actually done but to the things that one has wished for, flirted with or feared in oneself, and sometimes to the things one has merely glimpsed or heard about. Perhaps it's true, as war journalist Michael Herr wrote of his experiences in Vietnam, that in some strange way we are as responsible for everything that we see as we are for everything that we do.

Speak Bitterness works from a vast catalogue of confessions. It comes out of a culture (England, back end of the 90s) where every time there's a murder or a bombing the police get a dozen or more false calls — from people confessing or taking the blame, from people who, when questioned, know nothing at all of the atrocities committed. It comes out of a culture where the chat shows and the radio call-ins are filling up with people spilling the beans — weeping, laughing, stumbling for words — telling the truth about what they saw and what they did and how they did it, and why.

Writing this mid-way through rehearsals *Speak Bitterness* shows a group of seven penitents whose enormous task it is to confess to everything. They are by turns cowed, breezy, anguished, reluctant, jovial and of course determined. The text they work from lies somewhere between a mad catalogue of unlikely human infamy and the transcript perhaps of some strange and comical show-trial.

In a way it's also a throwback to those lovers we read about years ago — a public

summing up, an admission of complicity, a kicking over the traces and a way, in the end, of fixing a particular time and ones feelings for it.

We hope you enjoy our *Speak Bitterness* tonight.

Showtime (1996)

In a New York hotel room we prepare for a photo shoot—making a bomb using sections of sawn up broom handle covered in red tape, attaching wires, a clock, fragments of a smashed-up computer.

Over several days the performers will wear this bomb and be photographed in it—in Times Square in a sudden squall of rain, in the street, in the hotel lobby, on the roof against the skyline—and while we are photographing, thinking that we may as well grab rehearsal time while we can, I ask them to improvise—gestures, words, phrases.

On one of these days Richard is sitting on his hotel room bed, face covered in shaving foam, the bomb around his chest. He is making apologies, saying that he wishes things could've turned out better, playing small glances down to the ticking clock. He is talking about optimism, about how he should never have gone to Mexico, about a performance that we haven't even made, a performance that will be called *Showtime*.

It's there, in that room, that the show starts, in one sense at least and we feel sure we have a beginning, which will turn out, in the final event, to be the end…there are humans under duress and human bodies under the threat of unnecessary force. A clock ticking (amplified). Regrets, apologies. Small gestures of a body, fragments of voice and silences.

With this as an ending we are now in rehearsal working backwards and unfolding the ruins of a story. If our last theatre piece *Speak Bitterness* was all about openness—about the promise of confession and naked truth under white, exposing light, then *Showtime* may well be its opposite—a story emerging in darkness out of turmoil and shadow.

Filled with costumed thugs, surrounded by chain-link fencing and lit by a strange shifting gloom, *Showtime* bears the marks for me of three and half years of parenthood. These are the years in which the bathroom has half-filled with bright red and lime green plastic toys, in which the stories I have read feature talking mice and trees and in which our late-night motorway journeys are soundtracked by the delights of 'Heads, Shoulders, Knees and Toes'.

In New York we photograph Cathy stood amongst the most delicate snow-covered trees in midst of Central Park, as if to say, with the bomb strapped to her, that when she goes the trees will go too, and the snow will fall from the branches. It looks like something from a very strange fairy tale.

Showtime then is a strange colliding of adult and child worlds; brutality, sex and violence in all their adult manifestations finding expression in the inappropriate simple language of counting stories, alphabets, and pretended phone calls from a deserted storeroom late at night.

We hope you enjoy the performance.

Pleasure (1997)

We were reading this great quote from Fassbinder where he talks about how he hoped, in the end, that all of his films would make a house. How one film might be the bedroom, another might be the kitchen, another the garden and another the basement—each film in a different territory, with a different tone, but how he hoped in the end to make a whole house.

Thought of in this way we're pretty sure that *Pleasure* is the basement for us. Dark, slowed down, comical and very late night, it is not a piece that has much daylight in it.

Perhaps we knew where we were headed when a friend came into rehearsals in mid-summer 97 and, hearing the soundtrack of slowed-down tunes, told us how he and his sister had spent long scary nights together playing their parents' record collection slowed right down to 16 rpm, just as we had been doing for *Pleasure* —partly a kids' game of guessing the tracks and partly a matter of scaring each other with the voices, sounds and messages they could hear.

There's no doubt that *Pleasure* is something of a gear shift for us—a step back from the directness and intimacy of the confessions in *Speak Bitterness* and from the concern with place and history in our reflective lecture performance *A Decade of Forced Entertainment.*

Pleasure is, by comparison, an obsessive and mysterious piece where the images and texts connect or disconnect in quite unexpected ways, and where the world evoked is distant, and shadowy. Our concerns are with memory, with the body, with sexuality and its presentation, with romance, with sex itself. But the world of the piece is also obsessively night-time, drunken, disconnected.

Perhaps the key tone in the work so far is a kind of blankness—a list of words written on a blackboard, a man stripping brashly, a woman undressing slowly in the half-light, a woman dressed as a bride watching a record as it turns around and around. There's a just-so-ness to these moments which we're very much in love with without fully understanding it—a collection of images that are allowed in some strange way, to simply stand.

Between these images is the heart of *Pleasure*—a kind of late-night radio message picked up on some random scanning receiver—a portrait of a world where it is always after midnight, and where the dawn never comes.

We hope you enjoy the work.

Appendix

Forced Entertainment Personnel

Company members
Tim Etchells, Deborah Chadbourn,
Cathy Naden, Robin Arthur,
Richard Lowdon, Terry O'Connor
(since 1986), Claire Marshall (since
1989)

Other founder members
Susie Williams (1984–1987) and
Huw Chadbourn (1984–1986)

Associates
Tim Hall and Sue Marshall
(performers)

Regular collaborators
Hugo Glendinning (photographer),
John Avery (composer), Nigel Edwards
(lighting), Bytehaus (digital projects)

Administrator
Verity Leigh

Current board
Nicky Childs, Antonia Payne,
Colin Pons, Martin Harvey,
Simon Shibli

Past board members
Stella Hall, Philip Bernays,
Katy Sender, Alan Read,
Helen Marriage, Noel Greig

Also credit to
Andy Clarke, Martin Bailey, Johnny
Goodwin (technicians), Fred McVittie,
Jack Randle, Mark Etchells, Sarah Sin-
gleton, Nancy Reilly McVittie, Richard
Hawley, Sara De Roo (performers),
Nick Crowe and Ju Row Farr (assistant
directors), Julliet Sebley, Michelle
McGuire, Deveril Garagin, Tracey
Doxey (administrative assistants and
trainees), Gary Wraith, Mark Parkin,
Jo Cammack (film people), Marie
Clements at Communique (PR).

Forced Entertainment Past Projects

All the works are theatre performances
unless otherwise indicated. Dates refer to
the year of creation and original touring/
distribution. Many of the works have been
re-staged or re-presented in the years following their creation. Since 1986 Forced
Entertainment has received regular support
from the following funding bodies: Arts
Council of England, Yorkshire and Humber-
side Arts Board, Sheffield City Council and,
for overseas touring, the British Council.

1984

Jessica in the Room of Lights
First performance 14 December 1984,
Yorkshire Arts Space Society, Sheffield

1985

The Set-up
(National Review of Live Art)
First performance Spring 1985,
The Leadmill, Sheffield

Nighthawks
First performance 23 October 1985,
North Riding College, Scarborough

1986

*The Day that Serenity Returned to the
Ground*
(commissioned by The Zap Club)
Performances January 1986,
The Zap Club, Brighton

*(Let the Water Run its Course) to the Sea
that Made the Promise*
First performance 6 October 1986,
Trent Polytechnic, Nottingham

1987/88

200% & Bloody Thirsty
First performance 10 October 1988,
Trent Polytechnic, Nottingham

1989/90

Some Confusions in the Law about Love
First performance 19 February 1990,
The Leadmill, Sheffield

1991

Welcome to Dreamland
(Retrospecitve trilogy comprising
the previous three theatre works, spon-
sored by The Leadmill/Becks Bier)
Performances 15–18 July 1991

Marina & Lee
(Barclays New Stages Award)
First performance 18 March 1991,
Nuffield Studio, Lancaster

1992

Emanuelle Enchanted
(Barclays New Stages Award)
First performance 6 October 1992,
Nuffield Studio, Lancaster

1993

Club of No Regrets
First performance 5 October 1993,
Nuffield Studio, Lancaster

12 am: Awake and Looking Down
(durational performance/installation
commissioned by National Review of
Live Art)
First performance 22 October 1993

Red Room
(Performance installation with photographer Hugo Glendinning, commissioned by ICA Live Arts/Showroom
Gallery)
First presentation 30 November 1993
to 12 December 1993

1994

Ground Plans for Paradise
(Installation in collaboration with
Hugo Glendinning for Leeds Metro-
politan University Gallery)
First presentation 15 March 1994

Dreams' Winter
(Site-specific work, commissioned for
Manchester Central Library)
Performances 15–20 July 1994

Hidden J
First performance 10 October 1994,
Nuffield Studio, Lancaster

Speak Bitterness
(Durational performance/installation
commissioned by National Review of
Live Art)
First performance 23 October 1994,
Glasgow

1995

A Decade of Forced Entertainment
(Performance/Lecture)
First performance 4 February 1995,
ICA theatre London

Nights in This City
(Site-specific work, Sheffield)
Performances 16–21 May 1995

Speak Bitterness (theatre version)
First performance 26 September 1995,
Alsager Arts Centre, Stoke-on-Trent

1985

Break In!
(Children's project in collaboration
with Sheffield theatres)
Performances January 1996

Quizoola!
(Durational Work commissioned by
ICA Live Arts and National Review of
Live Art)
First performance 9 September 1996,
ICA London

List of Plates

Frozen Palaces R&D
(Digital media R&D, in collaboration
with Hugo Glendinning)

Showtime
First performance 25 September 1996,
Alsager Arts Centre, Stoke-on-Trent

1997

Nights in This City
(Rotterdam version commissioned by
Rotterdamse Shouwburg and R Festival)
Performances 23–27 September 1997

Pleasure
First performance 14 November 1997,
Arnolfini, Bristol

1998

Filthy Words & Phrases
(Seven-hour video installation, directed
by Tim Etchells and Hugo Glendinning)
Premiere 13 January 1998, International
Film Festival, Rotterdam

Paradise
(Internet project commissioned by
Love Bytes/Channel)
Launched on 23 April 1998

Nightwalks
(CD-ROM in collaboration with
Hugo Glendinning, commissioned by
Photo 98)
Launched 2 October 1998, Site Gallery,
Sheffield

Frozen Palaces (Chapter One)
Released on Artintact Edition 5,
November 1998

Dirty Work
First performance 12 November 1998,
Phoenix Arts, Leicester.

Cover: Cathy Naden
p. 2: Tim Etchells during rehearsals for *Marina & Lee*.
p. 26: *Hidden J* – Richard Lowdon & Claire Marshall.
p. 28: *Jessica in the Room of Lights* – Huw Chadbourn, Susie Williams.
p. 33: **top**: *The Day that Serenity Returned to the Ground* – Robin Arthur, Cathy Naden; **middle**: *200 & Bloody Thirsty* – Richard Lowdon, Cathy Naden, Robin Arthur with Sarah Singleton, Mark Etchells on video; **bottom**: *200 & Bloody Thirsty* – Richard Lowdon, Cathy Naden, Robin Arthur.
p. 37: **top**: *Showtime* – Claire Marshall, Richard Lowdon, Terry O'Connor; **middle**: *Marina & Lee* – Terry O'Connor, Mark Randle, Claire Marshall, Robin Arthur; **bottom**: *Showtime* – Cathy Naden, Claire Marshall, Terry O'Connor.
p. 41: **top**: *Speak Bitterness* – Richard Lowdon, Tim Hall, Terry O'Connor, Cathy Naden, Sue Marshall, Claire Marshall, Robin Arthur; **middle**: *Pleasure* – Terry O'Connor, Cathy Naden, Richard Lowdon, Claire Marshall, Robin Arthur; **bottom**: *Ground Plans for Paradise* – gallery performance to accompany model city installation: Robin Arthur, Richard Lowdon, Cathy Naden.
p. 47: UK maps from *A Decade of Forced Entertainment*, Tim Etchells.
p. 82: *Ground Plans for Paradise*, installation.
p. 83: *Nights in this City*, final installation, bus-garage, Sheffield.
p. 130: *12am Awake & Looking Down* – Richard Lowdon.
p. 132: *Some Confusions in the Law about Love* – Claire Marshall, Fred McVittie, Robin Arthur.
p. 140/1: **top row**: *(Let The Water Run its Course) to the Sea that Made the Promise* – **(1)** Robin Arthur, Richard Lowdon, **(2)** Cathy Naden, Richard Lowdon, Robin Arthur; **bottom row**: *Emanuelle Enchanted* – **(1)** Claire Marshall, Terry O'Connor, **(2)** Richard Lowdon, Terry O'Connor, **(3)** Richard Lowdon, Claire Marshall.
p. 177/8: **top row** – *Club of No Regrets* – **(1)** Robin Arthur, **(2)** Terry O'Connor, **(3)** Richard Lowdon; **bottom row**: *Speak Bitterness* – **(1)** Tim Hall, Claire Marshall, Cathy Naden, Robin Arthur, **(2)** Tim Hall, Claire Marshall, Robin Arthur, Richard Lowdon, **(3)** Richard Lowdon, Tim Hall.
p. 191: *Club of No Regrets* – Robin Arthur.
p. 192: *Marina & Lee* – Cathy Naden.
p. 193: *Pleasure* – Claire Marshall.
p. 194: *200% & Bloody Thirsty* – Richard Lowdon.
p. 195: *Dreams' Winter* – Terry O'Connor.
p. 196: *Filthy Words & Phrases* – Cathy Naden.
p. 198: *Hidden J* – Cathy Naden, Robin Arthur.

Acknowledgements

A shorter version of *A Decade Of Forced Entertainment* appears in *Performance Research* #1 (Routledge, 1996).

A version of 'On Risk and Investment' was presented at the ICA in May 1994, during Barclays New Stages in a season of ICA talks called *The Seven Ages of Performance*.

A version of 'Play On: Collaboration and Process' was first presented as part of a lecture series organised by Geert Opsomer/R.I.T.S in Leuven, Belgium, January 1998.

'On Documentation and Performance' was written in response to *Mind the Gaps*, 29–31 July 1994, a three-day conference on performance, process and documentation (Lancaster University Theatre Studies in conjunction with Centre for Performance Research). It was published in *Versus* magazine, 1994.

'Eight Fragments on Theatre and the City' was first published in *Theaterschrift 10: City/Art/Cultural Identity*, 1995.

A shorter version of 'Replaying the Tapes of the Twentieth Century: An Interview with Ron Vawter' was published in *Hybrid* magazine #3, July 1993.

A version of 'On Performance and Technology' was first presented at the Directors' Guild Conference, *Towards the Millennium* in Cambridge, December 1995.

A version of 'On Performance Writing' was first presented as a paper 'How to Write Words at the End of a Millennium: Instructions for Ghost Writers' at *Performance Writing*, an interdisciplinary symposium at Dartington College of Art organised by Writing Research Associates, 12–14 April, 1996.

An edited version of 'On Performance & Film: Tuning In' was first published in *Total Theatre* magazine, 1997.

A shorter version of 'I Wanna be Adored—ICA Live Arts on Tour in the USA' was published in the *Guardian* newspaper, 1996.

The reviews of 'Index Theatre: Recent Installation Works' and 'Peter Handke: The Hour in which We Knew Nothing of Each Other' were first published in *Frieze*. A version of the piece 'New

American Performance: Woosters, Wellman and Vawter' was published in *Hybrid* magazine. The review of 'Ann Teresa De Keersmaeker: *Stella*' was first published in *Performance* magazine # 61, 'Alan MacLean and Tony Mustoe: My Body Did Everything I Asked It' was first published in *Performance* Magazine # 64. The review of 'Steven Taylor Woodrow: Three Works' was first published in *Variant* magazine #10.

The programme note for *Some Confusions In The Law About Love* was first published in *City Limits*. The programme note on *Red Room* was first published as part of '*Red Room*, Photographic Documents: Hugo Glendinning and Tim Etchells' in *Art & Design*, October 1994, New Performance Issue. The programme note for *Dreams' Winter* was previously published in *Art Alive* Magazine #1.

Portions of the text for *Emanuelle Enchanted* have previously appeared in '*Emanuelle Enchanted*: Notes and Documents' by Richard Lowdon and Tim Etchells in Nick Kaye (ed.) *Contemporary Theatre Review British Live Art* (Harwood, 1994). Portions of the text for *Speak Bitterness* have previously appeared in *Language Alive*, Issue One (1996), published by Sound & Language. Portions of the text for *Club of No Regrets* have previously appeared in Nick Kaye (ed.) *Art Into Theatre*, Harwood, 1996.

Quotations from other people

p. 15, From 'Unpicking Kentucky Fried City' (review) by Claire MacDonald. *New Socialist* September 1986.

p. 16, From *Dispatches* by Michael Herr. 1968. ISBN 0-380-40196-7.

p. 18, From *Comedians* by Trevor Griffiths. Faber ISBN 0 571 10885 7.

p. 51, From unpublished article (1988) by John Ashford (The Place Theatre).

p. 102, From Sleeve notes *Totale's Turns (It's Now Or Never)*: The Fall. Sleeve notes by Mark E. Smith. LP number ROUGH 10 issued by Rough Trade.

Index